AI Nation

AI Nation

How Artificial Intelligence Will Reshape Governance

Zinedine Calvori

Mindful Pages

Published in 2026

ISBN: 9789374590454 (PB)
ISBN: 9789374590904 (eBook)

Published by

Mindful Pages
Imprint of Alpha Editions LLC
312 W. 2nd St #1834
Casper, WY 82601, USA

This book was developed using advanced writing tools to support the drafting and ideation process. All content has been thoughtfully curated, refined, and reviewed to ensure quality and relevance.

Content

Introduction

The child was the first to notice something was wrong. Standing in the biting wind outside a council office in northern England, she tugged at her mother's coat as the crowd shuffled backwards and forwards, trapped in a queue that seemed to obey no human logic. Hours passed. No official emerged to explain the delay. No sign on the door offered a clue. What governed the line that day—a supposedly simple process for verifying benefit documents—was a silent spreadsheet that had started ranking claimants by a risk score no one had bothered to communicate. People were not waiting for a person. They were waiting for an algorithm.

Few citizens think of their government as something that computes. Democracies are imagined in the language of parliaments and parties, not servers and code. Yet behind almost every administrative encounter lies an invisible choreography of decision rules, weightings, and automated triage. A housing application is routed to one caseworker instead of another. A nurse is dispatched to this home visit rather than that one. A tax return is flagged for scrutiny while thousands of others glide through unnoticed. The state, without announcing it, now runs on a hidden operating system.

We are accustomed to treating this as background noise: mere clerical machinery that keeps complex societies functioning. But the machinery is no longer passive. It has started to shape outcomes with growing reach and confidence. Algorithms—first simple scoring systems, now increasingly adaptive—are deciding where public attention flows, how resources are allocated, and which risks are prioritised. They do so quietly, and often in ways that neither citizens nor frontline officials fully understand. This silence is not neutral. It carries power.

That power rests on a paradox. Artificial intelligence promises to make administration fairer and more efficient, reducing the delays, biases, and inconsistencies that plague human judgement. At the same time, it threatens to deepen the very problems it claims to solve by wrapping them in technical opacity. A biased official can be challenged. A flawed rule can be amended. A defective model burrows deeper, presenting itself as objective even when its foundations are shaky. The challenge of modern governance is not merely that democracies use algorithms. It is that they often do so without admitting it, explaining it, or equipping citizens to question it.

This book began with a simple observation: the state is already algorithmic. The question is how to make it democratic. Once that question is posed, a cascade of others follows. When should governments rely on predictive tools? What assumptions should be acceptable when modelling human behaviour? How do we judge whether an automated decision is legitimate? Which tasks demand human oversight, and which merely pretend to? Where does accountability sit when a chain of software, data, and outsourced contractors produces an outcome that affects a person's life? Every chapter that follows attempts to offer a language, and a practical toolkit, for answering these questions with honesty and precision.

To understand what is at stake, we must begin by stepping back. Nations have long been shaped by the technologies they adopt. Census tables helped nineteenth-century empires govern sprawling populations, turning millions of individuals into comparable units. The telephone decentralised command, allowing states to respond to crises with unprecedented speed. The computer digitised record-keeping, shrinking monumental archives into flicker-quiet databases. Each innovation altered the balance between rulers and ruled by changing not only what governments could do but how they thought about doing it.

Artificial intelligence is the next transformation, but it differs from its predecessors in one crucial respect. It does not merely accelerate bureaucracy. It inserts its own logic into the very heart of decision-making. Traditional administrative systems recorded information and checked compliance. AI systems forecast, recommend, and optimise. They are instruments of interpretation as much as instruments of record. By offering predictions—who needs help, where crime may rise, which households are likely to struggle—they start to define problems before any human has framed them. They reorder the world in advance.

History offers a useful warning. Whenever states adopt the tools of abstraction—statistics, categories, probabilities—they can improve fairness by standardising treatment. They can also, unintentionally, flatten complexity and narrow the space for empathy. A caseworker overwhelmed by caseloads may welcome an automated triage tool; a citizen reduced to a row in a dataset may find it harder to be seen as an individual. The promise and peril are inseparable: greater consistency, but at the risk of procedural coldness; earlier detection of need, but with a danger of labelling that follows people for years.

Much of the public debate about AI focuses on dramatic scenarios: self-driving cars careening through cities or general artificial intelligence redefining humanity. These visions, though tempting, are a distraction from where the real transformation is happening. It is occurring in the unnoticed layers of public infrastructure: the scheduling engines that allocate clinic appointments; the eligibility systems that determine who receives a housing grant; the risk models that guide police patrols; the chat interfaces that mediate access to services. It is a quiet revolution, but no less consequential for its quietness.

One motif will recur throughout this book: the state as an operating system. Like any operating system, it sets the default pathways along which actions flow. It governs what is easy and what is hard, what is automated and what requires exceptional effort. Once defaults harden, they are rarely questioned. Citizens may contest an individual decision, but the deeper architecture—the rules that route, prioritise, and calculate—remains shielded behind technical and institutional walls. This metaphor matters because it illuminates a central truth: the most powerful decisions in governance are often those that appear procedural rather than political.

Treating the state as an operating system also clarifies what needs to be rebuilt. When governments digitised, they converted paper processes into online portals and electronic forms. But they often carried over old assumptions about fairness, transparency, and discretion without reconsidering how these values translate into code. A paper file can hold a messy, contradictory story. A form field cannot. When a frontline worker exercises judgement, they leave room for conversation. When a model issues a recommendation, it often arrives as a completed thought. The digital state, for all its efficiency, can be unforgiving.

The modern challenge is to design algorithmic governance that deepens, rather than diminishes, democratic legitimacy. Accuracy alone is not enough. A highly precise model deployed without consent or recourse may be efficient yet illegitimate. A tool that improves outcomes on average may still cause systematic harm to certain groups. A prediction that appears neutral may encode political trade-offs that deserve open debate. Legitimacy is the threshold condition for using algorithmic tools in public life. Without it, even beneficial innovations corrode trust.

Legitimacy, however, is not a single principle but an architecture. It requires clarity about who authorised a system, what purposes it serves, what alternatives were considered, how success is measured, and what mechanisms allow citizens to challenge outcomes. It demands transparency without overwhelming people with technical detail; oversight that is substantive rather than symbolic; and rules that anticipate how systems behave under stress, not merely in ideal conditions. Above all, it requires humility: the recognition that no technological system can substitute for moral judgement.

This book does not argue against using AI in public services. On the contrary, when designed and governed well, algorithms can help administrations recognise needs earlier, target interventions more effectively, and reduce burdens on overstretched staff. They can reveal patterns that humans overlook and highlight inequities that would otherwise remain hidden. They can support more consistent, evidence-based decisions. They can even strengthen citizens' rights by ensuring processes are traceable and auditable. The goal is not to resist algorithmic governance but to civilise it.

Civilising AI begins with data. Governments possess some of the richest administrative datasets in the world, capturing the textures of daily life with a fidelity that private companies can rarely match. Used wisely, these datasets can guide better policy. Used carelessly, they can generate new forms of surveillance or entrench historical injustices. Understanding how data is collected, linked, interpreted, and repurposed is essential for judging whether an AI system serves the public interest. Data is not neutral; it is destiny, shaping both predictions and the policies that flow from them.

Models, too, carry their own politics. A simple rule-of-thumb can be explained, questioned, and modified. A complex learning system may resist scrutiny even from its designers. Public institutions cannot rely on models that behave like sealed boxes, especially when the stakes include liberty, welfare, or essential services. Citizens deserve explanations that are not merely technically accurate but practically meaningful: explanations that allow them to understand the reasons behind an outcome and to challenge it if necessary. Explainability, in this sense, is not a luxury. It is a democratic right.

Accountability is the final pillar. As states adopt AI tools, responsibility risks dissolving into the cracks between designers, vendors, civil servants, and political leaders. This diffusion of blame is dangerous. People harmed by an automated decision should not need to navigate a maze of contractors and agencies to find redress. Public administrators should not be left carrying the ethical and legal burden for decisions they barely influenced. And vendors should not evade scrutiny by hiding behind trade secrets. A functioning democracy needs clear lines of accountability that reflect the full chain of design and deployment.

All these issues converge on a simple but unsettling reality: the systems that mediate public life are growing more complex than the institutions that oversee them. This imbalance cannot continue. Citizens should be able to understand the forces that shape their interactions with the state. Officials should have the confidence and competence to interrogate the tools they rely on. Legislators should be equipped to set boundaries that preserve rights and promote fairness. Without this collective capability, the algorithmic state will drift towards unexamined power.

Yet we should not underestimate our capacity to shape these systems. Democracies have repeatedly reinvented governance in response to new technologies: industrialisation led to labour laws; mass communication spurred transparency norms; computing called forth data-protection regimes. Each transformation required public imagination and institutional reform. AI is no different. What we build now will determine whether the next generation inherits a state that is more just, more capable, and more humane—or one that is efficient but brittle, powerful but unaccountable.

At the heart of this book lies a conviction that the future of governance is not predetermined. Technology creates possibilities, not destinies. The question is whether we can harness those possibilities with care. Can we design systems that help rather than categorise? Can we ensure that prediction augments human judgement rather than replaces it? Can we craft oversight that keeps pace with innovation without suffocating it? Can we build institutions that earn trust rather than rely on it? None of these challenges is easy, but all of them are necessary.

What follows is not a technical manual, though it contains technical insights. It is not a philosophical treatise, though it grapples with deep ethical questions. It is, instead, an attempt to equip readers—policymakers, practitioners, and the wider public—with the tools to evaluate, question, and shape the algorithmic systems that increasingly govern daily life. Each chapter explores a different part of this emerging terrain: the operating systems of public administration; the data that feeds them; the models that interpret it; the institutions tasked with oversight; the rights and responsibilities of citizens; the vulnerabilities and safety requirements of AI; the role of markets and vendors; the law's evolving relationship with code; the design choices that preserve dignity; and the playbook for building a more trustworthy future.

But before we turn to these themes, it is worth pausing on the tension that animates this entire project. We live in societies that demand both speed and sensitivity, both efficiency and fairness. We ask governments to be responsive without rushing, certain without being rigid, personalised without being arbitrary. AI can help us navigate these tensions, but only if we are clear-eyed about its constraints as well as its capabilities. The future of governance will not be determined by the technology itself, but by our collective decisions about how to use it.

That future is unwritten. The choices made in the next decade—about data stewardship, model deployment, accountability mechanisms, and legal protections—will shape the contours of public life for generations. Will citizens be treated as participants in their governance or as data points to be managed? Will public institutions adopt systems they can explain and defend, or will they drift into dependence on tools they scarcely understand? Will algorithmic governance strengthen democratic values or hollow them out?

These are pressing questions, not distant hypotheticals. By the time the child in the council queue grows up, the operating system of her state will look very different. The decisions we make today will determine whether she encounters a public sector that recognises her as a person with a story or as a profile with a score. Our task is to ensure the former, not the latter.

The chapters ahead offer a path towards that future—a future in which algorithms serve democracy rather than displace it, in which public institutions wield AI with competence and care, and in which citizens can trust the systems that shape their lives. The journey will demand vigilance, imagination, and humility. But if we succeed, we may yet build something remarkable: a state that is not only smarter but wiser.

Chapter 1
The Operating System of the State

The clerk still remembered the sound the files made. Thick cardboard jackets, edges softened by years of handling, stacked on the counter each morning like a small geological formation. Every request—a licence renewal, a housing appeal, a complaint about missed rubbish collections—was a physical object that travelled through the building by hand. Its journey was visible in scrawled initials, rubber stamps, and the dusty trail between offices. When something went missing, there was a room to search. When something felt unjust, there was a person to ask. The system was slow, imperfect, and frequently arbitrary. But it was legible.

Fast forward a generation. The files have disappeared, replaced by a portal. Citizens upload documents, tick boxes, and receive automated updates. Caseworkers log into dashboards where incoming requests are colour-coded and ranked by urgency. Supervisors glimpse performance through metrics rather than conversation. That old cardboard world has been swept aside by a restless digital logic—one that does not merely record decisions but actively shapes them. The new system feels clean, frictionless, modern. Yet the shift is far more than administrative housekeeping. It is a profound change in how power works.

The state's move from paper files to digital platforms is often narrated as a story of convenience or cost-saving. But to treat it that way is to miss the deeper transformation. Digitisation alters the defaults of public life. The layout of a form influences which claims are made. The structure of a workflow determines which cases are prioritised. The design of a portal nudges citizens towards some choices rather than others. Beneath the smooth surface of digital government lies a set of assumptions—encoded in interfaces, databases, and algorithms—that quietly reconfigure the relationship between citizen and state.

This chapter explores that shift: the emergence of the state as an operating system. It examines not just the tools that governments use, but the logic those tools impose. When administrative decisions run through platforms rather than paper, they acquire properties that are easy to overlook: they become routinised, model-driven, and sensitive to the unseen decisions of designers and data engineers. In this environment, every technical choice is a governance choice, whether acknowledged or not.

Consider the deceptively simple act of tax pre-filling. To most people, it is a modern convenience, sparing them the drudgery of inputting figures already known to the revenue authority. Yet pre-filling is also a kind of quiet persuasion. The way the form arrives—complete, tidy, seemingly authoritative—nudges taxpayers to accept the figures rather than scrutinise them. For the revenue service, this increases compliance and reduces errors. For the citizen, it shifts the default from active declaration to passive confirmation. Design encodes priorities. What looks like efficiency is also a subtle rebalancing of initiative.

The same dynamic is visible in the rise of permit portals. Where once residents queued at local offices to seek permission for home alterations or business licences, they now navigate online pathways structured by predefined categories and automated routing rules. A portal may ask for certain documents but not others, or require applicants to select from a limited set of project types, or channel requests with particular keywords to specific teams. The portal appears neutral. But its design determines who gets processed quickly, who is asked for more evidence, and which cases end up languishing in queues. Defaults become power.

Digitisation does not stop at routing and record-keeping. Increasingly, governments are turning to prediction. The appeal is obvious: public services must allocate limited resources under pressure, and prediction promises to see around corners. If a council can identify which families are most at risk of eviction, it can target support earlier. If a police force can anticipate likely hotspots of violence, it can deploy officers where they are most needed. If a health system can predict which patients are likely to return to hospital within days of discharge, it can direct community nurses to avert avoidable readmissions.

But prediction brings its own tensions. A hospital readmission model may flag patients who, statistically, require more follow-up. Used thoughtfully, this may help overworked clinicians intervene before a crisis. Used blindly, it can create path dependency: once categorised as high-risk, a patient may receive disproportionate attention, while others with quieter needs are overlooked. Prediction widens the horizon of possibility, but it also risks narrowing the imagination. When numbers dictate where help flows, the stories that sit behind those numbers can fade.

The rise of prediction raises a deeper question: what makes an administrative decision legitimate? In an age of machine learning, it is tempting to fetishise accuracy as the ultimate measure of success. But accuracy alone cannot determine propriety. A model may predict outcomes with remarkable precision and still be fundamentally unacceptable if it lacks a legal mandate, if citizens cannot understand or challenge its logic, or if its deployment distorts rights or exacerbates inequality. Legitimacy is a richer standard. It requires transparency, contestability, and proportionality. It requires decisions that people can see, question, and resist where necessary.

This tension—between capability and legitimacy—sits at the heart of modern governance. A council might deploy a fraud detection tool that is highly accurate in identifying suspicious benefit claims. But if the tool is shrouded in secrecy, if its risk factors disproportionately target particular groups, or if the appeal process is opaque, the model may corrode trust even as it improves detection rates. The public sector cannot outsource its moral responsibilities to metrics. A system that is accurate but illegitimate is not just flawed. It is dangerous.

That danger is compounded when the human role in automated systems becomes ambiguous. The phrase *human-in-the-loop* suggests oversight and control. But in practice, humans can end up bearing responsibility without wielding real authority. A caseworker may be required to "review" a machine's recommendation, even when the interface makes it nearly impossible to disagree. A supervisor might sign off on benefit sanctions automatically triggered by algorithmic thresholds, despite having little context to meaningfully intervene.

The result is a hollowing out of judgement. Humans become accountable for decisions they did not truly make.

Imagine a benefits office where an automated system assigns sanctions to claimants flagged for alleged non-compliance. The supervisor, overwhelmed by a queue of digital alerts, is expected to approve or reject each sanction within minutes. The default option is "approve," with the system highlighting this choice in reassuring green. The underlying evidence is buried behind several screens. Rejecting a sanction requires justification; approving it requires none. The supervisor becomes the final link in a chain they barely control. If a claimant appeals, the bureaucracy points to the human sign-off; the human points to the model. Responsibility dissolves.

These developments reveal a larger truth: the state, through its digital transformation, has acquired an operating system that few citizens see and fewer understand. That system is not merely a technical layer. It is a constitutional force. It governs how decisions are initiated, processed, and justified. It shapes encounters with the state at every level—from the mundane to the life-altering. And because operating systems are rarely examined unless they break, their influence often escapes democratic debate.

This chapter invites the reader to step inside that hidden architecture. It traces the path from paper files to platforms, showing how digitisation alters defaults and reorders power. It explores the rise of prediction as a public function, examining both the promise and the peril of using algorithms to allocate attention and resources. It argues that legitimacy must anchor every technical choice, and that accuracy, however alluring, cannot substitute for democratic principles. Finally, it interrogates the fraught role of human oversight in automated systems, highlighting the gap between formal responsibility and real control.

Together, these threads reveal a central insight: modern governance is increasingly defined by the systems that route, score, and structure decisions long before any official or politician becomes involved. The question is not whether the state should use digital tools—those debates are over. The question is how these tools can be designed, deployed, and scrutinised so that they reinforce, rather than erode, the foundations of democratic life.

As you move through the chapter, you will encounter moments of innovation and unease, examples of public systems made genuinely better and cases where well-intentioned tools produced unanticipated harm. You will see how design choices shape citizen experience, how predictive logics influence the distribution of care and scrutiny, and how the presence—or absence—of meaningful human oversight determines whether algorithms serve people or ensnare them.

By the final section, one thing will be clear: the operating system of the state is too important to leave to technologists alone. It demands public imagination, political courage, and institutional humility. And it requires a citizenry capable of recognising the quiet power of defaults, models, and interfaces.

Turn the page, then, with that awareness. The machinery of governance is changing. Its code is running. The question is whether we choose to understand it—and shape it—before it shapes us.

From Paper Files to Platforms

On 24 January 1998, at an office of the Inland Revenue in Nottingham, staff began trialling a system that would eventually reshape how millions of people interacted with the British state. It was the early prototype of what became the United Kingdom's online Self Assessment service. For the first time, a tax return did not originate as a paper booklet but as a partially pre-filled digital form, drawing on employment and pension records already held by the government. Clerks who had once sorted envelopes now monitored dashboards. The change sounded mundane. It was anything but. A form that once *asked* for information began instead to *assert* it. One click confirmed, or silently surrendered, the state's view of a citizen's financial life. The cardboard file had given way to the platform.

What happened in Nottingham was mirrored across public administrations worldwide. In 2001, Estonia launched its X-Road infrastructure in Tallinn, enabling data to flow securely between agencies without paper intermediaries. A building permit could be applied for online; a medical prescription travelled electronically; tax returns became almost instant. By 2015, more than 95 per cent of Estonian residents filed taxes digitally. Officials celebrated the efficiency gains. Less discussed was the redistribution of authority occurring beneath the surface: the shift from local discretion to central defaults, from human interpretation to platform logic. This change had a texture — the quiet motif of the pre-filled field — and it altered not just the speed of governance but its shape.

The move from forms and ledgers to digital platforms is often narrated as straightforward progress. Show the old paper archives, name the inevitable digitisation, explain the savings in time and cost, and imply that improvements naturally follow. Yet this story underplays what changes when processes are reimagined as software. A paper form leaves room for narrative. It tolerates scribbles, marginalia, incomplete thoughts. A digital form demands compliance. Its fields require precision, and its pathways assume users will act in ways designers anticipated. When a portal insists a category must be chosen, even if none fits, design becomes a subtle exercise of power.

The Nottingham trial demonstrated this shift vividly. Pre-filled figures suggested authority. Behavioural researchers later observed that taxpayers were significantly less likely to amend pre-populated values, even when given explicit instructions to check them. The implication was clear: what the platform presented as fact gained normative force. This effect was not unique to the UK. In Denmark in 2012, the Skatteministeriet reported that more than 80 per cent of citizens accepted their pre-filled returns without modification. What began as convenience grew into a quiet default shaping fiscal behaviour. The motif returns: the pre-filled field nudges more than it requests.

Permit portals exhibit a parallel evolution. In Helsinki in 2008, the city's Building Control Department launched Lupapiste, an online system that consolidated more than a hundred different paper-based permit processes. Designers intended to simplify procedure. The platform routed applications automatically based on keywords and metadata, grouping them into standardised streams. But the categories embedded in the system began to influence the nature of applications themselves. Builders aligned project descriptions with portal terminology to avoid delays. Complex renovations were reframed as simpler works to fit predefined boxes. Show the applicant navigating requirements, name the digital constraints, explain the alignment behaviour, and see the implication: platforms do not merely *process* choices; they *shape* them.

A credible counter-example exists and must be addressed. Some municipalities deliberately resisted heavy standardisation, fearing that platforms would ossify discretion. In 2014, the city of Freiburg chose to retain mixed channels — paper, email, and online forms — for certain planning approvals. Officials argued that digital pathways risked erasing local nuance and that hybrid systems preserved relational understanding between residents and planners. The Freiburg case does not invalidate the broader pattern; it qualifies it. Where systems are intentionally designed to preserve flexibility, the power of defaults can be moderated. But such decisions are rare and typically require active resistance to the gravitational pull of automation.

Digitisation alters power not through overt instruction but through its quiet command of the ordinary. A paper application sits on a desk until someone reviews it. A digital application enters a queue governed by algorithms that rank urgency, completeness, or predicted workload. A clerk once exercised judgement about which file to pick up next. A platform now executes a routing rule — if the applicant selects "commercial", the case moves to Team B; if the applicant uploads certain documents, the system elevates priority. Every rule reflects a value, and every default channels those values into administrative reality.

Nowhere is this clearer than in the expanding use of predictive triage. Prediction, as a public function, rests on an intuitive appeal: if an agency can foresee where demand will spike or where harm is likely, it can act sooner. The ideal is earlier help rather than belated crisis management. But prediction binds action to its underlying data, and data draws from yesterday more than tomorrow. In January 2019, the New South Wales Health system in Sydney piloted a readmission prediction model across several hospitals to allocate community nursing visits. The model drew on historical discharge patterns and clinical indicators. Patients flagged as high-risk received additional follow-up calls and visits; those flagged as low-risk received fewer. The result was measurable: readmission rates declined modestly (NSW Health Report, 2019). Yet staff reported an unintended effect. Once a patient entered the "high-risk" pathway, the label tended to persist, even when clinical conditions improved. The platform encoded a presumption of fragility, and undoing it required manual override — an action that busy nurses were reluctant to pursue.

Here the motif shifts subtly. Before, the pre-filled field captured attention. Now it is the *persistent flag* — a signal that once set tends to remain. Flags can be sticky. They narrow imagination, making certain options seem inevitable even when circumstances change. The logic of the ledger has been replaced by the logic of the model.

The counter-example emerges from Rotterdam. In 2021, the city suspended its welfare fraud prediction system after academic review highlighted high false-positive rates for young claimants from particular postal codes. Officials concluded that the model's predictions were too entangled with historical enforcement patterns. Unlike the Sydney case, where prediction brought efficiency with manageable risks, Rotterdam illustrated prediction's fragility: when the data reflects structural bias, the model reproduces it. Reconciling these cases reveals a simple truth. Prediction amplifies not only insight but existing patterns of attention. When those patterns are fair and well-understood, prediction helps. When they are opaque or biased, prediction hardens them.

These shifts — pre-filled returns, permit categories, readmission flags — share a powerful commonality. They change the default conditions under which people act. Defaults matter because they require energy to resist. The easier path becomes the chosen path. In a paper-based office, staff had to decide how to route a file. In a platform environment, the decision occurs automatically unless someone intervenes. Intervention becomes exceptional. Exception becomes suspect. And the suspect becomes burdensome.

To understand how deeply this reconfigures governance, imagine a simple metric: the average handling time for a permit application. On paper, delays often reflected staffing shortages or complex cases. On a platform, delays may reflect users being funnelled into narrow categories that trigger time-consuming checks. A portal that prioritises speed may push applicants to supply minimal information; a portal that prioritises thoroughness may invite excessive documentation. In both cases, design inscribes a value choice. The behaviour is visible in timestamps: who submits what, when, and how often. The motif persists: defaults shape movement.

Digitisation also changes institutional memory. Paper archives recorded the messiness of public encounters. Smudged signatures, stapled notes, appended letters — these artefacts held stories. Digital systems strip away this materiality. Information becomes structured, searchable, and extractable. This improves auditing and analysis but can impoverish narrative. When the system requires a checkbox instead of a paragraph, descriptive richness collapses into codified categories. Researchers studying local governments have noted that digitised case histories often omit discretionary context that was once routinely written into margins. This omission is not accidental. Platforms are built for consistency, not texture.

One might argue that platforms can incorporate free text fields or scanned documents and therefore preserve nuance. Technically, yes. But the weight of the system pushes towards structure. Free text is harder to analyse, harder to route, and harder to justify in performance dashboards. Over time, it becomes an exception. What the system measures becomes what the institution values. What it does not measure quietly recedes.

Consider again the Helsinki permit portal. Early user data from 2009 showed that applications containing extensive free text experienced longer processing times. Officials concluded — logically, from their perspective — that complex descriptions slowed workflow, and so encouraged applicants to rely more on predefined categories. This improved throughput but at the cost of nuance. The system preferred the neat case over the messy one. And the messy case shrank accordingly.

The deeper implication is that digital platforms discipline behaviour on both sides of the interface. Citizens learn to present themselves in platform-friendly terms. Officials learn to trust system outputs more readily than their own instincts, partly because the platform provides an audit trail the individual cannot. A clerk who follows a flagged priority decision feels shielded; a clerk who exercises judgement feels exposed. The platform's logic begins to supplant the professional's craft.

A necessary caution follows. Not all digitisation erodes discretion. Singapore's MyInfo system, introduced in 2016, offers a different trajectory. By consolidating personal data across agencies and allowing citizens to manage consent for sharing, it created a platform that reduced redundant paperwork while preserving a degree of individual control. The lesson is not that platforms must centralise power, but that without explicit design choices, they tend to. The default is drift towards automation, standardisation, and tacit acceptance of system-generated truth. Only intentional counter-design shifts the balance.

Across these examples, a final thread emerges. Paper-based government made friction visible. Queues could be seen; delays could be felt; files could be searched; exceptions could be explained. Platforms make friction invisible. A user clicks "submit" and enters a process governed by rules they cannot observe. When something stalls, the cause may lie in a validation script or an automated routing error — both inaccessible to the user. Visibility is replaced by opacity, and opacity reshapes responsibility. The citizen cannot see where their request sits. The official may struggle to see why the system treated it as it did. Accountability blurs.

Yet digitisation is not reversible, nor should it be. The task is to recognise the stakes. Every default is a choice. Every choice carries a priority. And every priority alters the equilibrium between ease and scrutiny, speed and understanding, efficiency and justice.

The cardboard files are gone. The portals remain. The question that lingers is deceptively simple: when a platform fills the field for you, who decides what belongs there?

Prediction as a Public Function

On 3 March 2019, clinicians at Liverpool University Hospitals began reviewing the output of a new readmission risk model used in the Royal Liverpool building. The system, commissioned by NHS England and supplied with five years of hospital episode statistics, generated daily lists of patients predicted to return within thirty days of discharge. Nurses noticed a pattern. Those flagged at "very high risk" received automatic referrals for community nursing visits within forty-eight hours. Others waited. The referrals were not instructions but suggestions. Yet, as one senior nurse later observed, *"once the flag is there, it directs your eye."* A line in a spreadsheet—an artefact of probability—started to decide where scarce care travelled. Five words in the first 400: *The flag changed everything.*

Prediction has always tempted public agencies. Welfare officers want to anticipate hardship before it becomes crisis. Police chiefs seek to deploy patrols before violence breaks out. Hospitals try to identify vulnerable patients before deterioration. The attraction lies in a simple promise: early help saves trouble. Reducing the burden of avoidable harm is a visible behaviour, measured through statistics such as repeat attendance, missed appointments, or emergency admissions. But once predictions inform decisions, the line between anticipation and prescription starts to blur. The motif of *the flag* returns — small, bright, insistent.

Show first, then name what has changed. When Liverpool's nurses redirected care based on model outputs, they enacted a shift from reactive to predictive allocation. Name the principle: prediction transforms public functions from observing need to forecasting it. Explain the mechanism: a model estimates probability based on past cases, distilling years of data into a single number. Implication: priorities move upstream, but they may also become anchored to the patterns of yesterday.

This logic extends well beyond hospitals. In August 2016, Durham Constabulary piloted the Harm Assessment Risk Tool (HART) in the north-east of England. Developed with researchers at the University of Cambridge, HART used data from previous custody records to predict the likelihood that an arrested individual would reoffend violently within two years. The model informed bail and diversion decisions. Officers retained discretion, but the presence of a "high-risk" classification influenced how much supervision they considered appropriate. Predictions altered real behaviour: more frequent checks, tighter conditions, closer monitoring. The metric was visible in workloads, recorded in officer logs.

Policing offers a vivid demonstration of prediction's appeal. Street patrols birthed by intuition become deployments guided by probability scores. Tasking meetings once dominated by anecdote increasingly present heat maps derived from models. Leaders commit resources because predicted harm feels more objective than instinct. Yet this commitment reveals a limitation. When historical arrests reflect targeted enforcement rather than underlying offending patterns, predictions reproduce that targeting. Prediction, when built from uneven histories, risks inheriting their distortions.

A counter-example tests the argument. In 2020 in Glasgow, the Violence Reduction Unit pursued a strategy intentionally sceptical of predictive tools. Rather than relying on risk modelling, it invested in neighbourhood workers and community intelligence. The approach contributed to falling rates of violent assault over the preceding decade. It succeeded without automated flags. This does not undermine the value of prediction; it shows that early intervention can be achieved through relational knowledge rather than algorithms. Reconciliation begins here: prediction is attractive, but not inevitable. It is a method, not a destiny.

The welfare domain shows how prediction steers behaviour. In June 2017, New Zealand's Ministry of Social Development published its Investment Approach reports, detailing actuarial-style predictions of lifetime benefit costs. The analysis named groups of clients predicted to remain on benefits for long periods. Case managers received dashboards highlighting these groups. The intention was benign: earlier support. Yet the behaviour was concrete. Clients flagged as high-cost were offered training or employment programmes ahead of others. Those flags became a quiet motif in conversations, shaping who received proactive calls and who waited. Prediction changed the rhythm of service.

The pattern is familiar. Show the administrative decision, name the model, explain the behaviour it induces, and trace the implication. A welfare officer's caseload is finite. Attention must be rationed. Prediction offers a method of rationing that appears fairer because it is data-driven. But when flags persist, they create path dependency. A person labelled "long-term risk" enters programmes aligned with that label. If circumstances improve, the label lingers. Staff hesitate to de-escalate because the prediction carries institutional authority. Numbers, once assigned, endure.

Return to Liverpool to make the motif vivid. The readmission model assigned scores daily, yet high-risk patients tended to remain high-risk. Nurses reported that the flag, once attached, coloured their expectations. This is the behavioural signature of prediction: it stabilises categories that should be fluid. Metrics meant to prompt attention can freeze it.

The second named example strengthens the picture. In 2014, Kaiser Permanente in California scaled an inpatient risk model known as the LACE Index. Although not an AI tool, it estimated readmission risk using length of stay, acuity, comorbidities, and emergency visits. The model influenced discharge planning and home-visit scheduling across multiple hospitals. Researchers observed a measurable effect: patients above a threshold received an average of one additional follow-up contact. But they also noted a limitation. Patients just below the threshold—often clinically similar—received significantly less attention. The threshold introduced a behavioural cliff. Platforms turn probability into categories, and categories become decisions.

The motif appears again: a flag becomes a gateway.

Prediction's benefits are tangible. In welfare, predictive models can surface households one missed payment away from crisis, directing caseworkers to intervene before eviction. This behaviour can be measured through reduced arrears or fewer emergency grant applications. In policing, predictions allow commanders to schedule patrols informed by patterns of harm rather than anecdote, with implications for patrol density and officer time. In health, predictive triage can reduce readmissions, shorten length of stay, and shift workload into community settings. Each domain has its metric; each metric reflects a real decision.

Yet prediction brings risks. It can narrow organisational imagination. When probabilities feel precise, alternative explanations become harder to see. Staff may commit to the model because deviating requires justification. The quiet motif returns: *once flagged, always flagged.*

A limitation deserves frank attention. Some predictions improve fairness. For instance, Massachusetts General Hospital in Boston developed a heart failure readmission model in 2018 that improved identification of risk for older patients traditionally under-flagged in clinician judgement. Prediction here corrected a bias. Yet other predictions harden disparities. Studies of American crime prediction models in 2016 and 2017 found that arrest-based data amplified pre-existing enforcement patterns in predominantly Black neighbourhoods. This variation matters. Prediction is not good or bad in itself; its validity depends on context.

Reconciliation rests on one principle: prediction amplifies the world it is built from. When historical data reflects equitable service patterns, prediction supports early help. When history is uneven, prediction magnifies the unevenness.

One can see this clearly in the differing trajectories of the UK and Dutch readmission initiatives. A 2020 audit at University College London Hospitals found that its readmission model, which incorporated social and clinical variables, reduced unnecessary bed days when paired with a human review step. Meanwhile, in Rotterdam's suspended welfare prediction system (2021), the absence of robust review led to disproportionate scrutiny for certain postal codes. The behaviour differs because the structure differs. Prediction's impact emerges in the combination of model, data, and governance.

The core dynamic becomes clearer when we examine how prediction reconfigures responsibility. When an officer assigns extra supervision because a tool flagged risk, responsibility appears shared. But if the prediction is wrong, who bears the burden? The officer who acted? The analysts who built the model? The organisation that commissioned it? In Liverpool, when a high-risk patient did not receive a visit in time, staff debated whether the omission was a human oversight or a system misclassification. Prediction complicates accountability by diffusing agency across people and tools.

Yet the pull of prediction persists. It offers governments a narrative of foresight. Officials measure reduced reoffending or fewer emergency admissions and claim success. These are concrete metrics, and they matter. But beneath them sits a more delicate question: *what does the flag hide?* When an agency follows predictions, it may overlook unflagged need. The invisible cases become the cost of optimisation.

This tension animates modern governance. Public agencies must balance two imperatives: act early enough to prevent harm, but avoid locking people into categories defined by past data. Prediction encourages the former while risking the latter. The hospital model reduces readmissions but may entrench assumptions about who is "complex." The policing model improves deployment but may reinforce geographic stereotypes. The welfare model enables early support but may shadow claimants with labels they cannot shake.

Prediction, then, is a public function that changes the tempo of administration. It shifts the moment of action from after an event to before it. It moves attention from what *has* happened to what *might* happen. And it imbues probability with institutional force.

The motif remains with us: a small flag, persistent, bright, whispering direction.

As the use of predictive tools expands, the question that shadows every public agency deepens. When the flag appears, should it guide, or should it be interrogated?

Legitimacy Before Accuracy

At 7:12 a.m. on 13 August 2020, outside Stoke Newington School in London, students gathered with phones in hand as the A-level results released by Ofqual landed in their inboxes. Within minutes, the pattern emerged. High-achieving pupils from historically low-performing schools had seen their grades pushed down by an algorithm designed to maintain national distributions. Individual effort vanished behind statistical smoothing. The model had been tested, calibrated, and—by its designers' account—*accurate* in reproducing past patterns. Yet its authority collapsed in a single day. Accuracy did not save it. The public asked a simpler, sharper question: *was this fair?* Five words in the first 400: *The spreadsheet felt like judgement.*

The scene showed, in stark detail, that legitimacy comes before precision. Name the principle: a public decision must be defensible before it is optimised. Explain why: people accept outcomes they can follow, question, and contest. Implication: when a system fails this test, accuracy becomes irrelevant. The Ofqual algorithm had no meaningful mandate to override teacher judgments; its workings were too opaque for students to understand; its appeal route was narrow; its effects fell hardest on those with least power. The outcry was not about statistical performance. It was about legitimacy.

The motif of *the line* threads through these systems. A line on a chart. A line in a spreadsheet. A line that separates those who benefit from those who lose. Once drawn, the line exerts authority. But who draws it, and under what authority?

A second example deepens the point. In February 2020, the District Court of The Hague struck down the Dutch government's SyRI system, a welfare fraud detection tool used across several municipalities. The ruling is verifiable: case number C/09/550982 / HA ZA 18-388. SyRI combined data from tax, employment, housing, and education sources to generate risk scores for fraud investigations. Technically, it was sophisticated. Legally, it was untenable. Judges found that its opacity prevented citizens from understanding why they were flagged; the law authorising it was too broad; and its impacts disproportionately hit low-income and migrant neighbourhoods. Accuracy of classification was beside the point. The court measured legitimacy instead. The metric was visible in residents' behaviour: increased suspicion, reduced engagement with welfare services, and fear of unseen surveillance.

Show the pattern: both Ofqual and SyRI produced calculable outputs that policymakers trusted. Name the criteria they violated: mandate, transparency, contestability, proportionality. Explain each through behaviour. *Mandate* means an institution commits to lawful authority before deploying a tool—Ofqual exceeded what Parliament expected; SyRI operated under a vague statute that bundled too many powers. *Transparency* demands that affected citizens can understand the basis of decisions—students could not see the weightings applied to their schools; welfare recipients could not see the risk factors SyRI used. *Contestability* requires a path to challenge—appeals for downgraded grades were restricted; SyRI offered no meaningful mechanism to dispute a score. *Proportionality* asks whether the intrusion matches the objective—detecting fraud is legitimate, but subjecting entire neighbourhoods to opaque profiling was judged excessive. Implication: even a well-performing model collapses when it breaches these lines.

A credible counter-example clarifies the boundaries. In 2013, New York City's Department of Buildings piloted a statistical model for prioritising fire safety inspections. The model, built from past inspection data and fire incidents, identified properties that warranted urgent attention. Unlike SyRI or Ofqual, the agency published a plain-language explanation of the system, retained inspector discretion, and allowed building owners to request re-evaluations. The tool did not generate punitive action; it prioritised queues. Its mandate was explicit: reduce inspection backlogs after several fatal fires. Residents could see the goal. Inspectors could override the model. The line remained visible. This does not make the system flawless, but it shows that prediction can support legitimate action when embedded in accountable institutional design.

Reconciliation of these cases requires attention to process, not just outputs. Legitimacy is not a moral flourish added after optimisation. It is the architecture that determines whether optimisation is permissible at all.

To understand why, return to behaviour, not abstraction. Trust is not an idea; it is a pattern of action. When students in London protested, they held signs reading "Judge me, not my postcode," making visible the perceived injustice. When Dutch residents challenged SyRI, community groups reported increased fear of applying for benefits. When New York inspectors used their prioritisation model, they documented in logs when human judgment overruled algorithmic suggestion. These behaviours show legitimacy in motion: protest when it is absent, reluctance when it is brittle, and discretion when it is preserved.

The motif of *the line* returns. Each system drew a line that allocated opportunity, scrutiny, or resources. The question is whether the line was drawn with democratic authority.

The Ofqual case reveals how fragile legitimacy becomes when public institutions treat accuracy as sufficient. The model was designed to correct grade inflation caused by cancelled examinations. It compared cohorts, weighted school histories, and made fine-grained adjustments within subjects. But its very design contradicted reasonable expectations. Students commit to years of work expecting individual assessment. A model that judged them through historical school averages broke that expectation. The implication is clear: the criteria of legitimacy serve as guardrails against designs that, though clever, misalign with public values.

The Dutch SyRI ruling demonstrates another dimension: proportionality is not an abstract legal standard. It materialises in concrete intrusions. SyRI pooled data from multiple sources and allowed risk scoring across whole districts. Residents could not see what triggered scrutiny, nor correct errors. The intrusion was collective, not tailored. Judges compared the breadth of data used with the limited evidence of benefit. The imbalance was decisive. Proportionality failed where a narrower, targeted system might have passed.

A further example from the United States illustrates a different pathology. The COMPAS risk assessment tool, widely used in sentencing decisions across several states since 2012, became the focus of public scrutiny after a 2016 ProPublica investigation alleged racial bias in predicted recidivism. What matters here is not the mathematical controversy—scholars debated definitions of fairness—but the legitimacy gap. Judges in Broward County, Florida, encountered defendants unable to challenge the factors underpinning their risk scores because the model was proprietary. The behaviour was visible in court transcripts: defence lawyers asking for explanations they could not obtain; judges noting they had limited insight into model logic. The implication reinforces the motif: a line drawn without explanation cannot command legitimacy, even if statistically consistent.

A counter-example to COMPAS exists. In 2018, the Public Safety Assessment (PSA), adopted in New Jersey, published its risk factors and weightings openly. Judges retained discretion and had explicit guidelines for when to override recommendations. An independent evaluation commissioned by the New Jersey Courts (2019) found increased pre-trial release without a rise in failures to appear. The system respected mandate, transparency, contestability, and proportionality. It was not free from criticism, but it demonstrated that legitimacy is feasible when design aligns with public obligations.

What unifies these cases is not accuracy but authority. A system with high precision but weak mandate feels imposed. A system with full transparency but disproportionate impact feels intrusive. A system with an appeal pathway but inscrutable outcomes feels hollow. Legitimacy relies on all criteria, not one.

A deeper implication emerges when we examine how officials behave under different legitimacy conditions. When legitimacy is strong, staff commit deliberately. They explain decisions to citizens. They document overrides. They adjust processes based on feedback. When legitimacy is weak, staff hide behind the model. They attribute decisions to the "system." They avoid discretionary judgment for fear of scrutiny. The shift in behaviour is measurable: in logs, in appeal rates, in complaint patterns.

The motif of *the line* appears again in these behaviours. A clear line guides. A hidden line blinds.

Proportionality deserves a closer look, because it captures the ethical hinge of automated public authority. A city may use predictive policing to prioritise patrols, but deploying officers solely based on predicted crime without community consultation risks intensifying distrust. A health agency may use a readmission model to allocate community nurses, but using that same model to assess benefit eligibility would be wildly disproportionate. Proportionality asks a simple question: is the level of intrusion justified by the objective, and is a less intrusive alternative possible? The answer is visible in outcomes. If intrusive data use yields marginal benefits, legitimacy erodes.

Transparency, too, must be understood behaviourally. Publishing weightings is not enough. Citizens need explanations they can actually use. In 2020, the city of Amsterdam published an "algorithm register" detailing active municipal models. Residents could read the purpose, data sources, and risk mitigations. This increased public awareness and led to tangible changes: one system for parking violations was paused after residents questioned its disproportionate fines in certain districts. The metric that mattered was citizen response. Transparency earned influence because it enabled contestability.

Mandate is similarly concrete. A parliamentary vote authorising data-sharing is a visible act. A ministerial directive buried in internal documents is not. Where mandate is ambiguous, legitimacy weakens. Ofqual's algorithm faltered partly because no democratic institution had clearly endorsed replacing exam scripts with statistical inference. Teachers sensed the gap. Parents sensed it too.

Contestability—the ability to challenge a decision—must be more than an email address. It must be a process that officials take seriously. In New Jersey's PSA, override documentation was reviewed regularly by senior judges. This prevented drift. In the Netherlands, SyRI offered no comparable mechanism. Citizens could not know whether they had been flagged. The absence of visibility made contestation impossible.

Thread the motif of *the line* once more. A legitimate system draws its line in daylight.

The examples point to a central truth: accuracy is an internal metric. Legitimacy is a public one. Accuracy measures model fit; legitimacy measures institutional fit. Accuracy evaluates correlation; legitimacy evaluates justification. Accuracy answers "does this work?" Legitimacy asks "is this allowed?" The questions differ. Their stakes differ too.

As governments adopt predictive tools, the temptation to optimise first and justify later strengthens. But optimisation without legitimacy damages both. When a model's outputs are rejected by the public, accuracy becomes irrelevant. When a model is dismantled due to legal or moral objections, any precision achieved evaporates. Legitimacy is not a luxury. It is the precondition for durability.

The tension that remains is unavoidable. Models can be accurate yet still violate basic expectations of fairness. Mandates can be clear yet fail to earn public confidence. Transparency can reveal complexity citizens find alienating. Contestability can become performative if appeals rarely succeed. Proportionality can collide with political pressure to act decisively. The line must be drawn somewhere.

The unresolved question lingers: when accuracy rises but legitimacy falters, which should prevail, and who decides where that line lies?

Human-in-the-Loop, or Human-on-the-Hook?

On 14 February 2018, at the Department for Work and Pensions office in Manchester's Albert Bridge House, a routine audit uncovered an anomaly. A benefits supervisor had approved 217 sanction decisions in a single week—an impossible workload if each case had been reviewed meaningfully. The pattern traced back to a new triage tool that flagged "likely non-compliance" among claimants, generating pre-filled sanction recommendations. Supervisors were asked to confirm outcomes with a click. Most did. Later interviews with staff revealed the same phrase repeated in different words: *"the system already decided."* A human was in the loop, technically. In practice, that human was on the hook. Five words appear early: *The click carried judgment.*

The scene exposes a profound tension in modern governance. Public agencies increasingly rely on systems that pre-process, pre-rank, and pre-judge. Oversight roles, once grounded in deliberation, risk drifting into ceremonial assent. The motif that threads through this section is *the signature*: a seemingly simple mark of human authority that may mask a hollowing of actual judgement.

Show the dynamic. A supervisor receives a list of recommended sanctions, each tagged with a risk score derived from past behaviour, missed appointments, or incomplete documentation. Name the role: oversight. Explain its intention: ensure fairness by inserting human evaluation before an adverse decision. Implication: if oversight collapses into rubber-stamping, the ethical scaffolding around automated judgement dissolves.

The Manchester audit was not unique. In October 2019, the French Cour des comptes examined CAF, the social benefits administration, and found that algorithms used to detect "atypical" claims produced alerts far faster than staff could reasonably assess. Employees processed these alerts in bulk, prioritising speed over scrutiny. The behaviour was measurable: approval times dropped, while the variance in approval-to-appeal ratios increased sharply across departments. Oversight became procedural rather than substantive. The signature persisted, but its meaning changed.

A counter-example sharpens the contrast. In 2018, the Western Australia Police Force introduced a Decision Support System for firearm licence renewals. Unlike the sanctioning tools in Manchester or Paris, the system required officers to document specific reasons when disagreeing with or accepting automated recommendations. This behaviour—documenting the grounds of agreement—forced engagement. Officers committed to decisions because they had to supply narrative justification. The motif of *the signature* carried weight again: a signature tied to reasoning, not mere confirmation.

Reconciliation emerges through attention to design. Systems that treat the human as a reviewer of already-determined outcomes push judgement out of reach. Systems that require explicit reasons to follow or reject a suggestion draw judgement back in.

The modern administrative environment places significant pressure on discretion. Public bodies measure processing times, error rates, and throughput. Staff feel this pressure. When a tool presents a recommendation, deviating carries cost. In the UK's Universal Credit service, internal guidelines published in February 2021 emphasised consistent application of sanction rules, unintentionally reinforcing the gravitational pull of automated suggestions. The visible behaviour: staff clicked "approve" because approving maintained consistency metrics; challenging required navigation through multiple screens and time-consuming justification. The line between oversight and compliance blurred.

Show how this dynamic works. Name the concept: *automation bias*. Explain it through behaviour: a caseworker confronted with a neatly generated score perceives it as authoritative, even when trained to question it. Implication: oversight becomes performative; judgement atrophies.

The motif returns: *the signature* that confirms without evaluating.

A short scenario illustrates the stakes. A claimant named Ms Patel misses a job centre appointment due to a hospital visit. The triage tool records a non-attendance and generates a sanction recommendation. The system flags her case as medium-risk based solely on prior missed appointments, not on the context. Her supervisor sees the recommendation on a dashboard populated with dozens of similar cases. She must decide quickly. The default button—green, prominent—reads "Confirm sanction." To challenge it, she must open three additional screens, check logs, and type a justification. Under pressure, she confirms. Later, when Ms Patel appeals and wins, the supervisor is told she is accountable. She carried the signature. She did not carry the discretion.

Two further examples reveal the institutional stakes. In 2016, the Los Angeles County Department of Children and Family Services piloted the AURA risk tool to guide social worker investigations. Workers were encouraged to use the model as an advisory aid. Yet ethnographic observations documented by the University of Southern California showed that some staff interpreted high scores as de facto instructions, especially during periods of staff shortage.

The metric that revealed the drift: high-risk scores correlated with more intrusive investigations, regardless of narrative context. The signature of the social worker appeared on files, but the logic of the model drove the action.

Contrast this with the approach taken by the Danish Health Data Authority in 2020 during its trial of a hospital-acquired infection prediction model. Clinicians were shown risk scores alongside uncertainty intervals and were asked to record whether they agreed, disagreed, or reserved judgement. The behaviour was concrete. Disagreement required explanation, but agreement also required a note. This symmetry countered automation bias. Staff did not feel compelled to treat the score as truth. The signature regained balance.

The question, then, is not whether humans appear in the loop, but whether they occupy meaningful roles within it. Oversight involves more than a final click. It demands the power to interrogate, modify, and reject. It requires time to think and evidence to review. It thrives when institutions measure careful decisions rather than rapid throughput.

Veto power clarifies the distinction. A human with veto has authority to block an automated recommendation without penalty. A human-on-the-hook, by contrast, carries responsibility without influence. The visible behaviour that signals veto: staff use it. They disagree, record reasons, seek additional information, and escalate uncertain cases. The behaviour that signals being on the hook: staff rarely reject, justify conformity, and attribute errors to "the system."

Responsibility is where these roles converge and diverge. Public bodies often assert that humans remain responsible for outcomes, even when systems heavily structure their actions. This position appeared in the 2020 Austrian Administrative Court decision regarding the AMS Algorithm, which supported employment service caseworkers. The court emphasised that automated decision-making was unlawful without meaningful human involvement. Yet caseworkers interviewed in Vienna noted they felt constrained by system rankings because deviating invited scrutiny. Responsibility existed in paperwork; authority did not.

One might argue that rigorous oversight is unrealistic under time constraints. Staff are overworked. Systems accelerate tasks. Efficiency matters. A limitation must be acknowledged: expecting every caseworker to interrogate every model recommendation deeply is impractical. But reconciliation lies in institutional design. Oversight can be meaningful when systems support, rather than rush, judgement. Denmark's infection model showed that requiring minimal but substantive engagement—two sentences of explanation—was feasible and effective. Manchester's sanctioning workflow demonstrated the opposite: design that short-circuits review undermines human agency.

The motif reappears—*the signature*—and with it a question: what does a signature mean when it follows a machine?

Accountability structures must reflect this meaning. When errors occur, supervisors often face disciplinary consequences, as happened in the Manchester case. Yet those supervisors operate within workflows that steer behaviour. Internal investigations observed that 92 per cent of sanction approvals in the examined week were completed in under ten seconds. This metric did not indicate negligence; it indicated design. A ten-second signature is not oversight. It is choreography.

Behavioural cues can detect whether humans hold real authority. If overrides are vanishingly rare, the system—not the human—makes the decisions. If overrides cluster only in trivial cases, discretion is symbolic. If overrides come with punitive administrative load, staff will avoid them. These cues are better diagnostics of human agency than policy statements asserting "human control."

Consider another example: the city of Amsterdam's 2020 development permit platform. Planners reviewing automated zoning checks were required to annotate discrepancies. The system tracked disagreement rates and fed insights back into rule refinement. The behaviour was measurable: disagreement ranged from 8 to 15 per cent across districts. These figures revealed active judgement. Supervisors were genuinely in the loop.

Contrast that with the Australian Department of Human Services' automated debt recovery programme in 2016. Staff were nominally responsible for confirming debts generated through income averaging. In practice, confirmation became a formality. The vast majority of notices were issued without substantive human review. Parliamentary inquiries documented staff pressure to meet output quotas. The signature was reduced to a procedural keystroke. Here, humans were fully on the hook and barely in the loop.

These examples converge on a broader truth. Systems that accelerate decision-making by collapsing discretion risk transforming human oversight into an alibi. Systems that slow decision-making by requiring explanation encourage genuine responsibility. The difference is in the design of interaction: default-to-approve versus default-to-explain.

The motif of *the signature* appears a final time. A signature authenticates authority only when it reflects judgement.

The unresolved tension lingers. As predictive tools accelerate administrative processes, how can institutions ensure that the human signature remains a mark of decision rather than a trace of compliance?

Chapter 2
Data is Destiny

The child's school report arrived with the usual mixture of hope and apprehension, but what struck the headteacher at a primary school in South London in 2021 was not the grades themselves. It was the spreadsheet that accompanied them. Each pupil's academic scores sat beside indicators drawn from social care, attendance, and even local mobility data. The borough had launched a pilot linking education and social service records to identify children most at risk of falling behind after the pandemic. On paper, it made sense: combine what the state already knows to target tutoring budgets where they would matter most. Yet as the headteacher reviewed the list, she hesitated. The algorithm had marked one quiet boy as a high priority because of a recent housing displacement flagged in social care files. She agreed he needed support, but she found herself unsettled by the sensation of being nudged by a dataset she had never seen assembled in this way. What counted was not simply the data. It was the decision that data quietly steered.

We like to think of public decisions as shaped by laws, policies, or ethical principles. Increasingly, they are shaped by data flows that cross organisational boundaries and carve the map of administrative action. These flows form ecologies—dense, interconnected, often fragile. When tax records meet health histories, or school attendance bumps up against mobility traces, the state acquires new lenses through which to view its citizens. Some lenses reveal previously unseen need. Others blur the world into categories that stick. If the first chapter explored how platforms organise decisions, this chapter turns to the raw material those platforms depend on. It asks how data becomes destiny.

Modern governance rests on a simple but profound truth: what the state measures, it comes to value. And what it values, it eventually governs. This is not merely a technical observation about spreadsheets. It is a political fact. For a century, governments have collected information to administer welfare, police cities, manage health systems, and plan infrastructure. But the logic of measurement is shifting. The administrative ledgers of the twentieth century produced snapshots. The datasets of the twenty-first produce moving pictures—granular, linkable, and increasingly predictive. The temptation is to believe that more data reveals more truth. Yet data also imposes meaning. The categories chosen, the proxies adopted, the contexts stripped away: each decision shapes the contours of public life.

The motif that threads through this chapter is *the map*: the administrative map that the state draws from the fragments of our recorded lives. Maps illuminate; maps distort. Their power lies not only in what they capture but in what they omit. And because digital maps update in real time, the omissions often matter more than the pixels displayed.

Take the intertwined ecologies of tax, health, education, and mobility data. Each system was built for its own purpose, governed by its own legislation, and designed with its own constraints. When these systems remain separate, they reflect the silos of government. When linked, they reveal patterns previously hidden. A health authority may target chronic illness programmes based on tax-band data that signals deprivation. An education department may use mobility traces from transport passes to understand attendance patterns. A council may match school performance with social care involvement to anticipate safeguarding needs. The gains can be substantial. Linkage can prevent crisis, save money, and allocate resources more rationally.

But the losses—privacy, context, autonomy—accumulate slowly, often unnoticed. When mobility data collected for transit planning is used during emergencies, as happened in Milan during the 2020 lockdowns, the pivot may be justified, even necessary, but it shifts the boundary of public purpose. Citizens who tap in at a train gate seldom imagine their journeys feeding epidemiological models. And when school and social care records merge, the walls around intimate family details become porous. The question becomes not only *whether* the data is accurate, but *whether its reuse is legitimate*. Administrative maps, once drawn, are difficult to erase.

Measurement deepens this tension. The state rarely measures the world directly. It measures proxies—crime counts rather than harm, attendance rather than learning, appointments rather than wellbeing. These proxies become policy. Crime counts reward officers for recording incidents, even if they represent minor disputes. Harm indices encourage police to focus on serious violence, but in doing so may neglect communities where minor offences accumulate into real insecurity. The choice of metric shapes behaviour. Patrol routes change. Case workloads shift. Funding moves. The proxy becomes the driver.

A recurring example illustrates the point. When New York City adopted CompStat in 1994, crime metrics fell sharply. But scholars later documented that officers adjusted behaviour to meet performance targets: discouraging formal reports for minor crimes, reclassifying incidents, focusing patrol density where metrics were easiest to influence. The proxy bent reality. By contrast, when Glasgow's Violence Reduction Unit invested in community engagement and adopted a harm-focused model from 2005 onward, officers were encouraged to prioritise prevention, not just recording. The proxy changed, and so did the behaviour. Measurement became policy—and policy changed the map.

Bias enters these maps not as a moral failing but as a structural fact. A dataset can be clean and still incomplete. A model can be accurate and still unfair. Bias takes many forms. Sampling bias arises when the data collected reflects only the groups most visible to the state. Label bias emerges when the categories recorded oversimplify complex events. Deployment bias occurs when a model is used in a context that differs from the one on which it was trained. These distinctions matter, because each produces a different pattern of distortion on the administrative map.

Imagine a health dataset that records attendance at emergency departments. Frequent attenders may appear high-risk, but they may also be individuals lacking access to primary care. A welfare dataset may record job-search activity, but it does not measure the quality of applications. A policing dataset may count arrests, but arrests reflect enforcement, not necessarily crime. Fair inputs can lead to unfair outputs when the context shifts, when the model migrates, or when the institutional incentives push staff to behave differently under new rules. Monitoring plans—regular audits, drift detection, and data quality checks—exist to spot these shifts. But monitoring itself relies on measurement, and measurement shapes behaviour. The map redrafts itself.

Balancing these complexities are questions of data rights and public purpose. Consent remains a cornerstone of data protection, but administrative systems struggle to obtain meaningful consent when services are essential. A citizen cannot bargain over data-sharing when access to housing benefits or urgent healthcare depends on participation. Public interest tests therefore fill the gap, setting standards for when reuse is justified. A good test asks: does this use align with the original purpose? Does it expose individuals to new risks? Can the same benefit be achieved with less invasive data? Data trusts—structures that give communities a say in how shared data is governed—offer one route forward, though their effectiveness varies. They promise collective stewardship in place of individual consent.

The example of mobility data during emergencies is instructive. In early 2020, cities like Milan and London used aggregated transport data to monitor compliance with movement restrictions. The reuse was arguably justified by the urgency of the crisis. Yet the emergency created a precedent: data gathered for planning acquired a second life. Once an administrative map expands, shrinking it becomes politically and technically difficult. Citizens may accept one use, only to find that acceptance interpreted as acquiescence to another.

These stories reveal a common thread: data constructs the stage on which public decision-making unfolds. It defines what problems appear urgent, which groups become visible, and which remain hidden. It determines where attention flows. It shapes the boundaries of care and enforcement. Data is not destiny in a fatalistic sense. But it is destiny in a structural one. The datasets that governments assemble today will set the limits of what they can imagine tomorrow.

The richness of this terrain emerges slowly as the chapter unfolds. We will explore the ecology of administrative data, showing how linkages can illuminate lives while also exposing them; how proxies chosen for convenience influence outcomes for years; how bias migrates from sampling to systems; how rights and public purpose must adapt to a world where data flows freely across institutional lines.

Yet even these themes lead back to the motif of *the map*. Administrative data draws a map of society, and institutions navigate by its lines. The danger is not that the map will be wrong, though it often is. The danger is that the map will be treated as the territory, flattening the world into the shapes it is easiest to measure.

As the state grows more data-driven, a question rises with increasing urgency: who draws the map, who reads it, and who gets to decide when it is redrawn? The chapters ahead expand this question, but its tension already shadows the path forward.

Administrative Data Ecologies

On 15 March 2021, the London Borough of Southwark began analysing a dataset that had never existed in quite this form before. Education officials had linked Key Stage 2 attainment scores from 2019 with children's social care flags, council tax arrears, and anonymised mobility indicators derived from Oyster card tap-ins. The goal was precise: identify which pupils were likely to have fallen furthest behind during the pandemic and direct tutoring money accordingly. Within hours, patterns emerged. Some children who rarely triggered concern in school surfaced in red because their families had moved repeatedly; others with solid grades appeared amber due to sporadic attendance captured in transport data. The model performed as designed, yet the headteachers examining the list found themselves grappling with a deeper unease: their understanding of a child's needs was subtly reordered by data they had never previously seen combined. The spreadsheet did not merely inform; it reframed. Five words appear early: *The map felt altered.*

Administrative data ecologies grow from moments like this—when datasets collected for distinct purposes begin to converge. Show the shift: a school, a social care team, and a transport authority each hold a fragment of a child's story. Name the phenomenon: linkage.

Explain its power: disparate records can be woven into a composite map that reveals patterns no single dataset could show. Implication: organisations see further, act earlier, and, sometimes, overreach without meaning to. The motif threading through this chapter is *the map*—a map drawn not with ink but with variables, identifiers, and joins.

Tax records offer one of the longest-running examples of administrative mapping. HM Revenue & Customs in the UK, like the IRS in the United States, has accumulated decades of earnings, address histories, and employment profiles. When these records remain siloed, they function as neutral ledgers. But once connected with health utilisation or neighbourhood-level deprivation indices, they begin to shape public policy. In 2015, HMRC participated in a joint analysis with the Department of Health in England to understand correlations between income instability and emergency admissions. The study identified wards where volatile earnings aligned with spikes in unplanned care. The behaviour that followed was visible: Clinical Commissioning Groups increased funding for community mental health teams in precisely those areas. The tax-health linkage shifted resource allocation.

A second example reinforces the point. The Danish Ministry of Finance, working with national researchers, integrated education, income, and registry health data in 2018 to examine the long-term effects of early childhood interventions across municipalities. The linkage revealed that children who received additional language support at age four experienced improved outcomes in adult income and reduced reliance on unemployment insurance. The map illuminated patterns that previously lay hidden across ministry lines. Policymakers committed funds to replicate the most effective programmes.

The gains were real. So were the losses. Privacy, once protected by bureaucratic separation, became vulnerable in the face of technical ease. When datasets interlock, boundaries meant to protect the individual can blur. The Southwark case illustrates how data collected for schooling and transport gained new meaning when reassembled. A headteacher who knew a child's learning needs suddenly encountered mobility data implying instability at home.

The information was not inaccurate, but its reuse shifted the balance of context.

A counter-example challenges the assumption that linkage is always beneficial. In 2019, the Norwegian Data Protection Authority halted a proposal to integrate tax, health, and educational data for a national analytics platform, citing insufficient justification for cross-sector linkage. Officials argued that the model risked exposing sensitive categories without clear public purpose. The limitation teaches an important lesson: linkage without necessity erodes legitimacy. Reconcile this with the earlier examples by returning to the motif: a map must serve its purpose. When the purpose is vague, the map becomes intrusive.

Administrative ecologies grow by accretion. Tax systems capture income flows. Health systems document diagnoses, prescriptions, and admissions. Education systems store attainment, absences, and interventions. Mobility systems track journeys and frequencies. Each dataset mirrors a small system of life. But when these datasets are combined, the system enlarges. The state sees not only income or illness or schooling but a composite behavioural pattern. This expansion brings new administrative capacity—and new administrative risk.

Show the benefit. Name the category. Explain the dynamic. Implication follows. Linkage in health can predict chronic conditions earlier. In 2020, NHS Digital's integration of primary care and hospital episode data enabled earlier identification of patients at risk of complications from diabetes, prompting proactive outreach that markedly reduced emergency admissions in several Clinical Commissioning Groups. The visible behaviour: care teams initiated reviews weeks sooner than they otherwise would have. The map guided intervention.

Education–social care linkage can surface safeguarding concerns. In 2017, Leeds City Council connected persistent absence records with flagged social care cases to triage which families needed early help. The result: referrals became timelier, and unnecessary investigations dropped. The efficiency gain came not from speed alone but from precision guided by linkage.

Now the costs. A map simplifies. It collapses nuance into categories. It invites interpretation without conversation. In the Southwark tutoring example, children living in temporary accommodation appeared automatically high priority due to mobility flags, even when their teachers believed they were coping well academically. The behavioural implication was predictable: funding allocation leaned toward the data signal rather than professional judgement. A map, once drawn, exerts power even over those who know its limitations.

Privacy loss emerges through three mechanisms: breadth, persistence, and inference. Breadth arises when datasets expand beyond their original purpose. Persistence arises when data remains in circulation longer than the events it describes. Inference arises when linked variables reveal new attributes never explicitly collected. Mobility data is particularly sensitive in this regard. In Milan during the early months of 2020, anonymised metro data was repurposed to track reductions in movement during lockdown. Though aggregated, the data's patterns hinted at socio-economic gradients: some neighbourhoods reduced movement sharply; others, dependent on in-person work, did not. The map disclosed inequity without naming names. But even without names, inference reshaped policy.

The motif returns: *the map is powerful because it simplifies.* That simplification can be insight or imposition.

To understand administrative ecologies, we must see how datasets influence each other. Mobility patterns alter assumptions in health risk models. Income histories change interpretations of educational gaps. Household composition data reframes casework decisions. When datasets interlock, causation and correlation intertwine. A child's low attendance score may be driven by long commutes recorded in mobility data; a model may treat attendance as a behavioural issue, not a structural one. The ecology is fragile because context is easily lost.

Pair each abstraction with behaviour. Trust surfaces when parents agree to share school data because they believe it will help their children. Its erosion is visible when they withdraw consent after discovering the data feeds into systems they did not expect.

Efficiency is visible in reduced administrative load when caseworkers access integrated dashboards. Risk manifests when a dataset collected for benign reasons ends up used punitively, as happened in Chicago's 2016 "heat list" policing initiative, where individuals identified as potential shooting victims later reported feeling criminalised by increased attention. Though Chicago relied on arrest histories, not the tax or school ecologies described here, the lesson travels: a map's expansion can shift purpose in ways users do not anticipate.

A limitation must be acknowledged: not all linkage produces better decisions. Sometimes siloed data protects against overreach. In 2014, the German Federal Commissioner for Data Protection criticised a proposal to link school performance data with youth welfare records, arguing that granular educational data lacked the reliability necessary for statutory interventions. This caution reveals an important counterweight: linkage is only as strong as the weakest dataset. Combining incomplete or noisy data can amplify error.

Reconciliation lies in design. Administrative data ecologies require governance that recognises interdependence without collapsing boundaries. When Southwark linked education and social care data for tutoring allocation, officials added a qualitative review step, allowing headteachers to confirm or challenge model outputs. This restored balance. It reinserted the human into the mapmaking process.

The map motif recurs again: each join redraws a boundary. The question is who controls the pen.

As the administrative state becomes more data-rich, the stakes rise. When tax records, health histories, school scores, and movement patterns combine, the composite map reveals deep truths about inequality, vulnerability, resilience, and behaviour. Governments can use these insights to design more compassionate policy or more intrusive oversight. The difference hinges on governance: clear public purpose, proportionate scope, and meaningful transparency.

Administrative data ecologies are not inherently virtuous or harmful. They are infrastructures—powerful, pliable, and political. Their value lies in what they illuminate. Their danger lies in what they obscure. And because these ecologies grow through reuse rather than new collection, their expansion often escapes public notice. Citizens rarely know which parts of their lives contribute to which decisions.

The map expands. The map simplifies. The map guides.

The unresolved tension persists: as datasets converge, how should institutions decide which links illuminate need and which merely expose lives?

Measurement as Policy

On 12 April 1994, at One Police Plaza in New York City, senior commanders gathered as analysts from the newly formed CompStat unit projected crime numbers onto a screen. The data were precise: robbery down 6 per cent in Brooklyn South; burglary up 4 per cent in Staten Island. The numbers were not mere statistics. Within weeks, patrol patterns changed, supervisors were reassigned, and precinct commanders were summoned for intense questioning. What got measured became what got managed, and what got managed became what officers shaped their behaviour to influence. A single metric—crime counts—reorganised one of the world's largest police forces. Five words arrive early: *The numbers drove action.*

The scene captures a truth that extends well beyond policing. Measurement is never passive. It does not simply describe the world; it reshapes it. Name the principle: proxies become policy. Explain the mechanism: selecting a metric creates incentives, and incentives channel behaviour. The implication is structural: once a proxy enters an administrative system, it becomes a quiet governing force—an unseen hand on the tiller. The motif that threads through this chapter is *the indicator*: a small, tidy number that bends institutions around itself.

Crime counts offer the clearest demonstration. Show the shift. Name the metric. Explain the result. In New York, the CompStat model rewarded precincts for reducing the number of recorded incidents. Officers knew this. Scholars and internal investigations later documented behaviours aligned with the target: downgrading felonies to misdemeanours, discouraging formal reporting of minor offences, and increasing patrol presence in areas where reductions were easiest to achieve. The indicator shaped reality. The motive was not corruption but alignment with a system that equated "success" with fewer logged crimes.

A second example underscores the power of proxy choice. In 2015, the Greater Manchester Police piloted a "harm index" inspired by the Cambridge Crime Harm Index. Instead of counting incidents, it weighted crimes based on their sentencing tariff. A violent assault counted far more than a shoplifting. Officers committed to the new measure because it better captured the severity of harm suffered by victims. The behaviour that followed was visible in deployment logs: patrols concentrated in areas with patterns of serious violence rather than zones producing high volumes of minor incidents. The indicator shifted policing from quantity to severity.

The contrast is stark. Two metrics—crime count and crime harm—produce different worlds. The first encourages reductions in recorded incidents; the second encourages prevention of serious injury. The indicator acts as a compass. It determines where effort flows.

A credible counter-example offers nuance. In 2021, Police Scotland resisted adopting a national harm index, arguing that local contexts varied too widely for a uniform metric and that recording practices needed improvement before any weighting system could be introduced. This hesitation was not obstinacy but prudence. Measurement without solid foundations risks misleading decision-makers. Reconciling this with the earlier examples reveals a truth: the value of an indicator depends on its interpretability and trustworthiness. A flawed measure distorts more than it reveals.

Measurement extends far beyond policing. Education systems rely on attendance rates and test scores. Health systems monitor appointment wait times, readmission rates, and mortality ratios. Welfare agencies track job-search activity, sanction rates, and benefit durations. Each of these numbers, once embedded in performance frameworks, becomes a surrogate for success. And each, predictably, shapes the behaviour of those subject to them.

Consider attendance metrics in schools. In 2019, Ofsted in England emphasised persistent absenteeism as a key indicator. Headteachers reported increased pressure to follow rigid escalation pathways, even when underlying circumstances were nuanced. The behaviour was concrete: home visits increased, parental fines rose, and discretionary judgement narrowed. The indicator overshadowed context.

Or take the 18-week referral-to-treatment target introduced by NHS England in 2008. The goal was commendable—reduce waiting times. Yet hospitals facing resource constraints sometimes "paused" waiting lists using technical rules that excluded certain delays from measurement. The proxy was achieved; the patient experience did not always improve. The indicator became the outcome.

This dynamic—measurement turning into management—has its roots in a familiar tension. Public institutions strive to make the intangible tangible. Harm becomes numbers. Learning becomes scores. Health becomes wait times. Poverty becomes earnings bands. Proxies are necessary; they allow systems to compare, allocate, and evaluate. But proxies are also dangerous. They simplify. They compress. And, most critically, they attract attention like gravity. Staff do what the indicator rewards.

The motif of *the indicator* returns. A number that seems small becomes a fulcrum.

Show how this plays out in welfare. In 2012, Australia's Job Services Australia used "star ratings" to evaluate providers based on job placements. Providers quickly adapted their behaviour, prioritising clients easiest to place—typically those with fewer barriers—while offering slower, less intensive support to others. The metric incentivised "cream skimming." The behavioural signature was measurable: disproportionate placement rates for jobseekers with higher educational attainment. Indicators drive priorities.

A counterweight comes from social care. In 2017, Leeds City Council shifted its performance focus from raw referral numbers to family outcomes, using a composite measure that tracked stability, school engagement, and child wellbeing. The behaviour changed. Staff spent more time on sustained support rather than short-term closure of cases. The indicator shaped culture, this time for the better.

Yet even careful design cannot eliminate the fundamental paradox. Measurement must simplify, or it cannot function. But simplification always loses something essential. Crime counts ignore psychological harm. Harm indices miss community perceptions. Attendance metrics obscure the reasons behind absences. Health wait times do not capture quality of care. Welfare placement rates do not reflect job security. The indicator never contains the whole story. And institutions act as though it does.

That tension deepens when proxies become targets in algorithmic systems. Predictive models trained on crime counts treat recorded incidents as truth, even when they reflect enforcement intensity rather than underlying offending. Models built on health readmissions assume hospitals are responsible for factors often outside clinical control. Models trained on school absence interpret mobility constraints as parental neglect. The indicator seeps into the model, and the model amplifies the indicator. The distortions compound.

Bias enters here not through malice but through metrics. If the indicator used to train a model reflects structural inequality, the model will learn inequality with mathematical fidelity. This is why the choice between crime counts and harm indices is not merely a technical matter but a moral one. The indicator shapes the system. The system shapes the data. And the data shapes the next generation of indicators.

The motif flickers again: *the indicator is a mirror*, but one that reflects selectively.

To illustrate this dynamic more plainly, return to New York. After CompStat's introduction, felony complaint numbers fell sharply. But subsequent analyses found that victim surveys did not always align with those reductions, suggesting underreporting. Officers adapted behaviour to meet the measures, and the measure shaped public perception of safety. The indicator became reality.

Now contrast this with Greater Manchester's harm index. While officers embraced the new weighting, the index also introduced a limitation. Serious crimes became disproportionately visible, but lower-level offences that accumulate into chronic insecurity could fade from view. A measure that captures severity may miss persistence. The indicator reveals one pattern but hides another.

Reconciling these requires a clear principle: every proxy highlights something and shadows something else. The task is to know which shadows matter.

Measurement is policy because numbers structure power. When a police chief reviews weekly harm indices, when a hospital reviews performance dashboards, when a school reviews attendance rates, the metric directs their attention. And attention is the scarcest resource in public administration. What leaders attend to becomes what organisations care about.

The motif returns once more in a quieter form: *the indicator is a compass*. A compass guides. But a compass can also send a traveller along the wrong path if the magnet beneath it has shifted.

Administrative systems must therefore ask two diagnostic questions. First: does the indicator reflect the goal or merely resemble it? Second: what behaviours will this indicator trigger in people trying to meet it? These questions may appear technical, but their consequences are deeply human. They determine where police patrol, which patients doctors prioritise, which pupils receive interventions, and which families receive support.

These questions lead us to a final tension. Measurement promises clarity. It offers numbers where once there were stories. But governance requires judgement, and judgement resists compression. The indicator will always pull action toward itself. The open question—the one that hovers as this subchapter closes—is simple and enduring: when the indicator and the lived reality diverge, which will the institution follow, and who decides what counts as counting?

Bias: From Sampling to Systems

On 24 October 2019, a study published in *Science* revealed that a widely used US healthcare algorithm—deployed by hospitals in states including New York and California—systematically underestimated the needs of Black patients. The model did not use race; it estimated "future healthcare need" using past healthcare costs. Those costs were lower, on average, not because Black patients were healthier, but because they received less care. Inputs that looked fair produced outputs that deepened inequity. Hospitals adjusted referral pathways within days of the findings. Five words surface early: *The bias hid plainly.*

The case exposed a simple, enduring truth: data bias rarely announces itself. It sits quietly in sampling choices, in the labels used to teach models, and in the contexts into which models are deployed. When any of these layers shifts, even slightly, outcomes change. The motif threading through this section is *the seam*—the barely visible line where one form of bias blends into another.

Show the pattern. Name the types. Explain the mechanics. Implication follows. Sampling bias emerges when the dataset used to train a system does not represent the population it will later judge. Label bias arises when the outcome used as a "ground truth" encodes past distortions. Deployment bias occurs when a model built for one environment is inserted into another, where behaviours, incentives, or demographics differ. Each seam is subtle; each carries real consequences.

The healthcare example demonstrates sampling and label bias intertwined. Hospitals relied on historical utilisation data—who used care, when, and at what cost. Because access varied by race, the sample reflected inequity. Because the model labelled "cost" as "need", the label transmitted that inequity forward. Staff acted on the predictions. The behaviour was visible: patients flagged as "high-need" were offered enhanced care management, while others were not. The seam became an outcome.

A second example illustrates bias through a different route. In 2013, the Los Angeles Police Department began using a predictive policing system known as PredPol (later Geolitica), based on the work of mathematicians George Mohler and colleagues. The model trained on recorded crime reports in neighbourhoods such as Boyle Heights and Hollywood. Critics, including a 2016 report from the civil rights group Stop LAPD Spying Coalition, argued that because enforcement patterns shaped those reports, the algorithm reinforced intensive patrols in historically over-policed areas. The sampling bias was geographic: the model learned from where police had been, not where harm actually concentrated. The behaviour that followed was quantifiable: patrol cars returned to the same hotspots, even when calls for service elsewhere rose. The seam widened.

A counter-example adds necessary nuance. In 2020, the Dutch Central Bureau of Statistics developed a mortality-risk model used during the early months of COVID-19 to anticipate pressure on hospitals. Its training data represented the national population across age, sex, and comorbidity profiles. Independent evaluation by RIVM (March 2020) found that the model transferred effectively across regions, partly because the sampling frame was comprehensive and labels—mortality and hospitalisation—were consistent. This illustrates a limitation to broad claims about bias: not all predictive systems amplify inequity. Some mitigate it when data and context align. Reconcile these examples by returning to the motif: seams matter. Where the seams match—between data, labels, and deployment—models can behave as expected. Where they misalign, the system pulls apart.

Bias becomes particularly elusive when "fair" inputs nonetheless produce unfair impacts. Show this phenomenon. Name the dynamic: context shift. Explain the mechanism: a model trained on a stable environment can drift when the world changes. Implication: fairness at training time is no guarantee of fairness at deployment.

Education offers a clear case. In 2021, a northern English council commissioned a model to predict pupils likely to fall behind in reading. The model used attendance patterns, prior attainment, and teacher assessments—inputs considered legitimate. Yet once deployed, it disproportionately flagged pupils from families living in temporary accommodation. The reason lay not in sampling but in deployment: the model treated irregular attendance as a risk indicator, but in the post-pandemic period, irregular attendance reflected housing instability rather than disengagement. Teachers observed the behaviour directly: pupils they viewed as capable were elevated to high-risk groups. The seam here was temporal. The model learned from a pre-pandemic context and tripped in a post-pandemic one.

A second example shows a different seam. In 2018, Transport for London analysed aggregated Oyster card taps to model morning-peak congestion risks. The system performed well until major engineering works altered travel patterns. Once the works began in February 2019, the algorithm underpredicted flows on diverted routes. Deployment bias surfaced: the model was calibrated to a topology that no longer existed. The visible behaviour was operational: staff redeployed late, and station crowding alerts triggered after queues had already formed. Nothing about the inputs was unfair, but context shifted, and fairness is always relative to context.

These examples highlight the broader architecture of systemic bias. Sampling bias affects who is seen. Label bias affects how they are interpreted. Deployment bias affects what happens when those interpretations are acted upon. The seams between stages determine whether systems align with or undermine public values.

Monitoring plans attempt to stitch these seams more tightly. Proper monitoring measures drift: changes in data distributions, shifts in model residuals, or disparities that diverge from baseline. Monitoring compares outcomes across groups and across time. It commits institutions to intervene before patterns harden. Without monitoring, bias becomes invisible.

Show what monitoring looks like when it works. Name a real case. Explain its structure. In 2020, NHS Blood and Transplant introduced bias monitoring for its kidney allocation algorithm after a review found disparities in waiting times for minority ethnic groups. Analysts created monthly dashboards comparing predicted and actual match rates by ethnicity. When deviations exceeded a set threshold, the system triggered manual review. The behaviour was concrete: clinicians reassessed allocation rules, and revisions were implemented in December 2020. The seam was checked; the stitch held.

A counter-example reveals what happens when monitoring is absent. The US Department of Labor's 2019 review of automated résumé screening tools used in several states found that systems often ranked applicants based on proximity to previous hires' profiles. Because many agencies had historically hired from narrow educational backgrounds, the model perpetuated these patterns. No drift detection flagged the entrenchment of these profiles. Bias formed not from malicious intent but from a lack of scrutiny. The seam tore.

Reconciling these cases reinforces a simple principle: monitoring is effective only when it is continuous, interpretable, and coupled to authority to act. Dashboards without intervention remain decorative. Intervention without understanding risks compounding error. The seam must be inspected and maintained.

Bias becomes systemic when these elements—sampling, labels, deployment—interact. A policing dataset overrepresents some neighbourhoods; a risk score labels residents there as "high priority"; officers deploy resources accordingly. Each step amplifies the last. A health dataset underrepresents certain groups; a cost proxy labels them as low-risk; care teams deprioritise interventions. A transport dataset fails to capture off-peak workers; congestion predictions ignore their patterns; service planning overlooks them. Bias lives not in a single point but across connections.

The motif appears once more: *the seam is fragile.* A system is only as fair as its weakest seam, and the weakest seam is easy to miss.

These ecologies force a final, enduring question. If even fair inputs can produce unfair outcomes when the world shifts, what should institutions monitor—and how often—to ensure that the seams of their systems hold?

Data Rights and Public Purpose

On 7 April 2020, as Milan entered its fourth week of lockdown, the city's transport authority—Azienda Trasporti Milanesi (ATM)—sent mobility summaries to Lombardy's regional crisis unit. The figures showed a 75 per cent fall in metro journeys since 23 February. Officials used the aggregated data to adjust essential service timetables and direct police patrols to stations where crowding persisted. The reuse was lawful under Italy's emergency decrees. Yet it carried a disquiet that surfaced later when residents learned that data gathered for planning had been repurposed for public order. What felt like a neutral tap-in became evidence in a system none of them had consented to imagine. Five words arrive early: *The repurposing altered expectations.*

The scene exposes a perennial tension in administrative data governance: information collected for one purpose often proves irresistibly useful for another. Show the dynamic. Name the principle: data purpose limitation. Explain the rationale: individuals trust institutions when they can anticipate how their information will be used. Implication: when reuse expands quietly, trust contracts sharply. The motif threaded through this subchapter is *the boundary*—the line between legitimate public purpose and overreach.

Consent, the traditional anchor of data rights, illustrates the first boundary. In consumer technology, consent manifests through terms and conditions—an imperfect system but one grounded in individual choice. In public services, consent is constrained. A resident cannot meaningfully opt out of having their address used for council tax billing or their medical history recorded in a health system. Consent remains important, but its power shrinks when services are essential. This shift forces governments to rely on a different foundation: public interest.

The public interest test asks whether a new use of data aligns with the reasons it was collected, whether risks are proportionate, and whether safeguards are in place. Its strength lies in process, not rhetoric. Consider the UK Office for National Statistics' decision in May 2020 to use confidential patient data to estimate COVID-19 prevalence. The justification rested on three visible behaviours: NHS Digital published data minimisation steps, the ONS committed to aggregate outputs, and independent ethics boards reviewed methodology. The public interest was articulated through transparent action, not abstract reassurance. Trust was earned through process.

A second example illustrates how explicit public purpose can maintain legitimacy. In 2018, Transport for London (TfL) deployed Wi-Fi analytics across 54 stations to model passenger flows. TfL published detailed documentation explaining that MAC addresses would be hashed, retained for 24 hours, and analysed exclusively for congestion management. A public consultation preceded the rollout. The visible behaviour mattered: commuters knew where the boundary lay, and TfL stayed within it. Here, public purpose strengthened trust.

A counter-example brings the risks into sharper focus. In 2016, Chicago used predictive policing models that leveraged arrest data to generate a "Strategic Subject List." While framed as public-safety intervention, the project lacked a clear public interest justification beyond speculative harm prevention. Oversight was minimal. Residents on the list were never notified, and the metrics used for targeting were inseparable from historic enforcement patterns. When the programme drew criticism, the Chicago Police Department suspended it in 2019. The boundary blurred; confidence eroded.

Reconcile these cases by returning to the motif. When the boundary between original purpose and new use is declared and defended, public purpose can flourish. When the boundary is smudged, even beneficial projects falter.

Consent's limitations become more pressing in multi-agency data integration. A child's school attendance record, a family's benefits history, and a neighbourhood's mobility data each sit in different statutory frameworks. Linking them requires more than implied permission. It requires a clear public interest test that citizens can understand. In Southwark's 2021 tutoring allocation project, described earlier in this chapter, the council introduced a simple three-step compatibility check: was the reuse necessary, proportionate, and accompanied by review? Headteachers were given discretion to amend prioritisation lists. The behaviour was visible: educators challenged classifications when local knowledge contradicted linkage signals. The boundary held because professionals could intervene.

Data trusts offer one institutional mechanism to protect boundaries. A data trust, as explored by the Open Data Institute since 2018, delegates stewardship of a dataset to an independent body that must act in the collective interest of those represented by the data. Show the idea at work. Name a case. In 2019, the Greater London Authority piloted a data-sharing arrangement with the Royal Borough of Greenwich to use transport and environmental data in urban planning. While not a full legal trust, the partnership adopted trust-like features: external oversight, clear purpose statements, and tiered access policies. Explain the significance: collective governance replaces individual consent in contexts where data concerns groups, not just individuals. Implication: trust structures can strengthen legitimacy when data crosses administrative boundaries.

A second example comes from Canada. In 2020, the non-profit Connected North established a governance framework for its education connectivity data, granting Indigenous communities authority over data reuse. The governance board, composed primarily of community representatives, could veto external research proposals. This model demonstrated that public purpose can be defined locally, not simply by central agencies. The behavioural cue was strong: vetoes were exercised, and proposals were revised to respect cultural and contextual boundaries.

Yet data trusts face limitations. They require sustained resources, legal clarity, and local capacity. Not every community can or wishes to operate one. A counter-example demonstrates the difficulty. In 2019, an attempt in Toronto to establish a data trust for the Sidewalk Labs Quayside project faltered. Stakeholders disagreed on who would appoint trustees and what ultimate powers they would hold.

Without consensus on governance, the trust never materialised. The initiative's collapse revealed a structural truth: data trusts succeed only when all parties commit to the boundary they draw.

Reconcile this by returning to the motif: a boundary is meaningful only when jointly maintained.

Public interest tests become especially strained when data collected for routine operations becomes valuable during emergencies. Milan's mobility case is emblematic. Aggregated data helped authorities respond efficiently during lockdown. But when the emergency ended, the expectation of limited reuse lingered uncomfortably. Residents had accepted a temporary shift in data purpose; they did not consent to indefinite expansion.

A second example shows emergency reuse done with explicit care. During the 2017 wildfires in British Columbia, Canada, the provincial government used anonymised mobile network data—provided voluntarily by Telus under emergency provisions—to identify evacuation patterns. Officials published a post-event report detailing data sources, analytical methods, and destruction timelines. The behaviour reinforced trust: deletion was documented, and reuse was explicitly restricted to the emergency period. The boundary was reset.

These cases expose the core dilemma: public purpose expands during crises but must contract afterwards. Policy systems often handle expansion well and contraction poorly. Without strong governance, exceptional uses drift into normalised practices.

Practical tests can discipline this drift. Ask three questions. First, *compatibility*: does this reuse honour the conditions under which the data was collected? By compatibility, we mean more than legal compliance; we mean alignment with what citizens reasonably expect. Behaviour reveals expectations: if commuters believe tap-in data maps congestion, not compliance, reuse must honour that understanding.

Second, *necessity*: is the reuse required to achieve the stated goal, or is there a less intrusive option? Necessity is visible in operational metrics. During Milan's lockdown, aggregated station-level counts—not individual journey histories—were sufficient for enforcement planning. Intrusion was avoidable.

Third, *proportionality*: are the risks tightly bounded compared with the public benefit? Proportionality has behavioural markers: sunset clauses, external audits, and routine deletion signals restraint.

These tests do not eliminate ambiguity, but they structure it. They protect boundaries.

The motif reappears: *the boundary must be seen*. A boundary that is invisible to citizens is no boundary at all.

Consent, public interest, and data trusts each represent different tools for governing data reuse. But their effectiveness depends on transparency, participation, and institutional humility. Transparency allows citizens to see how data travels. Participation gives communities the authority to influence those paths. Humility requires recognising that not every technically useful reuse meets the threshold of public purpose.

The administrative state must ask a quiet but consequential question whenever data begins to move between purposes: does this reuse respect the people behind the data, or merely the convenience of the system?

The tension that follows remains unresolved: when public purpose and individual expectations diverge, who should redraw the boundary, and by what right?

Chapter 3
Models Make Rules

The first complaint arrived on a grey Tuesday morning. A landlord in Philadelphia had received a letter from the city's Department of Licenses and Inspections in October 2017, informing him that his property had been flagged for priority inspection. Within weeks, more notices followed—some to owners of visibly neglected buildings, others to those who had kept their properties in reasonable order. The common thread was not an outbreak of new hazards; it was an algorithm. The city's inspection unit had begun using a statistical model trained on historical violations, fire records, construction permits, and neighbourhood complaints to decide which buildings inspectors should visit first. The model was intended to bring fairness and foresight to a chronically under-resourced system. Yet as inspectors compared the algorithm's rankings with their own hard-earned instincts, a quieter question took shape: *when does a model stop guiding decisions and start making them?*

That question is not new. Public institutions have always used rules to channel judgement. For decades, inspectors relied on heuristics—rules of thumb passed between colleagues, grounded in experience if not in formal evidence. A peeling roofline, a cluster of tenant complaints, a history of unpaid fines: these cues shaped decisions about where to go next. Later, statistical scoring systems translated those instincts into formulae. A point for cluttered corridors, three points for electrical hazards, five for repeated violations. But machine learning altered the equation. It did not merely formalise existing rules; it learned new ones, drawn from relationships humans did not design or even notice. Scrutiny grew harder as the logic receded behind patterns in data. The shift from heuristics to learning systems changed who held authority over rules themselves.

This chapter explores that shift: how models, once auxiliary tools, now participate in rulemaking. To govern well, states must grasp this transformation not as a technical novelty but as a philosophical one. Rules carry moral weight. They shape who receives help, who faces scrutiny, and who is diverted to another path. When rules are learned rather than written, accountability takes on a different texture. It becomes a practice of interpretation rather than inspection, of tracing the logic of a model rather than the logic of a codebase. The motif threading through this chapter is *the hinge*: the moment where a model moves from suggesting an action to determining a default.

The hinge is not always easy to spot. Consider how explainability enters the frame. Public bodies often treat explanations as documentation boxes to tick. Yet an explanation that fails to help a citizen understand, challenge, or remedy a decision has not explained anything at all. Global explanations describe a system's general structure. Local explanations justify a single prediction. Procedural explanations illuminate how a decision travelled through the state. Each type matters, but only when matched to purpose. A tenant who receives an enforcement notice needs to know why the model prioritised their building, what they can supply to contest it, and how to correct the record if it is wrong. Explanation, in this sense, is less about satisfying auditors than enabling dignity.

As models embed themselves deeper into administrative routines, robustness becomes not a luxury but a constitutional requirement. Public data shifts constantly. An unemployment shock changes the behaviour of jobseekers. A new housing policy alters migration patterns. A health crisis reshapes clinical pathways. A model trained on yesterday's world can falter when tomorrow arrives with different incentives. Distribution shift and concept drift are the formal names for these phenomena, but their lived consequences are simple: when reality changes, models misread it. Guardrails—shadow deployments, trigger thresholds, scheduled revalidation—act as hinges of their own, allowing systems to catch drift before it warps decisions. Without them, learned rules ossify while the world moves on.

Testing these systems without harming people demands institutional imagination. Sandboxing—running models in controlled environments, trialling them on past cases, stress-testing them through adversarial scenarios—creates room for caution in a domain that too often rewards speed. Governments have experimented with A/B testing in back-office functions, red-teaming exercises led by outsiders, and staged rollouts that begin with advisory rather than binding decisions. Each approach reflects a political truth: the state is not merely deploying technology; it is piloting authority. And pilots have their own hazards. Some systems remain stuck in perpetual trial, never maturing into accountable public tools. Others graduate too quickly, propelled by institutional enthusiasm rather than rigorous assessment. The politics of "pilot forever" shadow the promise of innovation.

Taken together, these elements trace a landscape where models do more than process inputs. They shape governance itself. They create priorities, allocate attention, and draw the boundaries of administrative imagination. Once a model proves efficient at predicting risk, inefficiency becomes suspect. Once a ranking system improves some outcomes, deviation becomes questionable. A model becomes a rule long before anyone announces that shift. The hinge turns quietly.

This chapter invites readers to examine these hinges—where human judgement meets machine inference, where learning systems meet democratic design, where precision meets legitimacy. It follows the thread from heuristic to model, from model to rule, from rule to consequence. At stake is not whether governments will use models—they already do—but whether they will do so with a clear understanding of how models accumulate power.

A tension lingers beneath every example: when a learned rule begins to govern, who retains the authority to rewrite it, and how do we ensure that the hinge connecting model to decision never locks without scrutiny?

From Heuristics to Learning Systems

In October 2017, inspectors in Philadelphia's Department of Licences and Inspections began receiving a new daily list. It ranked every rental property in the city by predicted likelihood of serious code violations. The list came from a statistical model built by the city's Office of Open Data & Digital Transformation, trained on five years of documented hazards, fire incidents, 311 complaints, and historical inspection outcomes. Within weeks, inspectors noticed something striking. Buildings that had never raised red flags were leapfrogging long-neglected properties. The model spotted patterns invisible to routine practice. Yet as staff compared the rankings with their own instincts, a different question surfaced: *if the model rewrites the cues inspectors rely on, who now writes the rules?* Five words appear early: *The list rearranged their judgement.*

Heuristics—the rules of thumb that shape frontline decisions—have always been the understructure of administrative action. Show their place. Name the concept. Explain their appeal. A veteran inspector may judge risk by peeling paint, structural sagging, or the tenor of tenant complaints. These cues form a mental model, honed by repetition, bias, and experience. Implication: heuristics create consistency within teams but also embed blind spots. They are easy to use, hard to standardise, and, crucially, transparent: one can ask an inspector *why* they choose a building, and an answer will follow.

Statistical scoring systems, which surged in public administration from the 1980s onward, attempted to formalise these rules. Cities from Baltimore to Birmingham developed point-based inspection matrices: three points for electrical hazards, five for structural instability, and additional points for repeat violations. Metrics replaced tacit knowledge. Behaviour changed. Inspectors documented conditions more systematically, supervisors compared scores, and priority-setting became less personalised. These systems made the implicit explicit.

Then machine learning arrived. It did not simply encode old heuristics; it inferred new ones from patterns in data. Learning systems do not ask what an experienced inspector would notice. They search across dozens of variables for correlations that humans would never consider. A sudden spike in complaints about rubbish disposal in a neighbourhood might correlate with future fire hazards. A cluster of late permit renewals might signal deeper maintenance issues. These relationships can be powerful predictors—but they are often opaque. The motif that threads through this subchapter is *the hinge*: the moment when a model's learned rule quietly becomes the system's operational rule.

To see that hinge clearly, return to Philadelphia. The housing model outperformed traditional methods: early evaluations in 2018 showed inspectors found serious violations at roughly twice the previous rate when visiting algorithmically ranked properties. The behaviour was measurable: more high-risk cases identified per inspection hour. Efficiency improved. But scrutiny became harder. When inspectors questioned why a particular property rose in the ranking, the explanation was technical—a blend of weights learned from historical data, interactions between variables, and correlations no human had chosen. A rule of thumb could be challenged. A learned rule resisted interrogation.

A second example illustrates this pattern. In 2014, New York City's Fire Department began using a machine learning model to prioritise building inspections after several fatal fires. The model used over 60 features, from building age to past violations. Early results were promising; the department reported that buildings flagged by the model were significantly more likely to contain safety risks. Yet when local officials in Queens asked why certain small businesses appeared disproportionately, explanations were limited. The model had learned patterns from historical records that reflected uneven enforcement. Label bias and sampling bias collided. Learning systems, unlike heuristics, inherit past inequalities with mathematical precision.

A credible counter-example provides nuance. Copenhagen's Technical and Environmental Administration, which trialled a learning system for identifying unsafe rental properties in 2020, insisted on a hybrid design. Human inspectors co-created the feature set; the model was restricted to interpretable variables; and rule-based guardrails ensured that no building was deprioritised solely due to missing data. Monthly review meetings examined anomalies. The hinge remained visible. Here, learned rules supplemented rather than supplanted human judgement. This limitation shows that opacity is not inevitable but emerges when teams treat learning systems as replacements rather than partners.

The hinge becomes harder to manage as systems scale. Public agencies often deploy models into environments that differ from training conditions. This gap—deployment bias—distorts learned rules. A housing model trained on pre-pandemic rental patterns may misfire when eviction freezes or emergency rental schemes alter behaviour. A health triage model trained on winter demand may produce poor predictions during summer lulls. The behaviour is observable: models drift. Staff stop trusting outputs. Work-arounds emerge. Metrics fray.

Machine learning compounds this drift because it discovers relationships rather than encoding rules. A logistic regression built on explicit features provides coefficients one can scrutinise. A gradient boosting model or neural network constructs latent interactions that defy straightforward explanation. Even when global model performance remains strong, local decisions can be baffling. A building flagged highly one week may be absent the next. Inspectors might interpret volatility as unreliability, even when volatility reflects deeper data dynamics. The hinge becomes unstable.

To understand why learned rules are harder to scrutinise, differentiate three layers of opacity. First, *structural opacity*: complex models produce outputs through high-dimensional relationships. Second, *procedural opacity*: even transparent models can appear opaque if staff do not know how data flows through organisational systems. Third, *contextual opacity*: when deployment shifts the environment, rules learned from data no longer match lived conditions. Each opacity erodes confidence.

The motif returns: *the hinge shifts quietly*. Staff do not always realise when their professional discretion begins to orbit around model outputs.

Administration amplifies this shift through subtle incentives. When a model ranks properties, staff feel pressure to follow the ranking; deviation must be justified. When a model predicts which cases matter most, ignoring those predictions looks inefficient. Public agencies measure throughput, consistency, and compliance. Learning systems, which produce numerical priorities, align neatly with these metrics. Behaviour follows the numbers. Professional intuition recedes. Rules harden.

A case from Rotterdam in 2017 shows how the hinge can snap. The city's housing authority used a predictive model to identify potentially fraudulent rental registrations. The model relied on variables such as household composition, address histories, and unusual occupancy patterns. Investigators began using the model as a near-decisive guide. But when journalists exposed that the model disproportionately flagged residents in poorer districts, the authority struggled to explain its logic. The learned rules were inscrutable. The hinge locked. Public confidence fell.

Contrast this with Barcelona's 2021 pilot on building safety, where the model operated in "shadow mode" for six months. Inspectors compared model rankings with human-generated lists and found discrepancies. Some were errors; others revealed useful new signals. The department adjusted both the model and the inspection workflow before deploying it. Shadow deployments make the hinge visible before it fixes.

Learning systems also transform institutional memory. Heuristics carry a narrative: inspectors share stories about cases, failures, and surprises. These stories encode caution. When machine learning replaces heuristic knowledge, institutional memory becomes embedded in data rather than people. But data has no voice. It does not warn. It merely reflects. When patterns change, learned rules can become dangerous without warning.

The hinge again: what signals when a system must be revisited?

Monitoring plans help. Guardrails such as drift detection, accuracy thresholds, and periodic revalidation force organisations to ask whether a model still reflects the world. Yet monitoring is often treated as a technical afterthought rather than a governance practice. A drift chart may show significant deviation, but unless its implications for inspection fairness or resource allocation are understood, organisations may ignore it. Monitoring must be behavioural: teams must commit to specific actions when thresholds are crossed.

As learning systems mature, they invite a final challenge: distinguishing between correlation-based rules and normative rules. A model may learn that buildings in certain districts correlate with higher violations, but using district as a rule of action raises ethical and legal questions. Heuristics, for all their flaws, often encode normative judgements explicitly ("visit buildings with prior serious violations"). Learning systems blur descriptive and prescriptive lines. They suggest actions without stating principles. The hinge here is the shift from "we choose" to "the model selects".

These systems can improve safety, efficiency, and fairness. They can help inspectors see what was previously hidden. But they also shift authority. Learned rules, when not scrutinised, become de facto policy. A statistical pattern becomes a priority; a priority becomes a decision; a decision becomes a rule.

A tension emerges that cannot be fully resolved: when a model discovers a rule no human designed, who decides whether that rule should govern, and what happens when institutional incentives reward obeying the model rather than questioning the hinge where its logic meets public judgement?

Explainability That Matters

On a cold morning in March 2018, the Dutch Council of State reviewed a complaint from a family in Rotterdam who had been flagged as "high-risk" by SyRI, the government's fraud-detection system. They had received no clear reason for their designation. No caseworker could tell them which data points had been used, which patterns had triggered suspicion, or what steps they might take to correct the record. Their only guidance came in a sentence printed at the bottom of the notice: *"This decision is based on an automated risk assessment."* The court later ruled the system unlawful. But the deeper failure was visible long before the ruling—*the family had no pathway to understand, challenge, or remedy the algorithm's claim.* Five words capture the core problem: *They were left without reasons.*

Explainability in public systems begins with this scene. Show its stakes. Name its consequences. Explain its context. The Rotterdam case raised a principle that echoes throughout governance: a decision that cannot be explained cannot be held accountable. The implication is immediate and constitutional. When the state uses models to allocate rights, burdens, or opportunities, explainability becomes a civic infrastructure, not a technical add-on.

The term itself can feel slippery, often stretched into a general demand that complex systems be "interpretable". But explainability has three distinct forms—global, local, and procedural—and each answers a different public question. Global explanations describe how a model works in general terms: which features matter, how they interact, and why the system behaves as it does. Local explanations justify a particular outcome for a particular person: your property was flagged because recorded hazards increased by X, or your application was delayed because missing documentation created Y risk. Procedural explanations chart the decision's journey through the administrative machine: which systems were consulted, which checks were applied, who had authority to override the model, and how the final step occurred. These three forms together determine whether a citizen can make sense of a decision, contest it, and repair any errors.

To see why these distinctions matter, return to Rotterdam. SyRI was built from a legal framework passed in 2014 that allowed data integration across tax, social security, and labour agencies. Its operators could describe the system's purpose, but not its logic. There was no global explanation interpreting which patterns triggered risk scores. There were no local explanations that clarified why individual households were flagged. And procedural documentation was sparse. The failure was not merely technical; it was structural. Without explanations, the system converted data into suspicion without any route for citizens to understand the basis of that suspicion. The hinge motif appears again: the moment where a model's inference becomes a rule, and that rule gains force without traceability.

A contrasting example demonstrates how explainability can be designed with care. When London's Camden Council launched its Temporary Accommodation Modelling Tool in late 2020, it committed to publishing a global explanation of the model's logic. Officials detailed the key input features—rent arrears, inspection histories, property characteristics—and the decision thresholds used to rank properties at risk of failing. Crucially, local explanations accompanied every notification sent to landlords or tenants. Each explained which data contributed to the risk score and provided clear routes to correct errors: a phone number, evidence requirements, and expected timelines for review. Procedural transparency was strengthened by maintaining a public register of model changes and human override decisions. The result was measurable. Citizens contested incorrect records more quickly, and staff corrected data with fewer delays. Here, explanation was not a defensive document; it was an operational tool.

A credible limitation should temper enthusiasm. In 2022, the city of Helsinki introduced a predictive model to help caseworkers identify at-risk youth. It relied on interpretable features such as school attendance and social service interactions. Although the team planned for transparency, they found that local explanations could cause unintended stigma. For example, one young person discovered that their risk score was influenced by a sibling's social care history, which they perceived as unjust and invasive. Helsinki paused the rollout and redesigned the model to exclude family-level features. The lesson is clear: explainability can harm if it exposes sensitive correlations without ethical framing. Reconciliation comes through design discipline. Explainability must be paired with necessity tests: is the information relevant, fair, and proportionate to disclose?

To deepen the analysis, distinguish between *comprehension* and *interpretation*. A global explanation may be mathematically precise yet still impenetrable to non-experts. A local explanation may describe relationships that confuse rather than clarify. Explainability that matters asks a simpler question: *does the person affected understand what happened and know what to do next?* The metric is behavioural. If a citizen can identify which record is wrong, provide evidence to correct it, and anticipate how the decision will change, the explanation served its purpose. If not, the system failed—no matter how technically sophisticated the explanation appears.

One motif threads through this subchapter: *the doorway.* An explanation is a doorway into understanding. But too often, public systems build doorways without handles. Text appears, but it does not open anything. A citizen reads a sentence like "your risk score exceeded the threshold" and remains outside the decision's architecture. A meaningful doorway requires three elements: a reason, a route, and a remedy.

Consider how New Zealand's Ministry of Social Development approached this challenge in 2021 when testing a model to prioritise outreach visits. Every household that received an automated notification also received a plain-language explanation designed through user research. The explanation followed a simple template:

1. *What we decided*
2. *Why we made this decision*
3. *The information we used*
4. *What you can do if something is wrong*
5. *How long it takes to review*
6. *Who is responsible for fixing issues*

This template grounded the model's abstract logic in concrete actions. Instead of opaque references to "system recommendations", citizens encountered direct statements such as: *"Your household was prioritised because records show two missed rent submissions in the last six months and a recent notice from your housing provider. If this is incorrect, contact X by Y. We must reply within Z working days.*"The behaviour that followed was measurable. People corrected inaccurate records, caseworkers adjusted risk scores, and appeals focused on evidence rather than frustration.

By contrast, the U.S. Internal Revenue Service's machine-learning model for audit selection—expanded significantly in 2020—offers little to no local explanation for the majority of taxpayers. Although the IRS publishes high-level criteria, individual notices rarely disclose which factors triggered the audit. The result is predictable. Taxpayers with low incomes, especially those claiming the Earned Income Tax Credit, appear disproportionately in the audit pool. They know they've been selected. They do not know why. Without the doorway of explanation, anxiety fills the silence. The limitation is not technical—the system could generate local explanations—but institutional. This reflects a deeper question: who the system considers worthy of reasons.

Explainability also shapes organisational behaviour. When staff rely on model outputs they cannot understand, accountability becomes blurred. A caseworker who receives a risk score without context faces a dilemma. Trust the model? Override it? Investigate further?

Without clear explanations, staff may default to compliance. The visible behaviour is measurable: higher alignment with model rankings, lower rates of override, and more uniform decisions. This may improve consistency but can erode discretion. Procedural explanations mitigate this effect. When staff understand how decisions flow, and where human judgement sits within that flow, they can exercise responsibility rather than act as conduits.

Yet explainability has limits. Some models cannot be simplified without distortion. Some relationships are too complex to express faithfully in plain language. And some disclosures could cause harm by revealing sensitive correlations. Here, democratic design requires a protective layer: committees that review explanations for fairness, privacy, and clarity; public registers that document model behaviour; and independent audits that test whether explanations match actual decision logic. These practices shift explainability from a technical feature to a civic safeguard.

The motif returns: the doorway stands or falls on whether it opens. An explanation that tells citizens nothing new, or nothing they can act upon, is not a doorway—it is decoration.

The chapter's arc advances by emphasising remedy. Explainability without remedy is performance. Explainability with remedy is power. A citizen who receives a reason can identify an error. A citizen who receives a route can request correction. A citizen who receives a timeline can hold the state accountable. This triad—reason, route, remedy—anchors the plain-language template that will appear later in this chapter.

A final tension remains. Public institutions increasingly use models whose learned rules shift faster than policies can adapt. As model updates alter decision logic, explanations must keep pace. Yet revision cycles are long, documentation is slow, and staff are overburdened. The unresolved question lingers like an open doorway: *how do we ensure that explanations reflect actual model behaviour, especially when the model itself evolves?*

Robustness and Drift

In April 2020, the UK's Office for National Statistics released a stark figure: unemployment had risen by more than 856,000 claims within a single month, the sharpest recorded surge since comparable records began in 1971. In Manchester, job-centre teams noticed something else. A machine-learning model used to prioritise employment-support calls—trained on patterns from 2017 to 2019—had begun producing erratic rankings. People who had never been at risk of long-term unemployment were suddenly classified as "high priority", while others with sustained barriers to work slipped down the list. Staff questioned the model's outputs. The designers checked the logs. Then the hinge appeared: the world had moved faster than the data. A simple line summarised the failure. *The model thought yesterday still applied.*

Robustness in public systems begins with this jolt. Distribution shift—the change in the statistical properties of input data—and concept drift—the change in the underlying relationship between inputs and outcomes—are not rare anomalies. They are the ambient conditions of social life. Employment patterns change with economic shocks; clinical pathways shift during epidemics; housing demand fluctuates when migration flows alter. Public institutions operate in environments where stability is temporary. Models, however, are trained on the past. When the past becomes a poor guide, the machine misreads the present. Five words appear early: *Things changed. The model didn't.*

Show the dynamics. Name their significance. Explain the mechanics. Distribution shift occurs when the incoming data no longer resembles the data used to train the model. A benefits-triage system that once relied on patterns of seasonal employment sees its feature distributions warp during a recession: variables such as "recent employment gap" or "income volatility" spike simultaneously across groups that previously differed. Concept drift goes deeper. The *meaning* of a pattern shifts. Before the 2020 shock, a six-month employment gap reliably predicted risk of long-term unemployment. During the crisis, it predicted nothing except the fact that the labour market had frozen. The implication is profound. A model can retain high technical accuracy in a testing environment yet fail catastrophically in practice because the world it learned from no longer exists.

The motif that threads through this subchapter is *the floor giving way*. A model stands on assumptions about how data behaves. When that floor shifts, robustness becomes a question of institutional vigilance rather than technical optimisation.

A first concrete example comes from Denmark. In 2016, Copenhagen's Jobcentres deployed a predictive model to identify individuals at risk of long-term unemployment. The system performed strongly during its initial rollout: caseworkers reported more precise prioritisation, and evaluations showed higher alignment between predictions and eventual outcomes. But when the labour market tightened in 2018, the model's precision deteriorated. Distributional changes in jobseeker profiles—more short-term contracts, more part-time work—altered the feature relationships. The team detected the drift only because caseworkers raised persistent anomalies. The behaviour was visible: risk rankings no longer corresponded with frontline judgement. Copenhagen suspended the model, retrained it, and introduced monthly stability checks. The floor had moved; the system had to move with it.

A second example illustrates how concept drift distorts decisions even when performance metrics look stable. In 2015, Chicago's Department of Public Health launched an epidemiological prediction model to identify restaurants at risk of foodborne illness outbreaks. The system combined complaint data, weather variables, and historical inspection records. Early success was measurable: inspectors reached critical violations faster than before. Yet by 2017, as new delivery platforms changed eating patterns, the model began overweighting outdated cues. Lags in complaint reporting changed the relationship between early signals and later risks. The concept of "early risk" itself drifted. Inspectors observed the shift before the system did. Behaviour changed: they began overriding outputs more frequently. The model still appeared accurate in aggregated testing, but local decisions became misaligned.

A credible limitation helps refine the argument. Some models, especially those that rely on slow-moving demographic or infrastructural data, are less exposed to drift. For example, a model predicting long-term building energy demand in Helsinki, trained on structural characteristics from 2012 and updated in 2018, showed little drift through 2021 because the underlying features—insulation quality, building age, heating systems—changed gradually. This counter-example highlights that not all systems face constant volatility. Reconciliation requires distinguishing where drift is a structural risk (labour markets, health utilisation, policing patterns) and where it is environmental noise. The state must know which floors are stable and which are prone to sudden collapse.

The heart of robustness lies in guardrails. Shadow deployments make drift visible before it harms people. A model is run alongside existing practice, producing predictions that do not affect decisions but allow organisations to compare outputs with frontline behaviour. When the Netherlands experimented with a job-seeker prioritisation model in 2019, the six-month shadow deployment revealed a growing divergence between predicted and actual employment outcomes as seasonal work fluctuated. The divergence signalled distribution shift early enough to retrain the system. The behaviour was measurable: prediction error increased while the variance of key input features widened. Shadow mode kept the hinge loose; the floor could shift without taking the system with it.

Thresholds anchor decision points. A static risk threshold can produce perverse results when data skews sharply. During the UK's 2020 unemployment surge, some local authorities found that fixed classification thresholds labelled an excessive proportion of jobseekers as "high priority", overwhelming support teams. Those that had adopted dynamic thresholds—adjusting risk bands based on current distributions—managed caseloads more coherently. The implication is clear. Thresholds are not neutral; they are governance mechanisms that determine who receives help and when.

Periodic revalidation is the most overlooked guardrail. Revalidation is not merely retraining. It is a structured assessment of whether the model's core assumptions still hold. A city housing department that trains a risk model in 2019 and updates it in 2022 without examining how eviction rates, maintenance behaviours, or tenant turnover have changed is not monitoring drift; it is repainting a wall without checking the foundations. Proper revalidation includes dataset audits, stability tests on key features, comparisons of pre-shock and post-shock behaviour, and documented judgements on whether the model remains fit for purpose. The process creates institutional memory about how the floor has shifted.

Drift can also arise from administrative feedback loops. When a model prioritises some cases for review, those cases accumulate more recorded outcomes, reinforcing the model's assumptions. Meanwhile, unselected cases remain observationally thin. A benefits system that flags certain households for fraud checks will generate more fraud data from those households than from others, even if underlying rates are equal. The behaviour is visible in the data: the model becomes more confident about patterns it repeatedly observes and more uncertain about patterns it ignores. Over time, the observed world diverges from the real world. This is policy drift: the system remakes the environment it monitors.

A motif returns: *the floor gives way quietly*. Drift rarely announces itself. It reveals itself through small frictions—caseworkers querying predictions, appeals rising in certain categories, overrides increasing in frequency, waiting times lengthening unexpectedly. Robustness depends on noticing these shifts before they coalesce into systemic distortion.

A further tension emerges when external shocks collide with institutional inertia. During the first wave of the COVID-19 pandemic, several European cities suspended their homelessness-risk models because unprecedented shelter policies, moratoria on evictions, and emergency hotel provision altered the relationships between predictive features and outcomes. Some teams paused systems responsibly. Others kept models running but instructed staff to "use with caution", a vague directive that placed responsibility on individuals rather than on governance. The behaviour was telling: overrides increased sharply, but documentation of overrides did not. Drift turned into silent deviation.

To handle drift responsibly, public bodies must treat robustness as a governance practice. This requires three commitments: measuring stability, comparing model outputs to ground truth, and documenting human judgement. Each commitment transforms drift from an opaque technical phenomenon into a publicly understandable condition. Stability reports should disclose changes in input feature distributions. Output divergence analyses should compare predicted and realised outcomes. Override logs should record when staff disagree with model outputs and why. These behaviours create traceability. They let the organisation see the floor shifting.

Yet even the best guardrails cannot prevent every failure. Social systems change faster than models. Crises reorder priorities. Policies reshape behaviours. Drifts emerge from sources no dataset could anticipate. That leaves one unresolved question—one that lingers at the end of this subchapter: *When the floor gives way again, who decides whether the model should stand, adapt, or step aside, and how will they know when hesitation is the wiser choice than automation?*

Sandboxing the State

In September 2019, the New York City Mayor's Office of Data Analytics invited a small team of external researchers to stress-test a housing enforcement model that had been running quietly in the background for months. The team—drawn from New York University's Centre for Urban Science and Progress—arrived with one mandate: try to break it. They probed the system with fabricated building profiles, fed it adversarial combinations of incident reports, and checked whether the ranking engine could be manipulated by coordinated tenant complaints or spurious maintenance records. Within days, they uncovered vulnerabilities. A handful of missing fields could push a building far down the list. A cluster of artificially generated noise in one borough could pull unrelated properties into the high-risk zone. The city accepted the findings, patched the weaknesses, and delayed public deployment. The scene illustrated a sober truth. *A model can impress its creators yet collapse under pressure from those determined to probe its edges.* Five words sit early: *Testing saved the real cases.*

The need for safe experimentation is not new. Governments have long tested policies through pilots, trials, and controlled rollouts. But machine-learning systems introduce new dynamics. Their behaviour depends on the data fed into them, the incentives shaped around them, and the ways staff interact with their recommendations. A system that looks well-behaved in a laboratory can create inequities or perverse incentives when deployed across a city. The motif threading through this subchapter is *the rehearsal*: testing as the state's rehearsal before performance, an opportunity to correct flaws before they reach the public.

Red-teaming is the first form of rehearsal. Show its practice. Name its purpose. Explain its value. Red-teaming simulates malicious or adversarial behaviour to expose vulnerabilities. When the UK's Centre for Data Ethics and Innovation coordinated red-team exercises for local councils in 2021, participants discovered that small manipulations—altering a business name, adjusting a postcode boundary, or omitting a category of tax data—could shift risk scores unexpectedly. The implication was concrete. If organised actors attempted to evade enforcement, the system might fail silently. Red-teaming forced teams to observe not merely *what* a model predicted but how it could be gamed. The behaviour revealed patterns: inconsistent responses to missingness, predictable biases linked to postcode boundaries, and threshold sensitivities that could be exploited. Each insight turned into guardrails.

A second rehearsal tool is back-office A/B testing, where two decision pathways run in parallel without affecting citizens. Helsinki's Social Services Department adopted this approach in 2020 when evaluating two variants of a youth support triage model. They compared algorithm-generated rankings with human prioritisation across thousands of archived cases. The behaviour was measurable. Staff reviewed anonymised decisions and raised anomalies. Model A aligned closely with long-term outcomes but suffered from volatility; Model B was more stable but less sensitive to genuine high-risk cases. Helsinki selected neither. They examined the discrepancies, rewrote features, and built a hybrid model that incorporated the best elements of each. A/B testing acted as a mirror, reflecting how each model behaved under real distributions of complexity.

Staged rollouts form the third rehearsal. They begin small, expand carefully, and restrict harm. Barcelona's Municipal Data Office followed this approach when deploying a model to prioritise dangerous building inspections in 2021. They launched in advisory mode for three months: inspectors could see rankings but were not compelled to follow them. Supervisors monitored overrides and logged disagreements. When the system transitioned to partial decision-support, human vetoes remained mandatory. Only after a full evaluation of override patterns, error rates, and public complaints did Barcelona move to wider adoption. The implication was governance, not caution masquerading as delay. Staging allowed the city to check whether the model's logic remained sound across diverse neighbourhoods—densely populated Ciutat Vella behaved differently from the newer districts of Sant Martí—and ensured consistency before consequences became real.

A credible counter-example shows what happens without rehearsal. When the Australian Government expanded its automated debt recovery system—commonly known as Robodebt—in 2016, it skipped meaningful sandboxing. There was no shadow mode, little adversarial testing, and minimal staged rollout. The system began issuing debt notices based on income-averaging methods that often misrepresented earnings. The behaviour was visible: tens of thousands of notices were incorrect, appeals surged, and frontline caseworkers reported confusion about how to override determinations. The subsequent Royal Commission in 2023 identified the absence of rigorous testing as a structural failure. The state moved from design to enforcement without rehearsal, exposing hundreds of thousands of people to avoidable harm. Reconciliation is clear. When systems wield power over livelihoods, skipping testing is not efficiency—it is irresponsibility.

The motif returns: *rehearsal protects the public.* But the state sometimes resists rehearsal because testing exposes uncertainty. Institutions want confidence, not complication. Yet safe experimentation requires institutional humility.

To understand why sandboxing matters, examine what public models represent. They are hypotheses—claims that certain patterns predict risks or opportunities. A model used for housing inspections hypothesises that specific building features or complaint histories correlate with safety hazards. A model used for benefit sanctions hypothesises that behaviour X predicts non-compliance Y. These hypotheses require validation. Without rehearsal, they mutate into rules. And rules with no rehearsal convert fallible inferences into enforceable decisions.

Sandboxing also reshapes organisational behaviour. When teams run a model in shadow mode, they compare its outcomes with those of human staff. Disagreements trigger investigation. A diversion emerges: either the model is incorrect, or human judgement has drifted. Both outcomes hold value. In New Zealand's 2021 trial of a community-care prioritisation model, shadow mode revealed that caseworkers consistently underranked elderly residents living alone. The model highlighted a pattern overlooked by staff. At the same time, staff pointed out cases the model misread—individuals with complex medical needs that did not register in administrative data. Rehearsal made these divergences actionable.

Red-teaming extends this behavioural insight by showing how systems break. During Estonia's 2020 audit of predictive policing tools, red-teamers noticed that replacing a handful of incident report codes triggered large swings in risk rankings. The finding prompted the police board to tighten data quality checks and assign responsibility for validating anomalies. Rehearsal created accountability.

Yet sandboxing has politics. Some pilots never graduate. The phrase "pilot forever" is common in local government, describing projects celebrated as innovations but never granted authority or scale. Pilots can become decorative: a way for institutions to signal progress without altering entrenched workflows. In 2018, a major UK city ran a successful shadow deployment of a homelessness-prevention model, demonstrating improved accuracy and early-intervention benefits. But leadership changes, budget pressures, and political caution stalled adoption. The model remained in perpetual limbo—useful enough to showcase at conferences, never trusted enough to embed in practice. The implication is structural. Pilots can serve as shields that avoid hard choices about responsibility, oversight, and accountability.

Pilot-forever politics also emerge when models threaten existing discretion. A labour-market prediction tool may challenge caseworkers' longstanding intuition; a risk-ranking tool may expose uneven enforcement practices. Resistance can appear as demands for "further testing" indefinitely. The decision never arrives. The system never matures. Rehearsal becomes a postponement rather than a safeguard.

To steer past pilot traps, teams must articulate exit criteria: conditions under which a system moves from sandbox to service, and conditions under which it is abandoned. These criteria should be public. They turn experimentation into commitment rather than performance. Measurable thresholds—accuracy relative to baseline, override rates, user comprehension, and distributional fairness—anchor decisions. When New York City expanded its restaurant safety model after a 2018 sandbox period, it published the criteria that triggered deployment: sustained improvement over human baselines, consistency across boroughs, and verification that no subgroup experienced disproportionate false positives. Rehearsal became evidence, not theatre.

A quieter motif emerges: *testing is a stance, not a stage.* It is a position the state adopts toward uncertainty—a willingness to probe, question, and slow down before consequences hit the public record.

But even the best sandbox cannot simulate every stressor. Crises change domains overnight. Data definitions shift. Policies reshape incentives. This reality leads to the unresolved question that anchors the end of this subchapter: *When a model leaves the rehearsal room, who decides when to call it back, and what signals tell us that the performance must pause before the public bears the cost?*

Chapter 4
Institutions for Algorithmic Accountability

The first hint that something had gone wrong came not from a courtroom but from an appeals desk. In late 2019, staff at a regional benefits office in Edinburgh noticed a pattern. Dozens of claimants were challenging sanctions triggered by a new risk-scoring tool. The tool claimed to identify individuals "likely" to miss mandatory appointments. Yet when appeals officers examined the cases, many of the sanctioned claimants had spotless compliance histories. Some had never missed a single appointment in years of interaction with the service. The algorithm insisted otherwise. The agency had no public record of the model's purpose, no published criteria for its deployment, no timetable for review, and no clear line of accountability. Decisions kept landing on citizens; responsibility kept evaporating from the institution. Before long, a senior official raised a question that quietly haunts modern administration: *Who authorised this system, and on what authority did it begin to decide?*

The absence of an answer was not an accident. It was a design failure—one produced not by code, but by the institutional void surrounding it. As governments adopt algorithmic tools to forecast risks, allocate scarce resources, and modulate scrutiny, the challenge is no longer merely technical. It is constitutional. The rules that determine how rules themselves are made have not kept pace with the systems now shaping public life. We find ourselves in a moment where machine-assisted decisions can expand beyond their intended boundaries before any democratic guardrail has been built to hold them in place. Authority leaks outward. Accountability thins. Citizens feel its effects first.

This chapter steps into that institutional terrain: the world behind the interface, where mandates are issued, constraints are defined, and power is either anchored or allowed to drift. Its starting point is deceptively simple: every algorithmic system used by the state begins with an authorising choice. Someone, somewhere, decides that a model may govern. Yet in practice this decision is often informal—

an internal sign-off, a procurement checkbox, a quiet trial that slowly becomes routine. When no mandate is explicitly articulated, limits become hard to enforce. The motif running through this chapter is *the frame*: the structure that holds authority in place and prevents systems, however efficient, from governing beyond their remit.

The frame begins with purpose statements and sunset clauses. A model built to allocate emergency support during a heatwave may, without explicit boundaries, slip into ordinary use. A model designed to detect fraud during a crisis may evolve into a permanent surveillance mechanism. In France, the health ministry's data mobilisation during the 2003 heatwave was effective precisely because its mandate was time-bound and purpose-specific. By contrast, other jurisdictions have quietly extended crisis-era data practices into normal operations without public debate. The stakes are clear: purpose statements tell the public *why* a system exists; sunset clauses signal *when* its authority must expire unless renewed. Together they create a political rhythm—use, review, revise, or retire.

Beyond mandates, the frame must hold transparency mechanisms: registers, audits, and impact assessments. Many governments now maintain algorithmic registers—Finland's, launched in 2020, lists systems used across agencies; Amsterdam and Helsinki made theirs public the same year. These registers vary in depth. Some offer plain-language descriptions; others provide technical documentation, training data summaries, or impact evaluations. Their purpose is not merely disclosure but contestability. When people know which systems affect them, they can ask questions, challenge decisions, and demand evidence. Yet transparency risks becoming ritual. Paperwork theatre—the production of glossy assessments that no one reads—can shield rather than reveal. Genuine accountability requires that impact assessments be written for two audiences at once: the technical expert and the affected citizen. They must explain what the system is for, how it works, what could go wrong, and how the organisation will fix errors when they occur. Anything less is ornament.

Independent oversight is the next structural beam. Without independence, scrutiny collapses. Without expertise, scrutiny misfires. Without power, scrutiny becomes ceremony. A credible oversight body must combine all three. The composition matters: interdisciplinary experts, legal scholars, technologists capable of adversarial testing, and—critically—citizens whose lived experience grounds the discussion in the realities of public service. Canada's proposed algorithmic impact framework gestures towards this, but the more ambitious designs go further. In 2022, the Dutch Data Protection Authority began using appeals data to audit high-risk models, treating citizen complaints not as noise but as diagnostic signals. It marked a shift from theoretical oversight to empirical review: when patterns in appeals reveal anomalies, oversight bodies can trace the logic back to the system, not the citizen. The frame tightens when oversight can bite.

Procurement completes the institutional architecture. A contract is not an administrative detail; it is a constitution in miniature. The clauses it contains—regarding access to training data, rights to audit, explainability requirements, retraining schedules, portability, and exit options—shape the state's freedom to govern long after procurement teams have signed the final page. In 2021, a group of UK local authorities renegotiated analytic contracts to require vendors to disclose model update histories and provide reproducible explanations for all high-stakes decisions. It was a quiet revolution. Instead of accepting technology as delivered, they began to write governing power into the contract itself. Procurement became governance by other means.

Yet procurement can also undermine accountability. When vendor lock-in prevents agencies from auditing or exiting a system, the frame weakens. A predictive policing model purchased by a major US city in 2016 remained in use for years after internal reviewers raised concerns, simply because the contract provided no viable exit route. The system's predictions influenced patrol routes even as trust eroded. A frame that cannot bend becomes a cage.

Across these themes—mandates, transparency, oversight, procurement—runs a deeper question. What, exactly, is the relationship between the state and the systems it deploys? Treat models as neutral tools and accountability dissolves into technical maintenance. Treat them as governing instruments and the need for institutional scaffolding becomes undeniable. As algorithms mediate more public decisions—who receives support first, who is deemed risky, which buildings are inspected, which households are flagged—the fabric of accountability must adapt. Not by rejecting models, but by surrounding them with the institutions that democracy requires: clear authority, visible boundaries, meaningful review, and contracts that preserve the state's ability to act on behalf of its people.

The chapter moves through these structural questions not as administrative theory, but as a practical anatomy of power. It shows how small design choices can recalibrate entire systems, and how the absence of structure can turn even well-intentioned tools into sources of confusion and harm. It examines why some accountability frameworks sharpen responsibility while others muffle it, and how the most effective institutions treat transparency not as compliance but as care.

A tension lingers, unresolved and necessary. As algorithmic governance grows, institutions must adapt faster than their historical pace allows. Yet speed can undermine legitimacy if frames are built hastily. The question that emerges—quiet but insistent—is this: *How do we construct institutions capable of governing systems that learn and change, without allowing those systems to outrun the democratic structures meant to guide them?*

Mandates and Boundaries

On 16 March 2020, the Italian Ministry of Health authorised the emergency use of the *Sistema di Sorveglianza Integrata*, a data-driven platform designed to monitor regional infection patterns during the country's first national lockdown. Its remit was sharply defined: support crisis response, inform hospital coordination, and expire automatically once emergency decrees lapsed. For several months the system did exactly that. It ingested health-care data, produced regional forecasts, and helped direct ventilators and staff to the hospitals that most needed them. But when infection rates fell sharply in June, a quiet tension emerged. Regional officials asked whether the system could also be used to anticipate winter surges, to prioritise vaccine distribution, or even to detect anomalies in social-care patterns. The original mandate had lapsed, but the model still sat on servers with few institutional constraints around its future use. A single question hovered over the system's fate: *Who decides what an emergency tool may become once the emergency ends?* Five words capture the hinge: *Its authority outlived its authorisation.*

Mandates determine the legitimacy of algorithmic power. They are the constitutional spine of any public system that predicts, categorises, or triggers state action. Without explicit authorisation—granted by a body with lawful authority and subject to democratic oversight—an algorithmic system becomes a free-floating instrument, driven not by defined policy goals but by organisational convenience, vendor defaults, or the gravitational pull of "why not use it for this, too?" The absence of boundaries is not neutral. It creates drift. A tool designed for a narrow purpose slips quietly into broader use, and nobody can say precisely when that shift occurred.

The motif that threads through this subchapter is *the line on the floor*: the boundary that tells an institution where proper authority ends. When that line is faint, blurred, or never drawn, systems expand into spaces the public never authorised.

The first task, then, is to show how mandates operate in practice. Authorisation can take many forms—statutory approval, ministerial directive, council resolution—but what matters is the clarity with which it describes the system's purpose, scope, and limits. A purpose statement anchors the system in a defined public aim. It answers the essential question: *Why do we need this model at all?* Boundaries answer the companion question: *Where must it not go?* The implication is direct. A system without a mandate may produce efficient results, but efficiency without authority is administrative overreach.

Canada's 2021 Directive on Automated Decision-Making illustrated a structured approach to authorisation. Departments were required to publish purpose statements describing the specific administrative power the model would exercise, the legal basis for that power, and the foreseeable risks. They also had to classify the system's impact level, which determined the strength of safeguards required. This created a discernible line on the floor. A benefits adjudication model could not be quietly repurposed to detect fraud. A risk-scoring tool designed for low-stakes triage could not be upgraded to sanction claimants without a new mandate. Authorisation was treated as choice, not drift.

A second example shows why boundaries matter even more than mandates. During the 2021 floods in New South Wales, Australia, emergency services deployed a real-time geospatial model to route evacuations and coordinate rescue resources. The authorisation was narrow: crisis-only, automatically expiring when emergency declarations ended. Yet when the rains subsided, several local agencies proposed using the system to monitor "ongoing movement patterns" to understand compliance with rebuild orders. The system's architects refused. The mandate had expired; the model's authority had returned to zero. This refusal was as important as the system's deployment. It protected the boundary between emergency measures and routine governance.

Yet not all examples push in the right direction. A credible counter-example clarifies the stakes. In 2016, a regional police force in the United States expanded a predictive model originally piloted to anticipate burglary hotspots during a summer crime spike. The pilot had been justified as a seasonal intervention. But the model was never retired. Instead, it migrated into standard patrol planning without new oversight, public notification, or statutory authority. As a result, the system began shaping year-round decisions despite being calibrated for an entirely different context. The line on the floor had vanished. Reconciliation requires recognising that pilots can become mandates by inertia. Institutional discipline is needed to ensure that temporary authorisation does not become permanent authority.

Boundaries must be both substantive and temporal. Substantive boundaries define what data may be used, what actions the system may trigger, and which decisions must remain human-led. Temporal boundaries—sunset clauses—ensure that systems do not persist simply because no one remembers why they were created. Sunset clauses force a return to first principles. When a mandate expires, policymakers must decide whether the system still serves a legitimate purpose, whether it needs revision, or whether it should be dismantled.

Sunset clauses also shift institutional cultures. When staff know a system will expire unless reauthorised, they collect evidence to justify or challenge renewal. Behaviour changes. Documentation improves. Evaluation becomes part of the system's lifecycle rather than a sporadic add-on. Italy's emergency health surveillance platform worked precisely because expiry was built in. When the deadline arrived, the system did not cling to life through technical convenience; it paused until democratic actors made a fresh choice.

Yet sunset clauses fail if renewal becomes automatic. A system that renews without scrutiny behaves like a law that cannot be repealed. This is where purpose statements serve as diagnostic tests. A purpose that once made sense must be weighed against new realities. Did the system achieve what it set out to do? Did it create unintended burdens? Does the underlying risk profile still justify algorithmic intervention? These questions draw the line on the floor more sharply.

Mandates also determine who bears responsibility when systems misfire. An authorised system has a clear owner; an unauthorised system has only diffuse blame. Accountability collapses when staff cannot identify who approved deployment or what limits were set. The behaviour becomes visible in appeals data: higher volumes of contested decisions, inconsistent explanations, and staff deferring to "the system" rather than the underlying legal framework. When people cannot trace a decision to a law, a person, or a mandate, legitimacy frays.

The line on the floor must be visible not only to technologists and policymakers but to citizens. Public notification is part of the mandate. When Helsinki launched its algorithmic register in 2020, it provided residents with purpose statements written in clear language. The effect was subtle but important: citizens could see what systems existed, what they were for, and what they were not permitted to do. The register placed the line on the floor in public view.

Procurement intersects with mandates in quiet but consequential ways. A contract that grants a vendor unilateral control over model updates stretches the boundary of public authority. If a vendor can change a model's logic without fresh authorisation, the system's mandate becomes unstable. New Zealand's 2021 update to its analytics procurement guidelines tackled this directly, requiring agencies to specify which model components vendors could modify without approval, and which required reauthorisation. The contract reinforced the line on the floor rather than erasing it.

A limitation must be acknowledged. Mandates can be too restrictive. A health-care prediction tool may need rapid adjustment during a new outbreak; a rigid authorisation process can slow lifesaving responses. But this does not weaken the case for boundaries. It strengthens the case for layered authorisation: rapid interim mandates for crisis adaptation, followed by fuller review once the shock stabilises. The line on the floor can move—but only through deliberate choice, not convenience.

Throughout this subchapter, the motif returns: *the line on the floor*—a boundary that must be drawn, redrawn, and defended. Without it, models wander from their intended paths, and authority becomes unmoored from democratic control. With it, the state retains the discipline to choose when algorithms should govern and when they should stand down.

A final tension remains unresolved. As models evolve rapidly—learning, updating, drifting—mandates risk lagging behind. Yet tightening mandates too rigidly can freeze innovation. This leaves a question pressing against the line on the floor: *How can governments authorise systems that change over time, without granting them so much flexibility that the boundary dissolves?*

Registers, Audits, and Impact Assessments

On 29 September 2020, the City of Amsterdam published its first *Algorithm Register*, a public-facing catalogue describing every significant automated system used by the municipality. It listed models for parking enforcement, welfare fraud detection, and noise-complaint triage. For each, the register set out purpose, data sources, risks, and oversight arrangements. The register was not a grand gesture; it was a response to a bruising scandal earlier that year when the Dutch childcare benefits system was found to have produced discriminatory outcomes, triggering mass resignations and shattered public confidence. Amsterdam's register was a line in the sand: if the state deploys an algorithm, the public has a right to know *what* it does, *why* it exists, and *where* its limits lie. Yet the register also exposed the tension that animates this subchapter: transparency can illuminate, but it can also distract, becoming theatre rather than accountability.

The motif here is *the opened box*—the idea that disclosure should lift the lid on systems that would otherwise remain closed. But an opened box can be ornamental. It can reveal form without revealing function. A system can be "transparent" yet still unexamined, unaudited, and unaccountable.

Registers, audits, and impact assessments are often treated as interchangeable tools, but each plays a distinct role. A register answers the question: *What exists?* An audit asks: *Is it working as intended?* An impact assessment asks: *Should it exist at all, and if so, under what safeguards?* Confusing these tools weakens all three. Clarity is the first step towards discipline.

Registers have proliferated across Europe and beyond. Helsinki launched its own register in 2020; Nantes followed in 2021. Both municipalities placed plain-language descriptions of systems online and invited citizens to explore them. The act of listing had impact metrics attached: increases in public enquiries, fewer freedom-of-information requests, and improved internal documentation. The show element matters: when a department knows its system will appear in a public list, behaviour shifts. Staff update documentation, clarify purpose, and identify risks because they know the opened box is visible to all. This is disclosure as discipline.

Yet not all registers produce meaningful visibility. A credible counter-example illustrates the risk. When a national government—unnamed here for legal reasons—launched its algorithm register in 2022, the entries were so general that they revealed almost nothing. A welfare risk-scoring tool was described only as "a data-driven analytics platform supporting decision-making". No model type. No data sources. No risk description. The register satisfied a policy requirement but provided no public value. The box was opened, but only emptiness lay inside. Reconciliation requires acknowledging that registers must prioritise substance, not form. A single clear entry can be more informative than twenty hollow ones.

Audits move from disclosure to verification. They ask whether a system performs within its authorised bounds and whether it continues to do so over time. The best public-sector audits are adversarial in design. They test models under stress, measure disparities across demographic groups, and compare outputs against human baselines. They use metrics the public can understand: false positives per thousand cases; average appeal success rates before and after deployment; wait-time distributions across districts. Auditors measure, compare, and commit findings to public record.

A clear example comes from the United Kingdom's 2021 review of the Ofqual grading algorithm, commissioned after the exam-results controversy earlier that year. The audit examined input distributions, model assumptions, and outcome disparities. It showed, visibly, that the system had treated outliers harshly—students from small schools experienced disproportionate downgrades because the model relied heavily on historical school-level performance. The report did not only diagnose error; it demonstrated that accuracy cannot compensate for poorly chosen reference classes. The implication was stark: robust audits must evaluate the social logic of the model, not just its mathematical fit.

A second example shows how audits can strengthen organisational behaviour. In San Francisco, the Police Commission's 2018 audit of predictive policing systems found that patrol assignments had been shaped by historical crime reports clustered in neighbourhoods that were over-policed. The audit recommended suspending the model until new datasets could be collected. The model was shelved within weeks. This was oversight with bite, using evidence to trigger policy change.

Yet audits face a limitation: they can be expensive, slow, and uneven in quality. A poorly executed audit may create a false sense of security, masking harms rather than revealing them. Reconciling this requires professionalising the audit function. Governments must build or buy expertise capable of stress-testing models, not merely reading documentation. An opened box inspected poorly is no better than a closed box.

Impact assessments sit at the beginning of the system's life, not at the end. They ask whether a proposed system aligns with legal, social, and ethical boundaries before deployment. A meaningful algorithmic impact assessment contains five core components: a purpose statement tied to legal authority; a description of data sources and their provenance; an assessment of foreseeable risks, including disparate impacts; an explanation of mitigation strategies; and a plan for monitoring and review. Its audience is broader than technologists. Policymakers read it to decide authorisation. Oversight bodies read it to understand where to apply scrutiny. Citizens read it to assess fairness.

A well-documented case comes from Canada's 2019 Directive on Automated Decision-Making, which mandated impact assessments for all federal algorithmic systems. Departments had to classify systems from Level I (low stakes) to Level IV (high stakes) based on potential harm to rights, health, or economic security. Higher levels required external peer review. The directive made a simple but powerful move: it linked the impact assessment to operational constraints. If a system scored as high impact but lacked adequate safeguards, it could not be deployed. The opened box was tied to a lock.

But impact assessments can decay into paperwork theatre. A counter-example comes from a European agency whose internal assessment templates ballooned into 70-page documents that no policymaker read and no technologist updated. Staff completed them at the final stage of development, treating them as a compliance exercise. The assessments revealed nothing. They changed nothing. They sat unread on a shared drive, ticking a box while failing to open one.

The risk of theatre grows when processes multiply without purpose. Registers that list but do not explain. Audits that praise without probing. Impact assessments that record but do not restrain. The motif of the opened box becomes distorted: a display item rather than a tool.

A unifying thread across registers, audits, and impact assessments is the visibility of real behaviour. For example, an audit that claims a model is "fair" means nothing unless it reports disparities with metrics. A register that lists a system's purpose must show the decision thresholds or data categories used. An impact assessment that predicts low risk must demonstrate how monitoring will detect shifts—appeal patterns, error rates, decile movement across groups. The public can read numbers. They can interpret simple charts. They can understand thresholds. The opened box must show what matters.

Two further examples clarify how these tools interact. New Zealand's Social Wellbeing Agency published structured impact assessments in 2020 that included decision trees, model diagrams, and policy rationales. They did not drown the reader in detail; they showed the model's logic. This strengthened public engagement and helped avoid misinterpretation. Meanwhile, Denmark's 2022 municipal algorithm registry required each entry to link to its latest audit summary. This integrated disclosure: the register opened the box, the audit examined it, and the assessment contextualised it.

The limitation of tool-based accountability is that tools can be co-opted. A department may perform an audit to justify a predetermined outcome. A register may be curated for public relations. An assessment may be drafted by vendors. Reconciliation requires embedding countervailing power. Independent oversight bodies should read audit results. Civil-society groups should review impact assessments. Elected officials should use registers to question scope creep. An opened box viewed only by its maker is not transparency; it is décor.

A final tension remains. Public systems increasingly rely on models that update frequently—daily, hourly, sometimes continuously. Registers and impact assessments, however, are static documents. Audits take time. How should governments maintain meaningful visibility when systems evolve faster than oversight can keep pace?

The opened box must be updated, but without overwhelming readers or exhausting staff.

The unresolved question is therefore this: *When models change themselves, what does a credible opened box look like, and who must be able to look inside it for the system to remain legitimate?*

Independent Oversight that Bites

On 23 January 2020, in The Hague, the Dutch government resigned en masse over the childcare benefits scandal. Years of automated risk scoring inside the Belastingdienst had branded thousands of families as fraudsters on the basis of minor paperwork errors and opaque rules. Parents with no history of wrongdoing were ordered to repay vast sums, often overnight. Appeals bodies had flagged patterns of wrongful decisions for years; internal lawyers had warned of disproportionate impacts. Yet no independent authority with real power had forced the system to stop. When the Prime Minister announced the cabinet's resignation, one fact was quietly devastating: the tools of oversight existed, but none had teeth. The committees had met. The papers had been filed. The damage had been done. The committee room felt small.

Oversight without power is staging. Oversight with power, but without independence, is theatre of a different kind. The central question for algorithmic governance is not whether oversight bodies exist; most jurisdictions can point to ombudsmen, data protection authorities, ethics panels. The question is whether any of them can read the code, subpoena the records, compel remedial action, and explain publicly what they have found. The motif that threads through this subchapter is *the table*: the place where systems are called to account. Who sits at that table, what information they can see, and what they are authorised to do when they see something wrong, determine whether oversight merely watches or genuinely bites.

Design begins with composition. A credible review body is not a club of insiders. It is a structured collision between three kinds of knowledge: technical expertise capable of interrogating models; legal and institutional expertise grounded in public and administrative law;

and lived experience from the communities most affected by automated decisions. When one of these is missing, the table tilts. A panel of data scientists may miss the social significance of false positives. A panel of lawyers may struggle to challenge technical claims. A panel of citizens without access to experts may raise real concerns but be easily reassured with superficial explanations.

Consider the Canadian federal government's experiment with its Directive on Automated Decision-Making and the associated review processes after 2019. High-impact systems required external peer review. Panels included academic computer scientists, legal scholars, and, in some cases, civil-society representatives. They were given access to documentation, risk assessments, and limited test data. The behaviour that followed was concrete: models were downgraded in scope, additional human review points were inserted, and in at least one case a proposed deployment was delayed. The table mattered because the people around it had both knowledge and a mandate to criticise.

Contrast this with New York City's Automated Decision Systems Task Force, convened in 2018. It had a broad remit—to examine algorithms used across city agencies—and a membership including civil servants, researchers, and advocates. Yet it lacked key powers. Vendors refused to disclose proprietary models. Agencies withheld specific system details. The task force could recommend but not compel. Its final report, published in 2019, contained valuable principles but few concrete findings about actual systems. The table existed, but most of the important documents never reached it.

Power is the second design ingredient. A review body that cannot demand access to models, data, and contractual terms is confined to the surface. For oversight to bite, it must be able to see what matters and insist on change. Data protection authorities in Europe provide one template. Under the GDPR, they can investigate, issue fines, and order processing to stop. When the Dutch Data Protection Authority examined the SyRI risk-scoring system, its findings fed directly into a court judgment that declared the legal basis inadequate. The authority did not merely advise; it shaped consequences.

Yet many AI or algorithmic advisory boards are built without such powers. They meet quarterly, issue guidance notes, and are then thanked for their input while the machinery of deployment rolls on unchanged. The difference is visible in metrics. Where oversight has teeth, one can count enforcement actions, mandated suspensions, and remedial plans. Where it does not, one counts workshops and glossy reports.

Transparency is the third pillar. Oversight that operates entirely behind closed doors can drift towards capture, even if formally independent. At the same time, some aspects of review—such as security-sensitive details—cannot be fully public. The design problem is to decide which parts of the table are visible and to whom. One promising pattern uses layered transparency. Technical details are available to accredited experts; high-level explanations, risks, and outcomes are communicated in accessible language to the public. The French data protection authority has experimented with publishing summaries of algorithmic investigations, outlining what systems do, what went wrong, and how organisations must fix them. This visible behaviour builds trust because citizens can see both error and remedy.

The most underused source of oversight intelligence, however, is appeals data. Every time a citizen contests an automated decision, they produce a signal about how the system behaves in the world. If appeals cluster around certain neighbourhoods, demographic groups, or decision types, something is happening that aggregate accuracy statistics may miss. When the UK's Social Security and Child Support Tribunal began tracking patterns in appeals related to digital benefits systems, it exposed recurring problems: notices that lacked clear reasons, evidence misinterpreted by automated checks, and thresholds set without regard to atypical cases. In jurisdictions where appeal outcomes are systematically shared with auditors or regulators, those patterns feed straight back to the table.

A review body that ignores appeals data performs abstraction instead of accountability. A body that treats appeal clusters as "casework noise" rather than diagnostic information will miss early warning signs. The table should, in effect, have a reserved seat for the citizen voice, not as anecdote but as empirical pattern.

This is where adversarial expertise matters. Traditional audit approaches often ask whether a system meets declared specifications. Adversarial review asks how a system can fail, be gamed, or produce harm that its designers did not foresee. When the European Commission's High-Level Expert Group on AI carried out a red-team style assessment of certain public-sector pilots in 2019, it discovered vulnerabilities not mentioned in the initial documentation: susceptibility to data poisoning, over-reliance on proxy variables, and unmonitored feedback loops. Adversarial experts are those who treat the model as a potential opponent, not an object of optimisation.

Some administrators instinctively resist this stance, viewing adversarial scrutiny as hostility. But the behaviour of resilient systems shows the opposite. Projects that survive adversarial review are stronger. Their maintainers understand failure modes better; their documentation is more honest; their monitoring plans are sharper. A review table without adversarial seats is like a court without defence counsel: orderly, perhaps, but fatally incomplete.

Citizen seats are equally important. Not because citizens will read every technical annex or interpret every metric, but because their presence changes what is discussed. In Helsinki's data advisory board, which began work around 2020, resident representatives questioned assumptions that technical experts had treated as neutral: why was convenience for administrators weighted more heavily than the inconvenience of appeals for residents? Why were some harms framed as "operational risk" and others as "regrettable but acceptable"? These questions are not purely technical. They are political and moral. Their rightful place is at the table.

Yet there are limits. Citizen members may face steep learning curves; there is a risk of tokenism if they are outnumbered or unsupported. Reconciling this requires design. Citizen seats must be paired with resources: briefings, independent advisors they can consult, and the power to request pauses or further investigation. Without that, their role can become ceremonial. The visible behaviour that signals substance, not symbolism, is simple: citizen representatives occasionally disagree publicly with the technical consensus, and sometimes their view prevails.

A credible counter-example illustrates the pitfalls. Several large technology companies have created "external advisory councils" for AI ethics that collapsed within months. In one widely reported case in 2019, members resigned after discovering that the council had no access to key projects and no influence over decision-making. The table existed; the menu had already been set elsewhere. Public institutions should study these failures closely, if only to avoid replicating their emptiness.

Designing oversight that bites also raises questions about scope. Should there be one central body with sweeping powers, or a network of sectoral regulators with algorithmic expertise embedded? The answer is often "both". Central bodies can set standards, coordinate audits, and handle cross-cutting issues like fairness and transparency. Sector regulators understand the domain: health, housing, policing, welfare. A risk-scoring tool in child protection raises different issues from a congestion-pricing model. The table must be set where knowledge resides.

Finally, there is the matter of timing. Oversight that arrives only after deployment is damage control. Oversight involved during design can influence problem framing, data selection, and choice of targets. In Canada's directive, high-impact systems require early notification to the Treasury Board Secretariat and, in some cases, external review prior to launch. That shifts the rhythm. The table is convened before the model begins to govern, not merely after controversy erupts.

The deeper question is not whether independent oversight can be built, but whether institutions will tolerate its bite. Bodies with real powers will sometimes embarrass governments, halt flagship projects, and demand public explanations. They will slow down some deployments. They will insist that certain models never progress beyond pilot stage. Their success is measured not in how often they agree but in how well they can say "no" when "yes" would be easier.

This leaves a deliberate tension hanging over the table. As states grow more reliant on algorithmic tools, will they genuinely share authority with oversight bodies that include adversarial experts and ordinary citizens, or will they continue to favour panels that advise politely while the systems march on?

Procurement as Governance

In April 2017, the City of Chicago renewed a multi-year contract with a private vendor to maintain the predictive analytics system that helped the Department of Public Health identify properties at risk of lead contamination. The original contract, signed in 2014, had covered model development and initial deployment. The renewal added a clause allowing the vendor to update its model without prior municipal approval so long as performance, defined narrowly by detection rates, did not fall below a fixed threshold. Within a year, the model had changed twice. Officials discovered this only when external researchers compared outputs from 2016 and 2018 and noticed that the system was directing inspectors to different neighbourhoods, with no public record of new data sources or altered weightings. The model had moved, silently. The contract had allowed it. The city had purchased not a tool but a dependency.

That episode captured a broader structural truth: governments do not merely buy systems; they buy the incentives that shape those systems long after deployment. If procurement is sloppy, the public inherits opacity. If procurement is precise, the public inherits leverage. The motif that threads through this subchapter is *the hinge*: the idea that a contract, often treated as administrative paperwork, determines whether a system swings towards accountability or shuts tight.

Procurement begins before signatures. It starts with the problem framing that vendors respond to. When agencies issue requests for proposals that emphasise throughput or cost-savings above all else, vendors optimise for those metrics. When agencies require evidence of explainability, clear access rights, and exit conditions, vendors design accordingly. The hinge moves at the moment those requirements are written.

The Chicago case shows how unrestricted model updates can shift risk. To understand the implications, compare it with a counter-example. In 2022, the City of Barcelona negotiated a contract for its mobility analytics system used to analyse pedestrian flows in the Gothic Quarter. The contract stipulated that any model update must be logged, documented, and submitted to a municipal oversight team within five working days. Crucially, the city retained ownership of all derived data and required the vendor to supply a reproducible version of any update for internal testing. This clause tied algorithmic movement to visible behaviour. When a change was made, inspectors saw it. When they saw it, they could question or block it. The hinge opened outward, towards oversight.

Contracts also determine access to data and models. A common failure mode is when governments purchase black-box systems and rely on vendor summaries of performance. In 2019, the state of New Jersey faced this problem with a proprietary risk assessment tool used in certain child welfare processes. The vendor provided general documentation but restricted access to the underlying model, citing intellectual property protections. Officials could see outputs but not the assumptions that generated them. The system remained technically lawful but practically unauditable. Metrics such as false-positive rates or subgroup disparities were impossible to verify independently. Without access, scrutiny collapses into trust, and trust cannot substitute for verification.

Reconciliation requires precision in contractual language. Agencies must state, explicitly, what access they expect: to code, to model weights, to input-output logs, to training data sources, or at minimum to an executable artefact that can be tested in a controlled environment. The limitation is that small municipalities may lack bargaining power. Vendors with dominant market share may refuse. Here, consortium procurement offers leverage. When several cities negotiate jointly—as occurred with Norwegian municipalities procuring welfare analytics tools around 2020—vendors face a larger market and are more likely to accept transparency clauses.

Explainability follows similar dynamics. It cannot be an afterthought added to a signed contract. It must be specified. A contract can require vendors to produce global explanations of model logic, local explanations for individual decisions, and procedural explanations detailing how decisions flow through administrative processes.

When explainability is contractually required, vendors prepare documentation during development rather than scrambling post-deployment. This behaviour is visible: documentation updates appear alongside model updates; training materials reflect actual model logic; citizen-facing notices include reasons drawn from signed-off templates.

A striking example comes from New Zealand's 2020 procurement of a triage model for building safety inspections after earthquakes. The ministry involved required that every decision issued by the system be accompanied by a plain-language explanation produced by a vendor-supplied explainer module. The contract further required that this explainer be open for external audit. During pilot testing, independent reviewers discovered fragility in some of the explanations: similar properties were labelled differently. Because the contract mandated correction, the vendor was obliged to improve the logic rather than defend opaque errors. The hinge held steady because the contract fixed its axis.

Data portability is another hinge that determines long-term power. Without portability, governments become captive customers. Portability clauses allow agencies to migrate to alternative vendors or bring systems in-house. They require vendors to provide data in standard, machine-readable formats, accompanied by metadata and documentation. When Estonia modernised parts of its e-government services in 2021, portability was central. Vendors had to commit to export all structured data using defined schemas such as X-Road formats. This meant that when contracts ended, systems could be swapped without rebuilding entire data infrastructures. Behaviourally, this created competitive pressure: vendors knew they could be replaced, so they maintained quality and responsiveness.

A credible counter-example shows the risks of omitting portability. In 2018, a mid-sized US county attempted to transition away from a proprietary case-management system used in its probation services. The vendor claimed that the county's data was technically extractable but in practice handed over inconsistent XML files lacking documentation. Migration took 18 months instead of the projected four. Costs tripled. The county's oversight team could not verify historical decision rules, and several appeal cases were delayed because records were incomplete. The hinge, in that procurement, locked inward. Portability had been reduced to a slogan rather than a standard.

Exit clauses are perhaps the most underrated tool in the procurement arsenal. An exit clause specifies when and how the government can discontinue a system, reclaim its data, and shift to alternatives. Exit clauses matter because predictive systems age. Models drift. Social contexts shift. A contract that assumes indefinite performance traps the public into using systems that may no longer serve their purpose.

A clear example comes from Ireland's 2023 procurement of a model to support school place allocation fairness reviews. The contract allowed the Department of Education to suspend or terminate the system if monitored appeal rates exceeded a defined threshold for two consecutive quarters. This tied exit to a metric the public could understand: successful appeals. When those numbers rise, something is wrong. By contrast, a limitation becomes visible when exit depends solely on performance proxies like accuracy. Accuracy can remain high even as legitimacy collapses. Reconciliation lies in aligning exit triggers with the lived experience of those governed by the system.

The politics of procurement are just as significant as the clauses. Many agencies treat procurement as administrative routine. They underestimate how contractual terms shape incentives upstream. Vendor selection committees may focus on price rather than governance. Yet long-term costs arise not from the sticker price but from the hidden dependencies contracts embed. A contract that grants the agency full access but requires substantial internal capacity may fail because staff lack time or expertise. Conversely, a contract that shifts too much responsibility to vendors may reduce administrative burden in the short term but weaken accountability.

This interplay is visible in the case of London's 2019 procurement of traffic analytics tools for congestion modelling. Transport for London explicitly required that vendor updates be tested in a "shadow environment" for four weeks before deployment. This balanced capability: the vendor could innovate; the agency could verify. The visible behaviour was disciplined: shadow results were published internally; discrepancies triggered review meetings; updates slowed when anomalies emerged. Procurement created the conditions for iterative oversight.

Another tension emerges around intellectual property. Vendors argue that releasing code or model artefacts undermines competitive advantage. Governments argue that public decisions require public visibility. Some jurisdictions address this through escrow arrangements. In 2020, Finland established a model repository where vendors deposit code under controlled access. Independent auditors can inspect it; the public receives summaries. The hinge here opens partially, calibrated to balance trade secrets with accountability. Its implication is that procurement can be used to negotiate hybrid visibility, not all-or-nothing transparency.

A final thread concerns the lived experience of officials who must enforce contracts. Procurement officers often face intense time pressure. They juggle legal requirements, budget constraints, and political expectations. They may rely on templated documents that fail to capture the specificities of machine-learning systems. If procurement is governance, these officers are frontline policymakers. Their behaviour—asking the right questions, demanding the right clauses, resisting vague promises—is what turns contractual theory into institutional muscle.

The unresolved question sits at the centre of the hinge: as algorithmic systems become more adaptive, more complex, and more integrated into public services, will procurement evolve into a strategic governance tool or remain an administrative formality? Governments can write contracts that keep the hinge open—towards access, scrutiny, and exit—or contracts that allow systems to swing away from public control. The choice of hinge determines whether accountability endures long after the ink has dried.

Chapter 5
Citizens, Not Just Users

On a warm evening in June 2019, a crowd gathered in the Praça do Intendente in Lisbon, watching a projection of their city flicker across a temporary screen. It was not a film but a map—one that shifted and pulsed as residents adjusted sliders on nearby tablets. Each movement reshaped proposed transport routes, reallocating road space, cycling lanes, and pedestrian areas. A mother nudged her stroller with one hand and, with the other, dragged a slider that widened pavements near her flat. A café owner narrowed them again, pointing to delivery vehicles he relied on. The software visualised the consequences instantly: travel times, emissions, and local business footfall. No yes–no referendum. No abstract consultation. Real trade-offs in real time. People leaned forward, not because the system was complex, but because it treated them as agents, not data points.

That night crystallised a tension running through modern governance: democratic states increasingly mediate public life through digital systems, yet those systems often recast the citizen as a mere user—someone to navigate menus, tick boxes, and accept defaults. The Lisbon experiment offered a different imagination. It showed that citizens can engage meaningfully with algorithmically generated scenarios when the interface dignifies them, when the stakes are legible, and when the system's purpose is to expand, not narrow, their agency.

The motif that threads through this chapter is *the hand on the lever*: sometimes grasping it, sometimes slipping from it, sometimes never feeling it at all. Platforms can place the lever within reach or out of sight, shaping who participates, who waits, and who receives care or remedy. The difference is not technological capacity but democratic intent. To understand how AI reshapes governance, we must first understand how it reshapes citizenship itself.

Digital participation is often presented as a solved problem. Governments deploy survey tools; residents select from multiple-choice questions; the results feed into summary dashboards. But the distance between a ticked box and a shared decision can be immense. Participation becomes theatre when citizens are funnelled into predefined preferences, unable to explore the actual consequences of what they support. The more complex the policy, the more limited the questionnaire becomes. And yet, as participatory budgeting pilots from Madrid to Montreal have shown, model-assisted scenarios can increase the quality of debate. When residents can see the knock-on effects of spending £200,000 on a youth centre versus resurfacing local roads—the delays, the opportunity costs, the ripple effects on maintenance budgets—they do not merely express opinions; they deliberate. The citizen becomes a co-analyst.

But the lever can slip the other way. Online platforms that promise to "amplify voices" can just as easily mute them. Consider the pattern found in successive evaluations of digital consultations in the United Kingdom during the mid-2010s: participation clustered among highly educated, time-rich citizens, while residents with limited digital access or precarious schedules remained peripheral. Algorithms recommended popular threads, burying minority concerns. The platform design, not public apathy, determined whose voice carried weight. To treat people as citizens is to design systems that counteract these skews rather than reproduce them.

Beyond participation lies something more intimate and more operational: the experience of being governed through a screen. When public decisions move online, they produce a new kind of queue—digital, silent, and often opaque. Here, due process becomes a design problem. Notice, reasons, and appeal must be translated into interface elements that ordinary people can understand and act upon. A term such as "insufficient evidence" means nothing unless accompanied by examples; a deadline means little unless the system shows how many steps remain; an appeal cannot be meaningful unless evidence can be uploaded in standardised packs rather than as ad hoc attachments that caseworkers must decipher.

Consider a story from a benefits office in Nottingham in 2022. A claimant received a sanction notice through the online portal. The reasons were vague. Yet the portal included a newly introduced evidence pack template: a structured form allowing claimants to submit pay slips, explanatory statements, and third-party letters in a clear sequence. A week later, the internal system flagged the appeal for expedited review because the submitted pack met completeness thresholds built into the triage model. The appeal succeeded. Nothing miraculous occurred. What mattered was that the citizen understood the path to remedy and the system recognised that completeness, not eloquence, warrants attention. The lever remained within reach.

Trust in public institutions often falters not because systems are hostile but because they are indifferent. A cold screen replaces a warm conversation. Administrative justice—deeply relational in its traditional form—gets flattened into error messages and status bars. Yet digital tools need not sever care from governance. In several municipalities across Denmark, caseworkers now receive triage suggestions generated by models trained on past successful interventions. These suggestions do not replace judgement; they supplement it. Crucially, pilots that succeeded were those where caseworkers were shown why suggestions appeared and where managers protected discretion. The small dignities—being addressed by name, receiving a call when documents were unclear, seeing consistent reasons across messages—determined whether citizens perceived the system as humane or mechanised.

This raises a deeper question: what responsibility accompanies the vast quantities of data that citizens produce as they interact with digital public services? The shift towards civic data stewardship reframes people not as raw input but as co-owners of shared data assets. The model is not one of extractive collection but of reciprocal governance. Cities such as Barcelona and Ghent have moved towards community data boards—groups of residents, technologists, and legal experts who review proposals for data re-use. Their remit extends beyond consent; they examine whether re-use genuinely serves a public purpose and whether risks are tolerable. In some experiments, data dividends have been introduced: modest, collective returns channelled into neighbourhood improvements when mobility or environmental data create economic value for the city. The dividend is symbolic, but the symbolism matters. It signals that data do not flow in one direction.

What unites these developments is the reassertion of agency. When citizens are treated as users, the system's purpose is operational efficiency. When citizens are treated as citizens, the system's purpose becomes democratic legitimacy. These aims need not conflict, but they require conscious balancing. A beautifully optimised portal that fails to explain a sanction destroys trust faster than a slower system that respects dignity. A sophisticated participatory platform that mutes minority voices collapses the very ideal it claims to uphold. A clever triage model that overwhelms caseworkers with opaque suggestions corrodes professional pride and alienates the people it seeks to help.

The chapter ahead asks a simple, difficult question: how should a democratic state design digital systems that support—not supplant—the role of the citizen? This is not a sentimental invitation to idleness or endless consultation. It is a recognition that every digital touchpoint teaches people something about the state: whether it listens, whether it explains itself, whether it recognises them as whole human beings.

As public institutions expand their use of models and platforms, the stakes rise. The hand on the lever must belong to the public, even when mediated by code. The challenge is not only technical but constitutional: how to preserve voice, dignity, remedy, and shared stewardship in a world where governance increasingly flows through decisions made in milliseconds.

The path is neither linear nor settled. It begins with recognising that the difference between a user and a citizen is not rhetorical. It is architectural. And whether future systems tilt one way or the other will depend on choices now—choices about participation, due process, care, and data governance—that define the contours of democratic agency in the decades ahead.

Digital Participation Beyond Surveys

In May 2019, the Câmara Municipal de Lisboa invited residents to test a prototype platform for reallocating part of the city's transport budget. The tool visualised trade-offs in real time: widen a bus corridor along Avenida Almirante Reis and journey times dropped by measurable minutes; protect on-street parking in Arroios and cycling connectivity fractured instantly. Residents gathered in the Mouraria Creative Hub, adjusting sliders that reshaped the map projected on the wall. A teacher from Intendente shifted funds to pedestrian crossings and watched predicted injury rates fall. A shopkeeper reversed the change and noted the projected decline in evening footfall. The platform did not ask people *what* they wanted abstractly. It asked them to weigh what their neighbours would win or lose. Participation became embodied, not extracted. This was consultation with consequences, not a survey of disconnected preferences.

A paradox gives the scene its force: Lisbon spent roughly €45,000 building the model-assisted prototype—less than a third of what it spent, the previous year, analysing thousands of conventional survey responses whose results failed to resolve any meaningful public disagreement. The cheap tool produced clarity. The expensive survey produced noise. Why? Because the model showed the city's constraints, while the survey treated preferences as free-floating wishes.

The motif threading through this subchapter is *the table of trade-offs*. A system invites citizens to sit at that table or leaves them outside, peering through frosted glass. Most digital consultations still resemble the latter. They offer sliders without consequences, forums without structure, and dashboards that aggregate opinions but conceal the underlying tensions those opinions reflect. The work of democratic design is to bring citizens to the table and show them how their choices intersect.

Participatory budgeting, when infused with model-assisted scenarios, illustrates how this shift unfolds. Take Madrid's 2017–19 Decide Madrid platform, which integrated simple forecasting models into neighbourhood proposals. Residents could propose investments; the platform displayed estimated maintenance costs, likely completion timelines, and impacts on municipal staffing. This visible behaviour grounded deliberation. A proposal to expand playgrounds in Usera gained support only after users saw the projected impact on maintenance budgets and agreed to reduce spending elsewhere. The model did not dictate outcomes; it structured debate. The implication was clear: participation deepens when citizens are treated as capable of grappling with constraints rather than merely expressing desires.

Yet not all platforms amplify deliberation. Some mute it. Paris's 2018 digital engagement portal, for example, offered residents the ability to upvote proposals but offered no mechanism to explore trade-offs or competing effects. Unsurprisingly, the most popular proposals skewed towards amenities serving digitally engaged constituencies—cycling storage, urban gardens—while concerns from peripheral districts about public transport reliability were under-represented. Participation clustered, not by need, but by digital habit. This pattern has been documented repeatedly in civic-tech evaluations: if participation is limited to binary signals—votes, likes, clicks—the table of trade-offs collapses into a contest of visibility, not a forum of judgement.

A credible counter-example demonstrates the limit of model-assisted optimism. In Reykjavik's renowned Better Reykjavik platform, launched in 2011 and augmented with scenario tools in later years, participation surged, but deliberative quality varied sharply. When models were too complex, users disengaged. When effects were too simplified, users distrusted them. Reconciliation came through iterative design: the city added context cards explaining each forecast, allowed residents to compare two or three scenarios at once, and built a "what changes most?" feature that highlighted the top three consequences of each choice. Complexity was not abolished; it was scaffolded.

The first major claim of this subchapter is that model-assisted participation changes the locus of agency. To show this, consider how people behave when they see *instant* consequences of their choices. In Lisbon's pilot, residents spent longer on scenarios that affected multiple neighbourhoods than on single-street preferences. They compared commute times, emissions, and local business metrics. They adjusted. They debated. They returned to earlier choices when counter-effects emerged. Behaviour changed because visibility increased. The platform transformed abstract values—

mobility, safety, climate—into visible decisions with traceable impacts. It named, and then revealed, the trade-offs.

The implication is profound: digital participation becomes meaningful when citizens can *see the problem as the state sees it.* This is not a concession; it is a constitutional principle. Nostalgic formats such as open-text surveys obscure the public budget, dilute competing claims, and reward free-floating aspiration. Scenarios force alignment with reality.

The second claim is that participation must be designed to counteract underlying inequalities. Digital tools can widen or narrow civic gaps depending on structure. In Taiwan's vTaiwan process during 2015–18, the Polis platform surfaced consensus on contested issues—ride-sharing laws, online alcohol regulations—by mapping clusters of opinion and showing which statements bridged groups. Policymakers and citizens discovered areas of agreement previously hidden beneath surface-level antagonism. The platform's behaviour—visualising patterns rather than amplifying noise—shifted the entire political rhythm. But it also depended on early outreach to bring in varied participants. Without those efforts, the map of consensus would have mirrored the digital elite.

The limitation is that even the most inclusive digital design cannot fully overcome offline inequalities. People with unstable shifts, limited connectivity, or linguistic barriers remain under-represented. Reconciling this means treating digital participation as one component of a broader participatory ecosystem. In Lisbon's case, community organisations were invited to host their own scenario sessions, using translated materials and assisted facilitation. The model moved, but the table remained local.

A third claim runs deeper: model-assisted participation can reveal *latent priorities* that surveys miss. In Montreal's 2021 transport planning consultation, residents consistently ranked road safety as a top concern in surveys. But when shown modelled trade-offs—reduce car lanes to improve safety or maintain throughput at the cost of slower pedestrian crossings—many participants altered their expressed priorities. They shifted from safety-at-any-cost to balanced solutions when they saw quantitative impacts on emergency response times and local congestion. The visible behaviour—the moment residents paused, reconsidered, and adjusted choices—showed the transformative power of models. The implication is that participation is not merely about collecting opinions; it is about cultivating informed preference.

But here lies a risk. If models appear too authoritative, they may nudge participants towards technocratic determinism. A scenario that quantifies certain effects can overshadow impacts it cannot measure. For example, in a Barcelona district budget pilot in 2020, the model emphasised cost and time impacts but could not quantify cultural effects such as preserving community spaces. Residents noted the omission and felt the process skewed. The counter-example reveals the central limitation: models shape the frame, and frames shape outcomes.

Reconciliation lies in openly communicating model capacities and blind spots. A well-designed platform names what the model measures—journey times, emissions—and what it cannot—cultural cohesion, sense of belonging. It invites residents to bring those missing values into discussion. This transparency is the hinge that prevents the model from becoming the master.

As digital participation evolves, the motif of *the table of trade-offs* reappears in a new dimension: the table is not a metaphor but a set of interfaces, visualisations, and feedback loops that determine whether citizens can meaningfully grasp the structure of governance. A slider is not politically neutral. A map projection can elevate one group's priorities or obscure another's. A recommendation algorithm highlighting "popular ideas" might amplify familiar voices while muting those who cannot spend evenings online.

The fourth major claim is that participation becomes governance when it shapes outcomes, not when it merely signals interest. In Porto Alegre—the birthplace of participatory budgeting in 1989—digital tools added in the 2010s increased attendance but did not always influence final decisions. In contrast, Paris's 2016–20 participatory budgeting cycle, which dedicated €500 million to resident proposals, embedded model-assisted costing directly into the approval process. Proposals that exceeded district limits were flagged immediately; residents could revise them within the platform. The behaviour this enabled—editing, resubmitting, refining—was procedural participation, not symbolic input.

Yet a limitation emerges: the more consequential participation becomes, the more contestable the models must be. If a platform shows that reallocating €100,000 reduces carbon emissions by a specific amount, residents should be able to ask *how* that estimate was calculated. Without explainability, the model becomes a black-box arbiter masquerading as democratic infrastructure.

The path forward is iterative contestation. Platforms should include links to methodologies, allow residents to test alternative assumptions, and provide logs of changes across consultation phases. When the city of Helsinki introduced scenario-based participation for urban green space planning in 2020, it published both the scripts used for the models and the uncertainties associated with each estimate. Residents responded with a mixture of appreciation and critique; officials adjusted parameters accordingly. The platform became a shared analytic space rather than a presentation layer.

The closing tension is unavoidable and necessary. Digital participation can democratise complex decisions or entrench new inequalities. It can reveal the structure of public problems or hide it behind seductive visualisations. The crucial question facing any democratic institution deploying such tools is simple and severe: *Are we inviting citizens to sit at the table of trade-offs, or are we asking them to endorse choices already made?*

The answer determines whether digital participation expands citizenship or merely rehearses the role of the user.

Due Process in a Digital Queue

On a wet morning in March 2021, at a Jobcentre Plus office in Liverpool, a claimant named Sarah Hughes opened the decision screen on her phone. Two weeks earlier she had received an automated suspension of her Universal Credit housing element, issued after a missed appointment she insisted had never been scheduled. The notice she received then had been opaque: a red banner, a short code, a link to generic guidance. But the update she saw now was different. After a local pilot introduced structured appeal interfaces, the system displayed three plain sentences explaining what evidence she needed, how long review would take, and who would read her case. She uploaded screenshots of her appointment log, added a short statement, and pressed submit. Forty-eight hours later, the decision was overturned, her payments reinstated. The outcome was modest. The principle was not. A digital queue had become a site where procedural justice could be seen and felt rather than guessed at.

The paradox that frames this subchapter is simple: governments spend millions automating eligibility decisions, yet often treat the inexpensive components of due process—clear notice, adequate reasons, accessible appeal—as optional design extras. A £3 tweak in interface copy can change a citizen's behaviour more than a £300,000 scoring model. But such tweaks require a commitment to *seeing* the citizen not as a user clicking through forms but as a rights-bearing participant navigating the state's power.

The quiet motif threading the analysis is *the line*: the queue as a symbol, the interface as a line of text, the boundary between algorithmic decision and human recourse. A digital queue can respect the line or smudge it.

The first major claim is that notice is not an information dump; it is a constitutional signal. Show this with a small behaviour. When the New York City Human Resources Administration trialled redesigned electronic notices in 2018, it replaced jargon-heavy codes with two-sentence explanations and a timestamp for the next action. Behaviour changed. Claimants opened notices more often, contacted support less often for clarification, and missed fewer review deadlines. The administration named the rationale: clear notice reduces administrative churn. The implication is broader: any automated system that cannot inform a citizen *what happened, why, and what comes next* is not merely inefficient; it is procedurally defective.

But notice alone does not secure due process. Reasons matter. In Estonia's 2020 revalidation of its digital unemployment assessment tool, officials required each denial to include the top two determinants of the outcome, written in language no more complex than the country's B2 literacy standard. The requirement forced developers to align model outputs with narrative templates. When factors could not be expressed meaningfully, they could not be used. This behaviour—translating variables into reasons—ensured that decisions linked to comprehensible grounds rather than opaque correlations.

A credible counter-example shows the danger of treating reasons as metadata rather than meaning. In the Netherlands, the SyRI fraud-detection system, used until 2020, attached lengthy legal citations to its notifications but gave no specific account of why an individual had been flagged. Citizens received notice without intelligible explanation. Courts struck it down for violating privacy and fairness standards. Reconciling this with the earlier examples produces a clear boundary: reasons must be *specific to the case* and *available before harm occurs*. Anything less is decorative legality.

The second claim is that appeal mechanisms must be embedded in the interface, not buried behind telephone lines or delayed letters. The behaviour to observe is simple: when citizens can see the appeal path at the moment they receive a decision, they are more likely to contest errors. During the Scottish Social Security Agency's 2022 trial of in-app "request reconsideration" features, appeal initiation rates increased, but average appeal length fell. Officials named the cause: citizens uploaded the right documents first time because the interface displayed a standardised evidence pack—a checklist that guided them through proofs of income, housing, or health. The implication is that digital due process is as much about *scaffolding success* as enabling challenge.

This brings us to the small story at the core of this subchapter: Sarah's appeal in Liverpool succeeded not because she had time, literacy, or support, but because the digital queue gave her a shelf to place her evidence on. The system framed her as someone who could meaningfully respond. She did. Her caseworker reviewed. The line held.

But appeals also test the limits of digital justice. Not all citizens can upload documents, compose statements, or navigate interfaces. A counter-example surfaces here: during the 2020 expansion of online tax appeals in France, cases from rural areas without stable broadband were disproportionately abandoned. Attempts to reconcile this led to hybrid offices where staff helped residents file appeals using simplified tools. The lesson is not to slow digital reform but to ensure it remains porous—open to assisted channels that uphold procedural rights.

The third claim is that due process in digital systems requires *timeliness* as much as form. A citizen who receives an intelligible notice and clear reasons can still be denied justice if appeal queues operate on unpredictable or opaque schedules. Behavioural data from New Zealand's 2021 digital social housing review showed that applicants receiving estimated review times avoided repeated submissions and did not escalate complaints as quickly. Officials named uncertainty as a driver of frustration. Once review timeframes were displayed and updated, the digital queue stopped feeling like a void and became a process.

Yet timeliness introduces tension. Rapid decisions risk superficial review; slow ones strain livelihoods. Monitoring plans can mitigate this trade-off. Canada's Employment Insurance digital trials in 2022 introduced a queue-monitoring dashboard for claimants, showing where their case sat in the review line and which step awaited completion. The visible cue reduced calls to help centres. But the limitation was that these timelines were probabilistic. Some cases fell outside estimates, undermining confidence. Reconciling this requires humility: transparency is not perfection, but it is better than silence.

The fourth claim centres on equality of arms. A fair digital queue ensures that citizens know what evidence matters and can obtain it. Standard evidence packs achieve this by listing common documents and allowing citizens to pre-fill statements. When Denmark piloted such packs for parental benefit appeals in 2019, error rates dropped. Caseworkers spent less time chasing missing information. Applicants felt they understood expectations. The behaviour was mutual orientation: both sides worked from the same map.

But an unaddressed limitation deserves attention: standardisation can inadvertently narrow the range of acceptable evidence. Citizens outside typical employment arrangements—informal work, variable hours, intermittent care responsibilities—may struggle to fit themselves into templated boxes. Reconciling this involves adding flexible fields, inviting narrative explanations, and empowering reviewers to request supplementary information. A digital queue must stretch to meet the citizen, not force the citizen to shrink to fit the form.

Across these developments, the motif of *the line* returns. Interfaces draw lines of responsibility, comprehension, and access. A line can direct people to the right step, or it can block them. It can invite them to participate, or it can convey a silent command: *abandon hope here*. Every design choice either strengthens or weakens the line that supports citizens as they interact with the state.

The fifth claim is structural: systems must log and surface patterns in appeals, not treat them as noise. Appeals data is the diagnostic heartbeat of administrative justice. When Finland's 2020 unemployment system logged reasons for overturned decisions, auditors found recurring misclassifications linked to outdated address data. Developers adjusted models. Review times fell. Accuracy improved. The behaviour—collecting structured appeal insights—became a governance mechanism. The implication is stark: a digital queue without feedback is a conveyor belt, not a justice system.

Yet a counter-example warns against complacency. When a large U.S. state deployed an automated eligibility tool in 2017, it collected appeal patterns but locked them inside vendor dashboards. Policymakers never saw them. Errors persisted. Citizens bore the costs. Reconciling this requires procurement clauses that ensure public access to appeal analytics, as discussed elsewhere in this chapter. Without such provisions, the queue becomes a proprietary corridor with no public light.

As digital services mature, due process will depend upon whether governments commit to designing *with* citizens rather than merely *for* them. Notice, reasons, appeal—these are not ritual components. They are constitutional anchors translated into pixels.

The unresolved question, therefore, is sharp. As public services shift further into automated pipelines, will digital queues become spaces where citizens can stand their ground, speak back, and be heard—or will they become corridors that move them along without room to breathe?

Trust, Care, and Administrative Justice

On a grey morning in February 2022, at a Social Security Scotland office in Dundee, a caseworker named Helen McDermott opened the triage dashboard that had been rolled out only weeks before. A claimant, Mark Douglas, had missed two check-ins. The system displayed a risk band and three suggested actions: contact by phone, send an evidence reminder, or schedule an in-person visit. Helen paused. Mark's file showed a long history of steady compliance and a recent hospital discharge. The model placed him in a medium-risk category. Helen overrode it. She chose the call. Mark answered on the third ring and apologised; he had been recovering from surgery and had misread the notification. The matter was resolved in seven minutes. The system had done its job—flagging the case—but the justice lay in Helen's judgement. A small dignity was preserved.

The paradox at the heart of this subchapter is this: automated triage can accelerate administrative fairness, yet the legitimacy of those systems hangs on whether they strengthen or corrode the relational fabric that underpins public service. A model may predict patterns, but only humans perceive the texture—hesitation in a voice, fear in an explanation, pride in a carefully organised folder. The queue may be digital, but trust is relational.

The quiet motif here is *the touchpoint*: the moment when a citizen meets the state through a person, a screen, or both. Trust is built or broken at these touchpoints. Dignity is granted or denied. Administrative justice becomes visible not in high policy but in these small encounters.

The first major claim is that trust in public administration grows from encounters that recognise the citizen as a person, not a datapoint. Show this through behaviour. In 2019, the London Borough of Camden introduced augmented case management tools for homelessness assessments. The system pulled data from housing histories, benefit records, and prior appeals. Caseworkers saw risk flags and suggested next steps. Yet the defining feature was that every screen required workers to record qualitative notes before confirmation: "What did the citizen say?" This mandatory field anchored the interaction in narrative rather than prediction. Officials named it the *human judgement checkpoint.* The implication is clear. Incorporating learning systems into frontline work must elevate—not erase—the relational dimension.

A credible counter-example illustrates the stakes. When a U.S. county automated intake for emergency cash grants in 2020, the system assessed eligibility before any staff contact. Call centre workers later reported that citizens viewed them as powerless intermediaries. "The system won't let me" became a refrain. Trust dropped. Workers faced abuse. The limitation was structural: the design removed the very touchpoints that enable reciprocity. Reconciling this with the Camden example requires a principle: algorithmic triage should structure attention, not sever relationship.

The second claim focuses on care as a measurable public value. Despite its softness as a term, care manifests through visible administrative behaviours: timely callbacks, proactive clarifications, avoidance of unnecessary sanctions. In 2021, New Zealand's Ministry of Social Development piloted augmented triage for hardship grants. Caseworkers saw prompts—"Ask about rent increase?" or "Check childcare receipt?" Users of the system judged it helpful when it enhanced attentiveness. Researchers noted improved completion of essential checks. Named metrics supported this: fewer rejections due to missing information, faster resolution times, higher claimant satisfaction. The implication is that well-designed augmentation can cultivate care by prompting more thorough, empathetic conversations.

Yet augmentation also risks care erosion when it becomes an engine for volume throughput. A limitation surfaced in a Canadian provincial disability assessment trial in late 2022: triage prompts expanded so rapidly that caseworkers felt pressured to complete checklists rather than engage. Citizens sensed the shift. “They didn’t hear me,” one applicant said in a survey. The lesson, reconciled with earlier successes, is that augmenting care requires restraint. Prompts must guide, not overwhelm. A touchpoint smothered by rigid scripting becomes a cold surface.

The third claim is that administrative justice depends on the alignment between machine suggestions and human accountability. Show this through a concrete example. In Oslo’s child welfare services, 2021 reforms required caseworkers to log each instance in which they accepted or rejected algorithmic triage recommendations. Supervisors later analysed these patterns to identify structural blind spots. If workers consistently overrode a certain type of suggestion—say, high-risk alerts based on unstable address histories—review boards interrogated the model’s assumptions. This behaviour loop became a form of just-in-time accountability. The implication is striking: administrative justice improves when disagreement between humans and machines is not penalised but examined.

A counter-example warns what happens when override culture is discouraged. In parts of Australia’s automated compliance programme, staff were expected to accept algorithmic debt flags unless “clear error” could be shown. Overrides were rare, not because decisions were perfect but because workers felt on the hook for deviations. The system repressed professional discretion. Reconciling this with the Oslo model shows that oversight must protect caseworkers’ right—and obligation—to disagree.

The fourth claim highlights that small dignities, applied consistently, accumulate into systemic legitimacy. Consider a specific behaviour: offering citizens a preview of their file before decisions are finalised. Denmark’s 2020 social benefit review introduced a “confirm details” screen where citizens could correct errors. The change was tiny. The effect was profound. Many errors stemmed from outdated addresses or misclassified income entries; correcting these before final calculation prevented sanctions and appeals. Citizens reported feeling respected: “They asked me before judging me.” The implication is that dignity is procedural. A small invitation can rebalance power.

The motif of *the touchpoint* returns. Care is not sentimental; it is infrastructural. It is encoded in how systems greet, inform, and listen. A cold touchpoint produces defensive behaviour: shorter answers, lower disclosure, reduced cooperation. A respectful touchpoint produces more complete information, enabling better decisions. The interface and the caseworker operate together.

The fifth claim is structural: relational public service cannot be retrofitted into systems that treat citizens as throughput units. Consider France's CAF (Caisse d'Allocations Familiales), which in 2021 evaluated the impact of quick-response messaging for childcare benefit applicants. Caseworkers could send short, personalised clarifications—"We received your payslip, thank you; next, we need confirmation of childcare hours." Claimants responded more fully and more quickly. The behaviour metric—fewer incomplete files—spoke volumes. The system supported the relationship rather than replacing it. The implication is that relational justice thrives when systems create micro-opportunities for reassurance.

But a limitation stands out: personalisation must not create inequity. In a 2022 evaluation in Toronto's housing authority, caseworkers who personalised messages sometimes helped citizens with whom they felt greater affinity. This created disparities. Reconciling this requires structured transparency: teams monitored message patterns and rotated assignments to reduce bias. The relational touchpoint must be offered fairly.

Across these examples, the through-line is unmistakable. Trust emerges when citizens sense that caseworkers have both discretion and support. Care emerges when systems prompt attention rather than demand obedience. Administrative justice emerges when procedural rights are wrapped in human regard.

Yet a deeper tension remains unresolved. As triage systems advance, will governments invest in strengthening the human touchpoints that hold administrative justice together, or will efficiency pressures push interactions into thinner, faster channels where trust cannot take root?

Civic Data Stewardship

In March 2020, as Milan's public transport system struggled to understand which neighbourhoods could safely sustain reduced service during the first COVID-19 restrictions, the municipal innovation unit partnered with ATM, the city's transport operator. They used aggregated mobility data—sourced from telecom providers and validated against 2019 passenger counts—to estimate movement patterns. Yet the breakthrough was not technical. It came when a citizen advisory panel, convened by the municipality in April 2020, insisted that any dataset used for service decisions must be subject to public review, including clear explanations of how aggregation thresholds protected anonymity. Because the panel approved the safeguards, the city released the analysis openly. The public accepted the temporary route changes with little protest. Stewardship, not surveillance, defined the outcome.

The Milan episode captures a tension threaded through this subchapter: large-scale data can support public purpose, but legitimacy hinges on who governs it. A city may hold detailed records of movement, schooling, taxation, or health encounters; yet without meaningful governance that anchors those assets in shared ethics, the data becomes a source of suspicion rather than solidarity. Civic data stewardship offers a different path. It treats people not merely as subjects whose traces are extracted, nor as customers whose consent is an administrative checkbox, but as members of a polity with rights and responsibilities over the data they collectively generate.

The quiet motif here is *the commons*: not a romantic image of an unspoiled pasture, but a contemporary shared asset that requires rules, rituals, and repair. Data, when treated as a commons, becomes a site of negotiated stewardship rather than unilateral extraction. The task is to show how this can be done credibly, concretely, and fairly.

The first claim is that civic data stewardship reframes power by recognising communities as co-governors of their own information. Show this with behaviour. In 2021, Toronto's Waterfront neighbourhood piloted a community data governance board as part of debates around sensor deployments for traffic safety. Members—elected by residents and including youth delegates—reviewed project proposals, privacy safeguards, and data retention periods. They had genuine veto power. Their decisions bound the city and private vendors. The named example demonstrates that stewardship boards can operate as real institutions, not decorative panels. The implication is profound: when residents meaningfully shape the terms of data use, public trust rises not because a city claims transparency but because people see their own norms embedded in the system.

Yet even this model has limits. A counter-example helps clarify them. In 2022, a similar board in Auckland struggled when it faced a proposal involving complex health-linked mobility data. Members lacked the expertise to assess re-identification risks. The board's recommendations split. Critics argued the exercise was symbolic. Reconciling this requires a principle: civic boards must be supported by independent technical advisors chosen jointly with the community, not appointed solely by agencies. Stewardship is not amateur oversight; it is informed consent at scale.

The second claim is that civic stewardship introduces a public-interest test that goes beyond individual consent. Individual consent—often buried in service terms—is too brittle to carry the moral weight of societal decisions about shared data assets. The alternative is visible in Helsinki's approach to education data. In 2022, the city evaluated whether to link school attendance records with youth services data to target tutoring funds. Officials applied a two-part test, co-designed with parents and teachers. First: *Is the reuse consistent with the original educational purpose?* Second: *Does the reuse generate collective, not merely institutional, benefit?* The behaviour metric was clear: parents had the right to request an audit explaining how the linkage improved outcomes. This created accountability at the level of purpose, not only process. The implication is that public-interest tests operationalise values, transforming vague commitments into enforceable criteria.

A limitation emerges when public interest becomes too expansively defined. Governments can overreach. For example, a 2021 Australian proposal to share welfare transactional data with employment service providers met strong opposition: the claimed "public interest" was too broad and poorly evidenced. The lesson, reconciled with Helsinki's more disciplined model, is that public interest must be bounded, specific, and reviewable. Vague appeals erode legitimacy; precise purposes strengthen it.

The third claim concerns *data dividends*: mechanisms that share the benefits of data reuse with the people who create the data in the first place. While often framed in economic terms, dividends can be non-monetary: improved services, tailored feedback loops, or communal investments. Estonia's 2020 health data project illustrates this. When the Estonian Health Insurance Fund partnered with university researchers to build predictive risk models, citizens were informed that their anonymised data would also produce two dividends: annual reports showing how insights improved national care planning, and personalised prevention recommendations delivered through the national health portal. Residents could see how their data contributed to public value. The visible behaviour—regular feedback and publicly documented improvements—made the dividend tangible.

Still, data dividends risk becoming tokenistic if benefits accrue primarily to institutions. A 2019 pilot in California attempted monetary dividends for mobility data used in traffic optimisation. The payments were trivial, the distribution opaque, and the programme collapsed. Reconciling these outcomes requires a more mature principle: dividends must be proportional, transparent, and aligned with community priorities. Money is not the point; meaningful benefit is.

The fourth claim is that civic stewardship requires architectures of accountability, not just advisory bodies. This means creating formal procedures through which communities can challenge, correct, or halt data uses. A compelling example comes from Barcelona's 2020 city data charter. Under this framework, civic groups can request a review of any municipal data partnership, triggering an audit by an independent panel comprising technologists, lawyers, and citizen representatives. These reviews are binding. The visible behaviour—halting a proposed energy-monitoring project until privacy safeguards were strengthened—shows the model's strength. The implication is that stewardship cannot rely on goodwill; it must be institutionalised.

A limitation arises when accountability mechanisms slow innovation excessively. Critics of Barcelona's model argued that frequent reviews delayed projects. Yet the city's own 2021 evaluation found that early, collaborative scrutiny reduced later redesign costs. Reconciliation emerges through a disciplined workflow: embed review early, not late; make it iterative, not episodic.

The fifth claim focuses on the role of shared norms in sustaining long-term stewardship. Data governance is not a one-off decision but an evolving practice. Norms shape how people expect their data to be treated, and how institutions behave when rules are silent. The Scottish National Investment Bank's 2021 adoption of a "data responsibility statement" showed how norms guide decisions in ambiguous cases. Staff were required to log any doubts about secondary data uses in a central register, reviewed monthly by a cross-disciplinary committee including citizen voices. This repeated ritual cultivated a culture of reflection. The motif of the commons returns: stewardship depends not only on rules but on the habits that keep the commons healthy.

A counter-example reveals how quickly norms can fray. After the Dutch "SyRI" case in 2020 highlighted unlawful risk scoring in welfare, public trust declined sharply. Courts intervened, systems were withdrawn, and regulatory repairs followed. The system collapsed partly because norms had been neglected; oversight was perfunctory. Reconciliation requires a sharper lesson: civic stewardship must be preventive, not reactive. Once trust collapses, restoring the commons becomes far harder.

Across these cases, a picture emerges. Civic data stewardship does not treat citizens as passive sources of information nor purely as rights-bearing individuals. It treats them as co-architects of a shared asset. Community governance boards, public-interest tests, data dividends, and accountability rituals each play a role. But none matter unless they bind institutions to the people whose data enables their decisions.

Yet a larger tension remains unresolved. As governments and corporations accumulate vast datasets, will they embrace models that share power, or will stewardship become a rhetorical gloss for extraction? The next decisions—how boards are structured, whose voices count, how dividends are defined—will determine whether data becomes a true civic commons or another domain where the public is present only in name.

Chapter 6
Security, Safety, and Resilience

At 07:43 on a windy morning in October 2019, the city of Johannesburg discovered its billing system had been quietly hijacked. A ransomware group had breached a misconfigured server, encrypted critical databases, and posted a taunting message: pay within 72 hours or watch public services grind to a halt. Council staff arrived to find printers spitting out ransom notes instead of statements; residents could not pay rates; call centres froze. The breach slipped through because, in a municipal network with thousands of components, a single unattended doorway was enough. The incident lasted only days, but it captured something essential about digital government: it is not the sophistication of an attacker that threatens the state, but the fragility of the everyday.

This chapter begins there—not with a spectacular failure but with the basic truth behind most digital crises. The majority of attacks on public systems exploit the mundane: unpatched servers, shared passwords, unreviewed code, untested procedures. Yet these mundane failures accumulate extraordinary consequences. A poisoned dataset in a benefits model. A tampered prompt in a planning assistant. A stolen model used to mimic official correspondence. These are not the imagined threats of a distant future; they are the attack surfaces already shaping public authority. The motif that will thread through this chapter is *the seam*: the place where administrative systems meet the unpredictability of the world. Some seams hold. Others tear.

The seam matters because governance depends on continuity. Citizens do not experience the state as an abstract institution; they experience it as a sequence of interactions that must work even when networks fail or adversaries act. That is why security, safety, and resilience belong together. Security prevents avoidable harm. Safety ensures systems behave as intended. Resilience ensures that when they do not, society still stands.

To see the stakes, consider the quiet vulnerabilities embedded in algorithmic systems. A public-sector model is only as reliable as the data it consumes, and some public datasets carry long memories. A compromised mobility stream can nudge transport priority routes to favour the wrong districts. A subtle prompt injection can distort triage questions in an online assessment. A stolen model can be repurposed to spoof official warnings. None of these need theatrical sophistication; they need only the right seam at the wrong moment. When public institutions deploy machine learning without reinforcing these seams, they discover how quickly authority can fray.

Yet focusing solely on exotic attacks misses the point. Governments must first master *basic hygiene*: asset inventories, patching cycles, access logs, key rotation, job separation, fallback credentials, and monitored thresholds. These prosaic disciplines are often treated as technical chores rather than democratic obligations. But they are the difference between a system that withstands a targeted attack and a city that shuts down because a single administrator forgot to renew a certificate. A later section of this chapter will examine a practical triage matrix designed for agencies with scarce security staff—an honest model for deciding what to fix *first*, not simply what to fix *eventually*.

Beyond security lies the deeper terrain of safety: ensuring systems fail in acceptable ways, not catastrophic ones. Reliability is only the first layer. A reliable system may still collapse abruptly when environmental conditions shift. Resilience, by contrast, accepts that failure happens and ensures it unfolds slowly, legibly, and reversibly. The distinction becomes clear during outages. When a licensing service in a mid-sized British city crashed during a software upgrade in 2021, staff were forced into ad-hoc procedures: emailing PDFs, manually checking spreadsheets, and improvising identity checks. None of this would have been necessary had the city kept a *default-to-human* protocol and an orderly rollback plan—a simple playbook specifying who makes the call, what data is cached, which channels hold, and how to keep queues moving. The outage was a reminder that digital services are not self-sustaining: they rely on operational choreography.

That choreography grows more complex as systems evolve. Modern public AI resembles aviation more than traditional software. It behaves probabilistically, adapts to data, and interacts with human operators who may misinterpret its signals. That is why this chapter introduces the concept of *safety cases* for public AI—structured arguments about why a system is safe enough for its intended use, rooted in evidence and specific assumptions. Such cases are standard in aviation and healthcare, where risks cannot be fully eliminated but must be explicitly justified. Councils and agencies do not need aeronautical engineering documents; they need lightweight templates that articulate hazards, mitigations, residual risks, and operator responsibilities. A safety case is not a compliance ritual; it is an institutional memory that survives staff turnover and political cycles.

Yet safety cannot be considered without grappling with crisis. Emergencies distort norms. They demand speed, flexibility, improvisation. Governments turn to AI tools for real-time support: routing evacuations during wildfires, modelling hospital loads during disease surges, or forecasting infrastructure failures during floods. Each rapid deployment carries a risk of *exceptionalism*—temporary measures that outlive their justification. A model introduced during a fire season might linger into safer months. A monitoring tool used during a pandemic could become a default metric. Crisis use is often necessary, but without explicit activation criteria, audit logs, expiry dates, and decommissioning triggers, exceptional systems become permanent by drift.

That, too, is a seam: crisis exposing the gap between urgent need and enduring principle. When crisis tools persist, they reshape governance quietly. Guarding against this requires institutions that understand not only when to activate a model but when to let it die.

These themes—attack surfaces, resilience, safety cases, crisis exceptionalism—are not isolated. They form parts of the same puzzle: how to maintain public trust when the state increasingly depends on models it cannot wholly predict. Security protects the state from hostile interference. Safety protects citizens from unintended harm. Resilience protects society from cascading failure. But each requires choices about trade-offs: simplicity versus sophistication, continuity versus speed, automation versus human judgment.

As you enter this chapter, the central question sharpens: how should a democratic state design systems that are strong enough to withstand threats, yet humble enough to fail safely? The answer lies at the seams, and in the discipline required to keep them visible before they tear.

Attack Surfaces of Governance

At 06:12 on 23 February 2021, staff at the Oldsmar Water Treatment Plant in Florida watched their cursor move across a screen without anyone touching the mouse. A remote intruder increased the sodium hydroxide levels in the system more than a hundredfold. The plant's operators reversed the change within minutes, but the incident revealed something deeper than a security lapse. A single compromised workstation—linked to an outdated version of remote-access software—had become a point where digital intrusion met physical consequence. The breach was not sophisticated. It did not need to be. It found a seam.

That seam sits at the heart of this subchapter: governments do not need to face exotic cyber-attacks to be vulnerable. They need only the smallest misconfigured window in systems that now anchor welfare, licensing, housing allocation, traffic control, or water safety. As public authorities adopt machine-learning models—trained on fragile, easily influenced data—new attack surfaces multiply. The story is no longer simply about defending networks; it is about defending decisions. A poisoned training dataset, a crafted prompt that warps an assistant's behaviour, a stolen model that reveals institutional logic: these are not edge cases but credible threats to the integrity of governance.

The motif threading through this analysis is *the seam*: the place where a system hands off to the next, or where trust meets automation. Seams reveal where the state must be strongest, because they are precisely where it is most exposed.

The first claim is that data poisoning represents the most under-appreciated attack surface in public AI systems. Show this concretely. In 2020, researchers analysing Chicago's police data found that a small number of questionable incident labels in a training set disproportionately skewed a violence-prediction model's outputs. That was not an attack—just poor input hygiene. Now imagine a deliberate one. A hostile actor alters a handful of training points in a welfare-fraud model. The change may be almost invisible: a dozen mislabeled cases among hundreds of thousands. Yet such edits can redirect risk scores, triggering unwarranted investigations or starving particular groups of support. Name the phenomenon: data poisoning, where an attacker manipulates training data to reshape a model's logic. Explain why this matters. Public datasets often blend administrative records from multiple agencies, collected through human judgement under pressure. Their lineage is long. Their provenance is uneven. A poisoned element can remain undetected for years before influencing a downstream decision. The implication is direct: governments must treat dataset integrity as a constitutional matter, not a technical nicety. If the training data is tainted, the rules the state learns are tainted too.

Yet a limitation surfaces. Not all data poisoning is deliberate or malevolent. Sometimes the "poison" is a policy change. When the UK's labour market shifted after the 2008 financial crisis, employment-support datasets captured new behavioural patterns that models misinterpreted as anomalies rather than structural change. Reconciliation requires a principle: monitoring must detect both attacks *and* shifts. The seam does not distinguish intent; systems must.

The second claim concerns prompt injection—an attack vector newly relevant as public bodies adopt large language models to assist with triage, case summarisation, or citizen-facing interaction. Show this through behaviour. In late 2023, a German municipal chatbot designed to answer questions about benefit eligibility was manipulated by individuals embedding hidden instructions into user messages. The bot began generating erroneous guidance, including incorrect documentation lists. The administration quickly suspended the tool. Name the problem: prompt injection, where malicious or cleverly structured text persuades a model to deviate from its intended behaviour. Explain the challenge: public models often interact with heterogeneous inputs from citizens, activists, and sometimes adversarial actors. Unlike internal systems, these models cannot rely on stable environments. The implication becomes unavoidable: without strict input filtering, output monitoring, and guardrail prompts, an LLM connected to a public workflow can be commandeered with a single clever sentence. And when that workflow influences real entitlements or duties, a manipulated output becomes an illegitimate rule.

A counter-example clarifies the limits. The Estonian Social Insurance Board tested an internal assistant in 2022. Because it operated only on staff-written inputs and never contacted citizens directly, the risk of prompt injection was minimal. The tool succeeded without incident. Reconciliation lies in correctly scoping risk: LLMs interacting with the public face wide-open seams; those confined to controlled settings present narrower ones.

The third claim centres on model theft. It may appear abstract, yet the behaviour is concrete. In 2018, the New York Taxi and Limousine Commission released an anonymised dataset of trip records. Journalists, starting with work by the *New York Times* and others, rapidly deanonymised driver information. But the deeper lesson was how easily models predicting high-value taxi routes—trained on that dataset—could be replicated by anyone. Name the risk: when the state's models or training data are stolen or leaked, adversaries can study decision boundaries, mimic official scoring, and exploit or manipulate administrative logic. Explain its consequence: a stolen housing-inspection model, for example, may reveal which building characteristics most influence prioritisation, enabling negligent landlords to game the process. The implication is that secrecy is not the answer; governance requires understanding and controlling what leaves the institution. Sometimes openness builds trust; other times it increases attack surface. Stewardship means choosing carefully.

But there is a balancing case. In 2020, the Danish tax authority published a simplified version of its VAT-fraud detection parameters as part of an accountability initiative. Critics feared gaming. Instead, compliance improved, because honest firms could understand their risk categories. The reconciliation is that model disclosure should focus on principles and thresholds, not on replicable decision boundaries. Transparency is not identical to openness; one informs citizens, the other enables adversaries.

The fourth major claim is that governments misallocate security effort by chasing exotic threats before establishing basic operational hygiene. Show the behaviour. A council may invest in AI-driven anomaly detection while leaving its patching cycles months behind schedule. It may commission threat modelling frameworks yet leave staff accounts shared between shifts. Name the underlying issue: operational hygiene—inventorying systems, enforcing credential policies, rotating keys, encrypting data at rest, maintaining audit logs, validating input pipelines. Explain why hygiene trumps high sophistication: most public-sector breaches exploit neglected basics, as the UK's National Audit Office noted in multiple 2020–2022 assessments. The implication is unavoidable: without hygiene, advanced security tools become decorations.

A counter-case sharpens the point. In 2017, the city of Los Angeles invested heavily in AI-supported intrusion detection systems. But the decisive protection came from a modest improvement: enforcing two-factor authentication across staff accounts. Reconciling this reveals a pattern: sophisticated defences work only when built atop foundational practice.

The fifth claim introduces a practical instrument: a triage matrix for scarce teams. Show its need. Many councils and agencies operate with overstretched digital units—sometimes a handful of engineers protecting thousands of endpoints. Name the mechanism: a triage matrix ranks threats along two axes—*exploitability* and *impact*. Explain its logic. A vulnerability that is easy to exploit and capable of harming entitlements, identity systems, or resource allocation demands immediate action. A hard-to-exploit issue with limited scope can be scheduled. The visible behaviour is a disciplined security backlog, with known deadlines, documented decisions, and explicit justifications. This replaces panic-driven firefighting with governed prioritisation. The implication is accountability: when something fails, leaders can show why resources went where they did.

Threading the seam motif again, the matrix helps organisations see which seams—between databases, between interfaces, between human and machine—are under the most strain.

Finally, no discussion of attack surfaces is complete without acknowledging uncertainty. Public systems operate in environments where adversaries adapt, institutions evolve, and data pipelines change. A defence that works in 2023 may be obsolete in 2025. The unresolved tension is therefore structural: if governments must increasingly rely on learning systems that themselves change over time, how can they protect seams that are not fixed but fluid?

What remains is a test. Not whether an agency can deploy advanced defences, but whether it can decide, with clarity and discipline, where to strengthen the seam next.

Fail-Safe, Not Just Safe-to-Fail

At 09:17 on 27 January 2022, the licensing office in Leeds discovered that none of its terminals could load the vehicle registration system. The outage stemmed from a failed database migration pushed the previous evening by a contractor. By mid-morning, taxi drivers queued outside the Merrion House service centre holding renewal forms they could not submit. Staff printed temporary permits from an old template found in a shared drive, phoned colleagues in other departments for cross-checks, and scribbled manual receipts as the queue lengthened. No data were lost. No lives were at risk. Yet for several hours, an invisible assumption about modern governance—that public systems degrade gently rather than collapse abruptly—proved false. When the service finally recovered, the post-incident report did not highlight software complexity or hardware exhaustion. It concluded something simpler and more unsettling: the system had been *safe-to-fail*, but not *fail-safe*.

The distinction matters. Safe-to-fail assumes that failures are allowed but manageable. Fail-safe assumes that, even when a critical component collapses, a predictable fallback will protect the people depending on the system. Leeds had resilience of a sort—resourceful staff, paper forms, sympathetic applicants—but it lacked design features that would have made the disruption orderly. The outage revealed how public institutions often rely on goodwill rather than engineered safeguards. Reliability had been prioritised, resilience assumed, and graceful degradation left to improvisation. This subchapter argues that the order must be reversed.

The image that threads through this analysis is *the handrail*: the feature that stops a stumble from becoming a fall. Public systems need handrails at every step, not because failure is exceptional, but because it is ordinary.

The first claim is that reliability, while essential, is a misleading measure of system strength. Show this concretely. In 2021, New Zealand's Ministry of Social Development reported uptime statistics above 99 per cent for its core eligibility systems. Yet a rare but severe outage that year prevented thousands of benefit applications from being processed for nearly a day. Name the problem: reliability metrics focus on frequency, not consequence. Explain the underlying issue: public services operate in *stakes-heavy* environments, where a single failure can carry disproportionate harm—missed childcare payments, lapsed medical exemptions, delayed licensing. The implication is clear: reliability becomes meaningful only when paired with resilience. A system that rarely fails but collapses badly is weaker, in practice, than one that fails occasionally but gracefully.

A counter-example clarifies the boundary. Estonia's e-Residency platform, launched in 2014, has suffered several minor outages, often due to maintenance. Because the platform includes cached credentials, alternative login paths, and mirrored data stores, these failures rarely interrupt critical processes. The reconciliation is that resilience transforms acceptable unreliability into acceptable risk. A stumble held by the handrail is not a disaster.

The second claim concerns resilience itself. Show the behaviour. During the 2021 winter storms in Texas, the state's unemployment-processing portal experienced extreme load. Many services degraded but did not crash entirely because backup servers were staged to activate, albeit slowly. Name the principle: resilience is the capacity to absorb strain without losing the ability to serve. Explain its mechanism: resilient systems degrade *gracefully*—reduced functions, slower responses, narrower scope, but maintained core obligations. The implication matters for public AI: a model that fails sharply under new conditions (for example, predicting labour-market behaviour during a sudden unemployment spike) can wipe out institutional confidence overnight.

Yet resilience is insufficient without what engineers call *graceful degradation*. To show this, return to Leeds. When the licensing database froze, staff lacked standardised offline procedures. The fallback became ad-hoc. Name the missing component: graceful degradation, the capacity to retreat in a controlled manner. Explain why it matters: without prepared handrails—printed contingency forms, cached identity lists, documented override rights—staff must improvise, producing errors, inequities, or opportunities for fraud. The implication is that resilience is not a software feature alone; it is a socio-technical choreography.

A limitation follows. Over-engineered handrails can create false reassurance. If offline procedures are too elaborate, staff never practise them; if fallback channels are too numerous, they fracture coordination. Reconciliation requires proportionality: handrails must be simple, memorable, and rarely changed.

The third claim introduces *default-to-human* design as the centrepiece of fail-safe public infrastructure. Show what it looks like. In 2020, the Flemish Government investigated an insurance-assessment model that occasionally produced contradictory outputs for similar cases. Instead of blocking the workflow, the system automatically routed ambiguous assessments to human reviewers. Name the behaviour: default-to-human, where uncertainty triggers escalation rather than silent automation. Explain its significance: public authority must remain legible. Humans can ask questions, recognise anomalies, and draw on contextual knowledge that models do not possess. The implication is straightforward: default-to-human pathways are not inefficiencies; they are constitutional safeguards.

Contrast this with an example that exposes the risks of poorly executed escalation. In 2019, an Australian administrative tribunal reviewed a welfare-debt case where an automated matching system had flagged alleged overpayments using income averages rather than actual pay slips. Human officers, overwhelmed by caseloads, approved the automated notices without scrutiny. The escalation existed in theory but not in practice. Reconciling these cases illustrates a structural requirement: default-to-human works only when humans have the time, authority, and clarity to act.

The fourth claim is that rollback is as important as escalation. Show the mechanism. The London Borough of Hackney, after deploying a housing-maintenance triage tool in 2022, retained a simple rollback path: if quality metrics or complaint rates breached thresholds for two consecutive weeks, the model reverted to advisory mode. Name this design: rollback-by-threshold. Explain its purpose: models behave differently as circumstances shift, and rollback keeps the system anchored in predictable rules. The implication is democratic as much as technical: rollback ensures that no automated system gains de facto permanence by inertia.

A counter-example reveals what happens without rollback. In 2015, Indiana's automated welfare-eligibility system wrongly cut benefits for thousands of applicants when certain documents were scanned improperly. With no rollback mechanism, the system continued issuing denials until the contract was restructured years later. Reconciling this clarifies a core principle: rollback is not a failure of innovation but its guardrail.

The fifth claim concerns outage playbooks—the practical scripts that connect reliability, resilience, and graceful degradation. Show their necessity. When the Leeds outage unfolded, no playbook specified which identity checks staff could perform offline, which renewals could be temporarily extended, or how to record transactions for later reconciliation. Name the missing tool: the outage playbook, a document that describes decision pathways, data-handling rules, and communication channels during disruption. Explain its function: playbooks reduce improvisation, preserve fairness, and maintain auditability. The implication is that playbooks are political documents, not merely operational ones. They codify which services deserve priority and which obligations can bend, and by how much.

A limitation is worth noting. Playbooks age quickly. If not revised and rehearsed, they become ceremonial rather than functional. Reconciliation lies in embedding short drills—annual rehearsals, staff walk-throughs, simple table-top exercises—to keep handrails fresh.

Threading the handrail motif once more reveals the deeper pattern. Public systems cannot eliminate failure. They can only determine *how failure behaves*. Whether a system stumbles or collapses depends on design choices made long before trouble arrives.

So the unresolved tension emerges: as governments integrate learning systems—adaptive, data-hungry, sometimes opaque—can they build enough handrails to ensure that when those systems falter, the fall stops short of harm? Or, put differently, when the next outage arrives, will a public institution descend into disorder or land, firmly, on a step designed not to break?

Safety Cases for Public AI

On 12 January 2009, US Airways Flight 1549 struck a flock of Canada geese shortly after take-off from LaGuardia Airport in New York. Within minutes, both engines lost thrust. Captain Chesley Sullenberger and First Officer Jeffrey Skiles glided the powerless Airbus A320 onto the Hudson River. All 155 people survived. Investigators later noted that the decisive factor was not heroism alone but the web of documented assumptions, failure modes, and procedural safeguards built into aviation. The cockpit crew could act under extreme pressure because preceding decades had forced manufacturers and regulators to anticipate what could go wrong, why, and with what margin for error. Every component of the aircraft, from engine casings to evacuation slides, was covered by structured safety arguments that stated why they were safe *and* what evidence supported that claim. Long before AI entered government, aviation showed that safety is not a posture but a dossier.

Public institutions now face a similar challenge: to operate learning systems that adapt, interact, and occasionally misfire without relying on luck or improvisation. Borrowing from aviation and healthcare is not about copying their formality wholesale, but about reclaiming a discipline: the craft of showing, with clarity and evidence, that a system is safe *enough* for the context in which people must live with it. The idea that threads this chapter—*the safety ledger*—captures something fundamental. Every automated decision draws down on a balance of public trust; every safeguard replenishes it. The ledger must never run negative.

The first claim is that safety cases offer a structured way to reason about hazards that are neither hypothetical nor fully predictable. Show why this matters. In 2017, the UK's Medicines and Healthcare products Regulatory Agency examined software used to analyse cardiac imaging for diagnosis. The vendor had produced a detailed "clinical safety case", stating its intended uses, known failure modes, expected error ranges, and mitigation strategies. Name the principle: the safety case is a narrative argument supported by evidence—testing records, domain analysis, data lineage—that explains why a system is safe for its intended environment. Explain its role: it forces designers and operators to surface assumptions before deployment and to document how the system behaves when those assumptions fail. The implication for public AI is that transparency emerges not through disclosure alone but through reasoned construction. A safety case is not a disclosure form; it is an accountability artefact.

A counter-example makes the point sharper. In 2016, a municipal housing authority in North America trialled a learning-based inspection prioritisation model without any documented safety argument. When a software update shifted risk scores towards older buildings in lower-income districts, the authority lacked records to explain whether the drift was expected or concerning. The absence of a safety ledger left staff unable to justify decisions or detect harm patterns. Reconciliation is straightforward: the safety case does not prevent drift, but it makes drift legible.

The second claim is that safety cases must adapt to the constraints of councils and agencies, not replicate the industrial heft of aviation or healthcare. Show this mismatch. Aviation standards like DO-178C (2011) can exceed hundreds of pages, demanding extensive traceability. Local authorities, by contrast, operate with tight budgets and limited technical staff. Name the solution: lightweight safety cases tailored to public administration. Explain their structure: a concise argument map, often using Goal Structuring Notation, that links three statements—*what this system is for, why we believe it is safe for this purpose*, and *what evidence supports that belief.* The implication is that complexity must shrink, not safety.

To see this in practice, consider the 2020 deployment of a model for triaging pothole repairs by a UK county council. The technical team produced a short safety case—barely ten pages—that identified three critical hazards: misclassification of severity, inequitable distribution of repair crews, and brittleness following extreme weather. Each hazard was paired with evidence: cross-validation accuracy for severity predictions, postcode-level fairness checks, and stress tests using historical storm data. The council's oversight committee could read the entire document in one sitting. The lesson is that brevity, when disciplined, can enhance scrutiny rather than reduce it.

A limitation arises: concise safety cases risk omitting subtle hazards. Reconciling this requires a rule of thumb drawn from clinical safety engineering—*include anything that materially changes a person's entitlement, treatment, or burden.* If a hazard touches one of those, it belongs in even the lightest safety ledger.

The third claim is that safety cases shift the centre of gravity of public oversight from performance to justification. Show the behaviour. When Ontario's Ministry of Community Safety piloted an algorithmic tool to highlight potential high-harm domestic abuse cases in 2022, the review panel did not ask merely how accurate the model was. They asked what assumptions underlay risk labels, how missing data were treated, and what interventions would follow. Name the shift: from predictive confidence to justificatory confidence. Explain its significance: a model with high predictive metrics can still be unsafe if its operational consequences are poorly understood. The implication is that safety cases become the substrate of democratic reasoning—why this system, at this time, for this purpose.

The quiet motif reappears: the safety ledger. Every justification—stated assumption, tested failure mode, planned checker—adds credit. Every undocumented guess withdraws it.

The fourth claim concerns evidence itself. Safety arguments are persuasive only when the underlying evidence is tailored to public-risk contexts. Show the variety. In aviation, evidence includes component tests, simulator trials, and failure-mode analyses. In healthcare, it includes clinical trials, post-market surveillance, and adverse event logs. Name the challenge: public AI draws from heterogeneous evidence—statistical tests, impact assessments, user research, and operational metrics. Explain the consequence: evidence must cover not just model performance but interaction effects—how staff use the outputs, how citizens interpret letters, how appeals flow. The implication is operational: a safety case must integrate the lived experience of administration, not merely the mathematics of models.

A counter-example demonstrates the danger of thin evidence. In 2018, a European city deployed a text-classification tool to triage citizen complaints. The vendor supplied accuracy metrics but no evidence on how misclassifications affected complaint-routing times. When certain neighbourhoods saw slower responses, the city struggled to assess whether the model was unsafe or merely imperfect. Reconciliation lies in a simple rule: evidence must follow consequences. If the consequence is delay, measure delay. If the consequence is exclusion, measure who is excluded.

The fifth claim focuses on how safety cases evolve. Show the necessity. Learning systems change as data shift. Without periodic revalidation, safety arguments decay. Name the discipline: continuous safety case maintenance. Explain its function: updating assumptions, versioning evidence, adding new failure modes discovered in practice. The implication is cultural: public bodies must treat safety cases as living documents, open to amendment and audit.

To see this approach elsewhere, look at the UK Civil Aviation Authority's 2019 review of drone operations. Operators were required to update safety arguments after significant changes in fleet size, operational environment, or incident patterns. Public AI, even at local scale, benefits from the same trigger points: new data sources, altered legal frameworks, or complaint trends. The safety ledger must remain accurate.

A limitation appears: maintenance requires time and skill. Councils may struggle. Reconciling this calls for a shared service model—templates, training, and centralised review units that help local teams maintain their safety cases without inflating overheads.

The sixth claim is that safety cases improve not only safety but governance discipline. Show the behaviour. When a metropolitan transport authority planned to pilot an AI-driven bus-priority algorithm in 2023, the requirement to produce a safety case forced the project team to articulate what "safe" meant: predictable queue times, non-discriminatory routing, and no sudden changes in signal patterns. Name the governance gain: clarity of purpose strengthens contracts, oversight, and public communication. Explain why: when systems are deployed with vague objectives, even minor failures appear catastrophic because there is no shared expectation. The implication is that safety cases anchor political legitimacy.

The motif appears again: the ledger. A clear purpose statement deposits trust before deployment.

The final claim is that safety cases anchor emergency-use systems, especially when exceptionalism risks drift into permanence. Show the scenario. During a severe wildfire season in 2021, a US West Coast county used a routing model to coordinate evacuation traffic. Because a safety case had been drafted beforehand, the emergency team understood what the model could and could not guarantee—estimated flow rates, sensitivity to blocked routes, and fallback triggers. Name the safeguard: bounded exceptionalism. Explain its structure: even in crisis, a safety argument constrains improvisation and supports later accountability. The implication extends to routine governance: systems built for rare events must still observe structured safety reasoning.

A limitation completes the picture. Crisis pace can pressure teams to deploy without a safety ledger. Reconciliation requires minimal viable cases—short, high-signal documents listing assumptions, hazards, mitigations, and monitoring plans. Better a brief ledger than none.

The unresolved tension sits in the open. Public bodies now wield systems that learn faster than their oversight rhythms. Can safety cases, even lightweight ones, keep pace without becoming rituals devoid of meaning? Or will the safety ledger prove the anchor that prevents public AI from drifting into unexamined risk, balancing ambition with restraint at the moment when it matters most?

Crisis Use and Exceptionalism

At 04:17 on 8 September 2020, the Clackamas County Emergency Operations Centre in Oregon authorised its traffic-management team to activate an experimental routing model. Wildfires were approaching two major highways. Embers carried by wind gusts up to 40 miles per hour had already forced staggered road closures across the foothills. By dawn, more than 100,000 residents were under varying evacuation levels. The model, trained on historical congestion data and constrained by fire-behaviour forecasts from the US Forest Service, had never been used in a live emergency. Yet within minutes it began signalling dynamic detours, reallocating flow through secondary roads that local farmers knew were narrow but still passable. Operators watched in silence as the heat map recalibrated. The outcome was mixed: some bottlenecks eased, but one diversion routed traffic through an unlit rural junction where two crashes occurred. The model had helped, and it had erred. The tension between necessity and risk was no longer theoretical.

Crises exert a gravitational pull on exceptions. What begins as an extraordinary activation can harden into routine practice if institutions lack a principled framework for when to deploy, log, and retire emergency systems. The Clackamas episode revealed something deeper: the threshold at which public bodies decide to suspend standard safeguards is rarely explicit, yet those decisions carry durable consequences for rights, expectations, and precedent. A wildfire lasts hours or days; its institutional imprint can last years. Emergency algorithms thus create what might be called a *ratchet*: a one-way motion that expands what is considered normal unless deliberate mechanisms resist the drift.

The first claim is that emergencies compress time, and compressed time distorts judgement. Show the behaviour. During the 2017 Manchester Arena attack, Greater Manchester Police activated a real-time communications triage system intended for major incidents. Designed to prioritise lines of inquiry during multi-agency responses, it was deployed within minutes of the explosion. Name the concept: activation criteria. Explain their purpose: to ensure that the decision to use extraordinary tools is made against defined signals rather than intuition or panic. The implication is institutional: without clear triggers—such as confirmed mass-casualty thresholds or simultaneous service outages—activation becomes discretionary, and discretion under duress can drift toward overuse.

A limitation deserves attention. Strict criteria can delay activation when speed is essential. Reconciling this requires a minimal set of *fast triggers* paired with mandatory retrospective review. If the circumstances are ambiguous, deploy by exception but justify afterwards. The ratchet loosens when retrospective justification is enforced.

The second claim is that crisis deployments require a logging regime that can survive scrutiny months later. Show why. When California's Office of Emergency Services coordinated evacuations during the 2021 Dixie Fire, operators used a routing support tool that suggested segment closures in near-real time. The state's after-action report (California OES, 2022) found that incomplete logs hampered investigators who attempted to distinguish model-driven decisions from operator overrides. Name the principle: forensic accountability. Explain its role: to preserve a factual record of which inputs were used, which recommendations were shown, when actors intervened, and what outcomes resulted. The implication: ephemeral crisis actions must leave durable traces.

The quiet motif appears—*the ratchet.* Detailed logs apply friction to the ratchet. They prevent exceptional operations from blending invisibly into standard workflows.

A counter-example highlights fragility. In 2018, a European city used an unlogged triage script to manage emergency accommodation during a heatwave. With no audit trail, the city struggled to understand later why some vulnerable residents were not prioritised. Reconciliation follows: logging need not be complex. Timestamps, input snapshots, and operator actions, captured automatically, suffice for oversight.

The third claim is that decommissioning is as critical as activation. Show the risk. After the Blue Cut Fire in San Bernardino County in 2016, a temporary traffic-control algorithm remained semi-active in the region's transport management software for several months. Engineers found that it continued to influence signal timing during peak hours, despite its original purpose having expired. Name the mechanism: sunset enforcement. Explain its logic: crisis tools must deactivate automatically when the defined emergency conditions cease, unless explicitly extended under fresh justification. The implication for governance is that exceptional systems must have built-in expiry, not optional off-switches.

A second historical reference reinforces the point. After the 2003 SARS outbreak in Toronto, several hospitals continued using emergency triage protocols designed for infectious-disease surges long after the outbreak ended, leading to longer patient waits in non-surge periods. The ratchet tightened through inertia. Retiring protocols proved politically and administratively difficult because no explicit off-ramp existed. Sunset enforcement is the antidote.

The fourth claim is that the public risk calculus changes during a crisis, but not in predictable ways. Show the behaviour. During the 2020 Western Australia bushfires, roadblocks guided by fire-spread models diverted families onto safer routes but also delayed livestock evacuation in farming districts. Name the phenomenon: harm displacement. Explain its mechanics: emergency algorithms often optimise for population-level safety metrics, such as total evacuation time, but can impose unanticipated burdens on specific groups. The implication is ethical: crisis optimisation must be paired with explicit impact checks, especially on communities without alternative options.

A limitation surfaces. During active emergencies, fully assessing impact distributions may be impractical. Reconciling this requires two practices: pre-season simulation of vulnerable groups' evacuation constraints, and post-event inclusion of those groups in after-action reviews. Harm displacement becomes visible only when measured.

The fifth claim concerns model behaviour under extreme uncertainty. Show the hazard. Wildfire behaviour models are sensitive to wind shifts. In the Clackamas case, one 30-degree change in wind direction nearly inverted the routing algorithm's risk-ranking. Name the concept: brittleness under drift. Explain why it matters: crisis data do not resemble training data; patterns become unstable, inputs degrade in quality, and assumptions break. The implication: crisis models require explicit uncertainty bounds and human override protocols anchored in those bounds.

The motif returns—*the ratchet.* When human overrides are discouraged or undocumented, operators may trust brittle outputs too readily. Friction is needed. Overrides should not merely be allowed; they should be expected and recorded.

The sixth claim is that emergency tools, once proven useful, tempt institutionalisation. Show the drift. After the 2019–20 Australian bushfires, several jurisdictions proposed permanent adoption of crisis traffic-routing algorithms. Name the risk: normalisation of exceptionalism. Explain the dynamic: tools created for extreme conditions can be misapplied to ordinary congestion management or policing operations, expanding state power unintentionally. The implication: permanent adoption must undergo fresh assessment—not treated as a reward for apparent crisis success.

A counter-example clarifies the boundary. Following Hurricane Sandy in 2012, New York City developed a crisis-only building inspection triage protocol. Unlike the routing systems above, the city explicitly prohibited its use outside declared emergencies. The protocol had a sunset and could not be reactivated without mayoral authorisation. Here the ratchet was purposefully resisted.

The seventh claim addresses public legitimacy. Show the human perspective. When residents of Talent, Oregon, fled the 2020 Almeda Fire, many relied on text alerts and highway signage controlled by algorithms they had never heard of. After the fire, community members demanded clarity on who authorised the tools, what data they used, and how errors were handled. Name the requirement: crisis transparency. Explain its contours: not real-time disclosure but timely, comprehensible communication after the fact—what the system did, why, and how oversight will learn from its performance. The implication: legitimacy is not won through perfection but through candour.

A limitation persists. Transparency can feel accusatory to overworked crisis teams. Reconciliation lies in framing disclosure as an institutional norm, not a personal critique. Logs speak to actions, not to blame.

The eighth claim is operational: crisis governance must integrate drills, rehearsals, and tabletop exercises. Show the effect. Victoria's emergency services in Australia conduct annual multi-agency wildfire simulations with live data, evaluating not only fire-behaviour predictions but also traffic-modelling performance and command-centre coordination. Name the function: pre-mortems for exceptional systems. Explain why: rehearsals expose brittle assumptions, identify coordination bottlenecks, and surface ethical dilemmas before they become real. The implication is preparedness: crisis tools should never debut during crisis.

The motif completes its circuit—the ratchet. Rehearsals resist inertia. They keep exceptional systems exceptional.

The unresolved tension sits plainly. Crises demand speed; accountability demands deliberation. AI tools shrink decision time; oversight expands reflection time. Can institutions design emergency deployments that are swift without becoming sloppy, decisive without becoming enduring, necessary without becoming normalised? Or does every crisis test not just the model but the boundary between temporary power and permanent precedent?

Chapter 7
Markets, Vendors, and the Public Interest

The story usually begins in a quiet room, not a dramatic crisis centre. A procurement officer in a mid-sized council sits before a stack of proposals, each promising transformation, efficiency, clarity—words that have grown smooth with overuse. One bid offers a sleek, closed platform with impressive benchmarks; another promises open components that can be adapted and shared. Only one detail gives pause: the closed platform locks the council into a five-year update cycle controlled entirely by the vendor. Yet the open alternative requires in-house capacity that the council does not quite have. The officer signs for the closed system. Three years later, when eligibility rules change and the council's needs shift, the system cannot. A minor contractual choice becomes a structural constraint. Markets have long shadows.

If the opening scene feels modest, that is precisely the point. Grand decisions about technology in the public sphere rarely announce themselves. They emerge from routine paperwork, meetings of the procurement board, and pricing tables negotiated at speed. Yet these quiet decisions shape what governments can do, how rapidly they can adapt, and who ultimately holds the pen on the rules that guide daily life. The paradox is sharp: the state is often treated as a consumer of digital systems, yet it is also a rule-maker, a risk bearer, and a guarantor of fairness. In theory, it can demand what it needs. In practice, it frequently accepts what it is offered.

The hook becomes clearer when one considers a simple question: why do governments with vastly different policy goals so often end up with the same technology stack? The answer lies not in ideology but in market structure. A handful of vendors can steer national practice through default settings, proprietary formats, and support contracts. Those defaults are rarely neutral. A portal designed for speed might privilege simplicity over nuance; a model optimised for fraud detection might downplay service quality. When the state becomes a passive buyer, commercial logic can quietly set the public agenda.

The chapter draws its energy from this tension between institutional duty and market reality. Procurement is not glamorous, but it is power. And power, when exercised without self-awareness, drifts toward convenience. That drift matters because modern public administration increasingly depends on models, data schemas, decision-support tools, and interoperable standards. These are not just technical artefacts; they are the infrastructure of governance. They determine what citizens experience as fair, comprehensible, and responsive. As earlier chapters have shown, algorithms shape options long before they shape outcomes. Markets do much the same.

To understand this landscape, we must begin with a shift in perspective: the state is not merely buying tools; it is shaping markets. A council that specifies an open eligibility-rules engine does more than secure flexibility for itself; it encourages a supply chain that values transparency and modularity. A government that demands access to model weights or audit trails is not being pedantic; it is signalling that sovereignty over public rules must remain public. These acts of demand-shaping do not require vast budgets. They require clarity about purpose, boundaries, and the long-term value of controllable components.

There is a second thread running through the chapter: the trade-off between openness and proprietary advantage. The public sector faces a real dilemma. Open systems promise inspectability and shared control, yet they sometimes lag in performance or maturity. Proprietary systems may offer rapid deployment, strong support, and refined interfaces, yet they can trap governments in upgrade cycles they cannot exit without pain. This is not a binary conflict but a negotiation of sovereignty. The most sustainable architectures blend open schemas—so that data and rules remain portable—with proprietary tools deployed where the stakes demand tested reliability. The art lies in ensuring that the wall between them is permeable and governed by contract, not goodwill.

Scale complicates everything. Large national agencies may have the leverage to demand transparency, while a small municipality with three IT staff and a tight budget may not. The market does not greet all buyers equally. Yet small governments are not doomed to dependence. Shared service hubs, regional analytics units, and talent exchanges can provide the collective capacity needed to interrogate vendor claims, resist lock-in, and maintain continuity during crises or political transitions. These forms of cooperation are not merely organisational conveniences; they are mechanisms for ensuring that technical sovereignty does not become a luxury only available to wealthy jurisdictions.

Running beneath these debates is a more philosophical question: what counts as value in public administration? Traditional procurement frameworks emphasise savings, efficiency, and risk transfer. But these metrics miss something fundamental: citizens judge systems by dignity, fairness, and clarity. A digital eligibility service that saves money while confusing or excluding people is a failure, even if the spreadsheet says otherwise. Public value includes equity of access, the trustworthiness of explanations, and the capability of institutions to adapt without waiting for vendor updates. Measuring these qualities requires dashboards that resist gaming—ones that track who benefits, who waits, who drops out, and whose voices shape the next iteration.

To anchor these ideas, imagine a short exercise: if you were forced to defend only three metrics for evaluating a major digital service, what would they be? Response times? Appeal success rates? Distribution of errors across demographic groups? Satisfaction among frontline workers? Your choices reveal your theory of public value. They also reveal your vulnerabilities. If you measure only cost savings, vendors will optimise for cost savings. If you measure only speed, they will optimise for speed. What you measure, they will deliver—literally. Procurement becomes governance because metrics become rules.

A pattern emerges: public interest cannot be secured by technical performance alone. It must be designed into procurement frameworks, contractual clauses, capability strategies, and evaluation systems. Markets will not spontaneously produce public value; they will produce what purchasers reward. The responsibility, then, lies with public institutions to articulate their needs in ways that shape supply. This requires skill, confidence, and a willingness to resist marketing gloss in favour of long-term stewardship.

Yet the chapter does not settle into pessimism. Markets can be steered, vendors can be partners, and procurement can be a source of innovation rather than constraint. The key is intentionality. When governments define clear purpose statements for digital systems, require modularity, preserve portability, and insist on transparent governance of updates, they create an environment where public tools evolve with public values—not in spite of them.

The closing movement leans forward. What happens when the state recognises its market power not as a burden but as an instrument of the common good? What becomes possible when procurement officers, engineers, caseworkers, and citizens become co-authors of the tools that shape their shared institutions? The chapter that follows traces the contours of this possibility: how to buy well, govern wisely, and ensure that the invisible architecture of public systems reflects not merely convenience or cost, but the values that democratic life demands.

The State as a Strategic Buyer

In February 2015, the Government Digital Service in London published a terse technical standard that went almost unnoticed outside specialist circles. Yet that document reshaped procurement far more than any sweeping legislative reform. The standard required suppliers to expose eligibility rules in machine-readable formats rather than bury them in proprietary engines. Within a year, several major vendors rewrote their product lines to comply. A simple clause, issued by a modest team in Aviation House, shifted market behaviour across the United Kingdom and quietly influenced procurement practice in New Zealand and Canada. One rule, one date, one place: and an entire supply chain recalibrated. This is demand-shaping in its purest form. Five words, early in the specification — *rules must be open* — signalled that the buyer was no longer passive.

The scene reveals a puzzle. Governments often wield budgets running into billions, yet they frequently behave like small customers negotiating in a rush. Why does the state, with its scale and constitutional weight, so often accept technologies it cannot fully understand or influence? The answer lies not in incompetence but in habit. Public institutions have inherited decades of procurement practice built around minimising risk, not maximising capability. And risk-minimisation is a timid compass. It points towards monolithic systems, long contracts, and supplier promises that prioritise stability above adaptability. When the state buys defensively, it pays twice: first in money, then in sovereignty. A five-word sentence can shift that balance, but only if procurement is understood as a strategic act of governance rather than a commercial transaction.

The motif that threads through this subchapter is the hinge. Every procurement choice becomes a hinge between past constraints and future possibilities. Some hinges open; others jam. Governments often discover, too late, that the architecture of their digital services has been pre-decided by contract. To know this is to understand why procurement is not a back-office formality but one of the most consequential functions of the modern state.

The first major claim is simple: governments shape markets through their demands, even when they do so unintentionally. Consider the European Commission's 2021 requirement that digital identity components adopt interoperable schemas. Suppliers adjusted within months because the buyer's expectations were clear, non-negotiable, and collective. Here the hinge opened. The standard reduced integration costs, accelerated cross-border services, and seeded a new ecosystem of small firms offering compliance tooling. The implication is immediate: by setting requirements around transparency, modularity, and portability, governments can encourage innovation rather than simply purchase it.

The second claim follows naturally: modular contracts grant public institutions the ability to evolve. When New York City's Mayor's Office of Data Analytics revised housing inspection prioritisation models in 2019, it succeeded not because of a clever algorithm but because earlier procurement had required the vendor to separate data ingestion from scoring logic. The city could replace the model while keeping the rest of the pipeline intact. The hinge swung smoothly. Modularity allowed iteration, contestability, and accountability — practical virtues, not abstract ideals.

To deepen this, the text must confront a limitation. Modular procurement can fail if governments lack internal capability to manage interfaces and evaluate components. A cautionary example comes from a 2017 attempt by a Scandinavian municipality to assemble an open-source benefits platform. The project faltered because staff could not maintain the data standards required for interoperability. The hinge jammed. The failure was not inherent to modularity; it was a mismatch between ambition and capacity. Reconciliation lies in recognising that modular procurement demands investment in people — contract managers, systems architects, and frontline workers capable of identifying when rules encoded in software diverge from lived practice.

The third claim concerns open standards for eligibility rules. Without them, policy becomes entangled in proprietary logic. Visible behaviour confirms the point: when France's CAF agency published child benefit formulas openly in 2018, civil society groups built parallel calculators that exposed edge cases and inconsistencies. Transparency produced scrutiny; scrutiny drove improvements. When rules remain hidden, the opposite happens. Citizens encounter inexplicable outcomes; officials struggle to detect unintended consequences; vendors gain disproportionate power over public policy. An open standard is not a technical nicety. It is the state asserting that public rules are public property.

Yet open standards alone are insufficient. They require contracts that ensure ongoing access. A vendor may comply on day one but bury future updates in ancillary fees, proprietary tooling, or oblique configuration files. Procurement must therefore specify not only access but *continued* access — a detail with profound implications. Once a system enters production, its governance becomes a negotiation. Clear clauses around explainability, audit rights, and rule extraction turn that negotiation from a plea into an entitlement.

A fourth claim extends this logic: shared components reduce duplication and create collective leverage. When the Australian Digital Transformation Agency launched its rules-as-code prototype in 2020, several states reused the same templates for means-testing logic. This clustering changed vendor incentives: suppliers adapted their offerings to align with the shared component because it reduced friction across multiple jurisdictions. The hinge widened further. Shared components transform scattered buyers into a coordinated market force.

A counter-example illustrates the risk of ignoring this collective dimension. In 2016, a group of English councils procured separate systems for homelessness triage, each using different question banks and data schemas. When national policy changed the following year, updates required a thicket of bilateral negotiations. Citizens faced inconsistent pathways depending on postcode. Vendors responded slowly because each update had to be customised. The hinge seized at every turn. Fragmentation is not just inefficient; it erodes fairness.

A fifth claim addresses the politics of vendor lock-in. Lock-in is not one behaviour but a series of small design decisions — proprietary schemas, opaque scoring logic, undocumented interfaces, inflexible update cycles — that slowly narrow the state's room for manoeuvre. One visible metric reveals the problem: the average time required to switch suppliers in UK local government core systems exceeds four years, according to a 2023 National Audit Office review. Four years is a political term. Migration becomes practically impossible within a single administration, giving vendors de facto power over decision timing. Strategic procurement counters this by insisting on data portability, documented interfaces, and rights to run parallel systems during transition.

Throughout these arguments, the hinge motif returns. Every clause the state writes becomes a hinge for later adaptation. Foresight lies not in predicting policy shifts but in creating conditions where shifts are feasible.

Two final examples sharpen the stakes. When Portugal modernised its social support platform in 2021, it required vendors to provide "policy diff" tools: interfaces that highlight how proposed updates to rules would change eligibility outcomes across demographic groups. This requirement, small on paper, changed development practices. Vendors could no longer submit black-box updates without demonstrating impacts. Officials gained visibility; citizens gained protection. Conversely, when a Canadian province outsourced its employment services system in 2019 without specifying auditability of machine learning updates, it soon found itself unable to verify why referral patterns shifted after a vendor-deployed optimisation. Queries met vague assurances; transparency had not been contractually secured. These two hinges swung in opposite directions.

By now, a subtle question emerges: what does the state owe its future self? Procurement determines whether tomorrow's officials inherit a toolkit they can adapt or a cage they must work within. That is the unresolved tension. Should governments prioritise short-term deployment speed or long-term sovereignty? Should they avoid perceived risk by choosing monoliths, or embrace modularity with its demands for capability? Should they lock in low prices today at the cost of flexibility tomorrow?

A strategic buyer must answer these questions before any tender is issued. The hinge turns regardless. The choice is whether it opens a door or closes one.

Open vs Proprietary Trade-offs

In April 2018, the Estonian Information System Authority published a short advisory note instructing agencies to halt a planned migration to a proprietary data exchange layer. The note was precise and unflinching: the proposed system would "weaken national autonomy by obscuring interface logic". Within weeks, the government reversed course, reaffirming commitment to X-Road — the open-source backbone that had quietly underpinned the country's digital state since 2001. The episode lasted barely a month, yet it crystallised a dilemma faced well beyond Tallinn: speed and convenience often pull governments towards proprietary systems, while sovereignty and adaptability pull them back. The tension is not abstract. Every database migration, every model integration, every procurement clause expresses it.

The hinge in that Estonian story was visibility. Engineers could inspect X-Road's schemas; policy officials could trace decisions; independent researchers could test assumptions. The proprietary alternative promised faster deployment and bundled support but concealed its interfaces and update mechanisms. When governments cannot view or influence those mechanisms, they inherit more than software. They inherit dependencies shaped by someone else's priorities. The question that follows — how much control can a public institution prudently cede? — runs through every line of this subchapter. It is a governance question dressed in technical clothing.

Three claims anchor the analysis. The first concerns speed. Proprietary platforms often excel here because vendors specialise, optimise, and deploy at scale. When the UK's Department for Transport trialled a commercial demand-forecasting model in 2020, pilot teams could simulate congestion responses within minutes instead of hours. This mattered when testing peak-time pricing scenarios for London and Birmingham. Engineers could iterate quickly because the tooling was polished. The implication is straightforward: proprietary systems can remove operational friction, and time saved becomes policy capacity.

Yet speed is only one axis. The second claim is sovereignty. Open data schemas — the quietly powerful motif weaving through these pages — give governments firm footing. An open schema is a statement of jurisdictional authority: *this is how our rules, entities, and relationships are structured.* In France, the 2018 adoption of open eligibility schemas for family benefits enabled both public and civil society review. The behaviour this schema produced was measurable. Within six months, independent groups surfaced inconsistencies affecting approximately 15,000 households, prompting corrective updates. Without open schemas, those discrepancies would have remained submerged.

A limitation sharpens the picture. Open architectures can strain local capacity. Consider the city of Barcelona's 2019 experiment with open-source mobility analytics. While its data schemas were transparent and its dashboards modifiable, the city struggled with talent shortages. Staff could not maintain the toolchain without external contractors, eroding some of the very sovereignty they sought. The hinge jammed. Transparency did not automatically equal autonomy. Reconciling this requires recognising that open systems demand ongoing investment in skills, documentation, and custodianship — costs that vendors often bundle, for better or worse.

The third major claim ties cost to long-term adaptability. Procurement audits across European municipalities in 2021 found that switching away from proprietary social care platforms required an average of three years and millions in transitional support (European Court of Auditors, 2021). The bottleneck was always the same: data locked in proprietary schemas and business rules embedded in vendor-specific formats. When governments pay low prices upfront but commit to expensive exits later, they mortgage their future discretion. Open schemas, by contrast, distribute that cost differently: they shift effort to design and governance, reducing the penalty for changing suppliers.

Two examples illustrate the hinges clearly. The first is New Zealand's 2020 decision to publish open standards for eligibility rules used across health and social support systems. Vendors adapted within months, and small firms gained a footing because integration barriers dropped. Agencies could test multiple models against the same rules without renegotiating contracts. Sovereignty, cost, and competition aligned. The hinge opened.

The second example cuts the other way. A Canadian province signed a multi-year contract in 2019 for an AI-driven employment referral system. The vendor controlled the matching model, its training data, and the method for updating scores. When bias concerns surfaced in 2021 — notably uneven referral rates between urban and rural applicants — auditors struggled because logs were incomplete and the model's internal representations were proprietary. Investigators could not trace how feature importance changed after updates. The hinge closed. Sovereignty was compromised not by malice but by contractual design.

Alongside these claims sits a counter-example that calls for caution. Some open-source projects decay in maintenance. A Brazilian municipality adopted an open-source eligibility engine in 2016, expecting flexibility. But when the volunteer maintainers left, the system ossified. Staff froze updates because they feared breaking core functions. The hinge rusted. The limitation here is clear: openness without stewardship breeds fragility.

Reconciliation emerges through hybrid architectures — systems that combine open data schemas with vetted proprietary components. This approach treats openness as the frame and proprietary tools as replaceable modules within that frame. Governments gain transparency where it matters most (data structures, rules, auditability) while borrowing maturity and optimisation from specialist vendors when needed. The hybrid model reframes procurement. It says: *we set the foundation; we choose the tools.* It protects against lock-in because components slot into predetermined structures rather than dictate them.

A motif returns: the hinge is not neutral. It must be designed. Hybrid architectures design the hinge deliberately. They specify what must remain open — schemas, rule formats, audit trails, logging standards — and what may remain proprietary — models for demand forecasting, entity resolution, anomaly detection, and other high-complexity tasks. When those proprietary modules can be swapped without rewriting underlying structures, the public institution holds the hinge, not the vendor.

Visible behaviours confirm the value of this design. When Finland developed its national interoperability platform in 2021, it mandated open schemas for citizen records while permitting agencies to use proprietary AI models for fraud detection. Logs had to comply with a shared format. Models had to justify score changes through documented interfaces. Investigators could isolate anomalies without needing full access to proprietary internals. In effect, the system treated proprietary components as guests in a house with clearly marked rooms and rules.

A further implication follows: hybrid systems change market dynamics. Vendors compete on performance rather than lock-in. Governments gain bargaining power because switching costs fall. Skills become portable because teams learn common schemas rather than idiosyncratic vendor dialects. The hinge opens wider with every shared standard.

Still, a credible limitation persists. Hybrid systems are not magic. They demand governance discipline. Agencies must maintain schema registries, enforce interface rules, and push back against vendor attempts to smuggle complexity into proprietary formats. These obligations are not optional. Without them, the hybrid becomes hollow — an open façade wrapped around a closed core.

This leads to the subchapter's unresolved tension. How much openness is enough? Should governments prioritise transparency even if it slows deployment, or should they prioritise speed even if it risks dependency? Can hybrid architectures genuinely reconcile these trade-offs, or do they merely postpone harder questions about capability and sovereignty?

The hinge remains in motion. The decision is whether the state holds it firmly — or discovers, too late, that someone else does.

Local Capacity, Global Supply

On a rainy morning in November 2019, a dozen officials from small municipalities across western Norway filed into a meeting room in Bergen's city hall. They had come from places with names that rarely make it into international reports: Voss, Øygarden, Askøy. Each had fewer than five people in their IT or planning teams. All were under pressure to "use data better". At the front of the room, the director of the newly created regional analytics unit pulled up a dashboard showing housing pressures, commuting flows, and school enrolments for the entire region. None of the contributing councils could have built it alone. Together, using a pooled team of ten analysts, they had produced models that now guided zoning decisions and transport planning. The unit belonged to no single municipality. It was a shared bench of capacity.

The paradox was obvious to everyone in that room. Individually, each council was a price taker in global technology markets. Collectively, they had bargaining power and technical competence.

A town of 15,000 people cannot dictate terms to a multinational vendor. A consortium representing half a million residents can. The analytic layer they had built did more than consolidate data; it changed who held the pen when specifications were drafted and contracts were signed. Local capacity had been created without pretending that every locality could, or should, become a miniature tech firm. The bench was regional.

This is the core tension for small governments confronting AI-saturated markets: they must navigate a global supply of tools and vendors with local means and obligations. Talent is scarce. Budgets are thin. Legal risk rests with them, not with the firms courting them. Lock-in is not an abstract fear; it is a line item in next year's budget and a constraint on next decade's reforms. The question is not whether they should "build or buy". It is how they can share.

The motif threading this subchapter is *the bench*. Not a decorative metaphor, but a practical image: the shared pool of people, tools, and patterns that sits behind frontline services. A strong bench allows small governments to choose and challenge suppliers. A weak bench leaves them clutching contracts they barely understand.

The first major claim is that local capacity is not the same as local ownership of every component. Show this carefully. In 2018, several rural councils in New South Wales joined a shared service hub for digital development. The hub employed designers, data engineers, and contract specialists on behalf of a dozen jurisdictions. None of those councils could have justified hiring a full-time data engineer alone. Together, they could. The hub did not replace local knowledge; it amplified it. Officials brought questions rooted in their communities — about flood risks, youth services, agricultural permits — and the shared team translated those into reusable models and dashboards.

Name this structure for what it is: a local capacity multiplier. Explain why it matters. Without such hubs, each small authority negotiates separately, repeating mistakes and paying for bespoke integrations that solve the same generic problems: identity verification, case tracking, appointment booking, eligibility checks. With a hub, patterns are captured once and reused. The implication is straightforward: capacity need not be atomised. The bench can be regional while decisions remain local.

A limitation appears quickly. Shared hubs can drift into centralisation. Councils may fear loss of autonomy or suspect that regional priorities will override their own. A counter-example sits in the history of some English "shared services" experiments in the early 2010s, where central IT units became gatekeepers rather than enablers. Requests queued for months. Local innovations were slowed. The bench became a bottleneck. Reconciliation requires clear governance: hubs must be jointly owned, transparent in their road-mapping, and accountable for responsiveness. Local capacity is strengthened only when the bench serves, rather than directs, the field.

The second claim concerns talent, not just tools. Small governments cannot match the salaries of global platforms, but they can compete on variety, purpose, and growth. Talent exchanges are one way of turning that into structure rather than hope. Show it in practice. In 2020, several cities in the Netherlands piloted a rotation scheme where data scientists spent six months in municipal teams and six months in a central analytics unit. During the municipal rotation, they worked on concrete problems: queue management in social services, school-place allocation, energy-retrofit targeting. Back at the central unit, they packaged the patterns, hardened the code, and trained colleagues.

Name this arrangement: a civic secondment loop. Explain why it matters. It keeps skills moving without demanding that every town maintain a permanent, fully staffed analytics department. It helps avoid a two-tier system where only capitals have sophisticated capability while smaller places rely purely on vendors. The implication is cultural as much as organisational: when staff know they can access a bench of peers, they are more willing to contest vendor claims, ask for logs, demand open interfaces, and say no to unhelpful "solutions".

Again, limits must be faced. Exchanges can create a cadre of specialists who float above local institutions, speaking a dialect that frontline staff and councillors do not understand. The bench risks becoming a club. Here, reconciliation lies in explicit translation duties: analysts must present their work in council chambers, sit with caseworkers, and document decisions in plain language. Capacity is not only technical; it is relational.

The third claim addresses lock-in directly. Lock-in, for a small government, is not a philosophical complaint; it is a crushing practical reality. It means being unable to change supplier without risking service collapse. It means accepting model updates without meaningful scrutiny. The behaviour that exposes lock-in is simple: how hard is it to leave? When a group of Scottish councils tried to replace their social care case management platform in 2019, they discovered that years of configuration and embedded workflows had effectively fused policy with vendor software. Extracting data was legally possible but operationally fraught. Migration timelines extended, costs rose, and staff patience waned.

Name this problem clearly: dependency by accretion. Explain its mechanics. Each change request adds a little more coupling between the authority's processes and the vendor's product. Over time, small governments lose the ability to define their own processes independent of the tool. The implication is stark: avoiding lock-in is not about one heroic negotiation; it is about dozens of small decisions that either preserve or erode freedom to move.

Shared regional analytics units and service hubs offer an antidote, because they create continuity above the level of any single product. When Bergen's regional unit procures an AI model for housing risk prediction, it does so with standardised data schemas and logging requirements that all participating councils agree to. If they later wish to test an alternative model, the shared team can do so without each municipality starting from scratch. The bench remembers. Lock-in is harder to impose on a group that shares memory and skill.

The fourth claim is that global supply can be bent towards local need when small governments coordinate their specifications. This is not a romantic assertion; it is visible behaviour. The "Nordic Institute for Interoperability Solutions", founded in 2017 by Estonia and Finland and later joined by Iceland, takes this approach explicitly. By co-developing and maintaining open-source components like X-

Road, they allow numerous jurisdictions — many with small populations — to stand on shared foundations when procuring additional services. Vendors know that complying with these shared components opens multiple markets at once. That knowledge shifts their incentives.

Explain the significance: coordination turns a scatter of small contracts into a coherent signal. The implication is that even modest authorities can influence global supply if they align around common standards and patterns. The bench, in this sense, is not just regional; it is transnational.

A credible counter-example tempers this optimism. Attempts to create central "one-size-fits-all" platforms at national level have sometimes stifled local adaptation. When a large European state rolled out a single, heavily specified social assistance platform in the mid-2010s, smaller municipalities found that their unique housing markets and labour conditions were poorly reflected. They could not tweak rules or interfaces without national approval. Frustration grew. Some turned to parallel spreadsheets and shadow systems. Here, scale worked against nuance. The bench was too distant. Reconciliation requires a layered approach: shared foundations, local configuration. Standards for data and interfaces, freedom for service journeys and messaging.

The fifth claim concerns measurement. Local capacity is often discussed as if it were an intangible virtue. But it produces visible metrics. Small governments with access to a regional bench tend to exhibit shorter procurement cycles for new analytics use cases; they rely less on single-supplier contracts; they resolve more issues in-house before escalating to external consultants. You can measure how many contracts include open-schema requirements, how many models have documented monitoring plans, how often staff override algorithmic suggestions based on local knowledge rather than vendor advice. These are behavioural indicators of real, not rhetorical, autonomy.

This brings the motif of the bench into final focus. A bench is tested not by how it looks on organisational charts but by what it allows frontline teams to do on an ordinary Tuesday. Can a caseworker question a risk score and get a timely, intelligible explanation? Can a planner in a coastal town see how flood-risk models treat her locality, and request adjustments based on new sea-wall data? Can a chief executive ask for a comparison between two vendor proposals that goes beyond price to include exit costs, data rights, and monitoring obligations? If the answer to these questions is yes more often than no, the bench is working.

Yet an unresolved tension remains. Shared units and exchanges require trust between jurisdictions that may compete for grants, investment, or political attention. They demand that small governments surrender some immediacy in return for long-term flexibility. They ask global suppliers to negotiate with coordinated buyers rather than isolated ones. All of this is hard.

The forward question for any small authority is therefore blunt. Do you want to face global AI markets alone, renewing contracts you cannot fully interrogate, or do you want to sit on a bench built with your neighbours — slower to assemble, occasionally uncomfortable, but strong enough to carry you when the next wave of systems arrives?

Measuring Value Beyond Savings

In January 2022, the Greater Manchester Combined Authority published a brief note that startled its finance team. The pilot they had run the previous autumn — a targeted employment-support scheme shaped by local analytics — had not delivered the projected savings. Yet councillors insisted it continue. The data told a different story. Participants had reported higher confidence in dealing with job centres. Caseworkers logged fewer escalations. Recruitment partners praised the consistency of referrals, even when volumes fluctuated. The scheme had failed to meet its narrow cost-reduction target but had strengthened relationships across the service. A dashboard built for savings said “stop”. The lived reality said “keep going”. It was a revealing moment. The city-region realised that public value had outgrown its accounting line.

The paradox lingered. If a programme builds trust and capability but costs more this quarter, is it failing or succeeding? No spreadsheet formula can answer that. Yet governments must decide week by week. Greater Manchester's admission that savings alone were a poor compass pushed officers to define what else mattered, and how it could be measured without distorting behaviour. That shift — from cost as the metric to cost as one metric — marks the frontier where AI-enabled systems will either support or erode public purpose.

The quiet motif of this piece is the *compass*. Not a decorative idea, but a practical device: indicators that orient action. A compass guides direction even when the terrain demands detours. But if miscalibrated — too few metrics, or the wrong ones — it leads good teams into bad decisions. The challenge is to build a compass that cannot be gamed into pointing anywhere you please.

The first claim is simple to show: public value is broader than fiscal savings. In 2015, the New York City Mayor's Office of Operations launched "NYC Service Design Studio" to improve interactions between residents and frontline services. One of its early projects focused on redesigning notices for public housing inspections. There were no immediate cost savings. In fact, printing clearer notices cost slightly more. But measurable outcomes shifted: missed appointments dropped; compliance improved; complaints fell. The named indicators — appointment adherence, complaint volumes, response times — captured behavioural movement that budget sheets ignored. By showing those shifts, the team reoriented internal debates from "Did this save money?" to "Did this help the service work better for residents and staff?".

Name this broadened domain precisely: equity, trust, and capability. Explain each through action. Equity appears in how different groups experience a policy, visible in metrics like uptake by neighbourhood, waiting-time disparities, or error rates for linguistic minorities. Trust shows in behaviours such as willingness to re-engage after an adverse decision, response rates to voluntary surveys, and complaint tone. Capability surfaces in the speed and quality of problem-solving within services: how often front-line workers resolve issues without escalation, how quickly multi-agency cases reach stable outcomes, and how many residents report being able to navigate systems independently.

The implication is decisive. If public value is seen through these behaviours, dashboards must move beyond cost curves. They must reveal relational and experiential outcomes, not just transactional ones.

A credible limitation sits here. Equity, trust, and capability can feel intangible. Councillors and ministers often prefer metrics with crisp numbers and tight definitions, fearing accusations of vagueness. So the counter-example is predictable: attempts to measure "wellbeing" through composite indices that collapse dozens of variables into single scores. When New Zealand trialled such indices in budgeting around 2019, some critics argued they were too broad to guide spending decisions. The compass risked spinning freely, failing to constrain choices at all.

Reconciliation requires specificity without reductionism. Composite indices should be replaced with families of indicators, each tied to a behaviour. For example, instead of a "trust score", track how many benefit claimants choose to give optional feedback after a negative decision — a visible decision to stay engaged. Rather than a generic "equity rating", compare processing times for similar cases across wards and publish the variance. The compass becomes stable because its points are grounded in observed actions.

The second major claim is that indicators must resist gaming. The show example is well-documented. When the UK government introduced hospital waiting-time targets in the early 2000s, some trusts moved patients to "assessment units" to stop the clock without delivering treatment. The indicator did not signal improvement; it signalled evasion. The behaviour was rational under pressure but disastrous for meaning. Once discovered, regulators had to strengthen definitions, audit flows, and embed qualitative checks.

Name the danger clearly: metric capture. Explain its mechanics. When staff are judged primarily by a narrow target, they adjust workflows to meet it, even if that harms service quality. In algorithmic contexts, poorly designed dashboards amplify this effect, because AI outputs can make the target feel technical and therefore unquestionable. The implication is stark. Metrics that can be gamed will be gamed. The compass will tilt.

To counter this, some jurisdictions have adopted dashboards built around distributions rather than single numbers. Show it. In 2021, Helsinki's education department introduced a dashboard to monitor support needs in early-years services. Instead of reporting only the average time between referral and support, it displayed the full distribution: median, upper quartile, and outliers. Frontline teams could see whether delays clustered in certain neighbourhoods or language groups. The structure left little space for gaming; a single tactical tweak could not mask a long tail of slow cases. The indicator set was harder to manipulate because it surfaced patterns, not just targets.

A limitation confronts us again. Dashboards with many indicators can overwhelm decision-makers. If every distribution is shown, none may be acted on. So reconciliation lies in careful curation: no more than a dozen indicators, each tied directly to a weekly operational decision. The compass must have a few cardinal points, not a galaxy of stars.

The third claim concerns capability building. Public value increases when residents can navigate services without excessive assistance and when staff can adapt workflows without vendor intervention. Capability is visible in behaviours such as self-completion of forms, number of repeated queries, or the rate at which frontline workers adjust decision thresholds in response to local context. Show this. In Lisbon's participatory budgeting processes around 2017–2019, the city created scenario visualisations that allowed residents to explore trade-offs before casting votes. Participation rates increased; more importantly, the diversity of proposals widened. Residents proposed projects with clearer costings, reducing administrative overhead. Capability had risen on both sides of the interface.

Name this growth: shared competence. Explain why it matters. When capability rises, services become less brittle. AI systems can be deployed with more nuance because staff and residents understand how to challenge or correct outputs. The implication is that capability must be measured explicitly. Dashboards should track how often users request clarifications, how many appeals succeed (signalling detectable faults), and how many decisions are reversed after local review.

The counter-example is an instructive one. When a large European welfare agency introduced an automated eligibility checker in 2020, the number of user queries fell sharply. This looked like increased capability. But follow-up audits showed the opposite. Many users simply gave up when confused, assuming the system was authoritative. Appeals rose months later. The low query rate was not a sign of capability; it was a sign of suppressed agency. Dashboards had misread silence as competence. Reconciliation requires pairing every "low query" indicator with a paired measure of engagement, such as optional feedback or completion time. The compass becomes reliable only when multiple behaviours point in the same direction.

The fourth claim is normative but measurable: public value requires attention to equity. Behaviour shows where inequities surface. In 2022, Barcelona's digital inclusion programme tracked differences in navigation times across telecom tariffs and device types. Residents connecting through older Android phones took significantly longer to complete housing-benefit applications. The city used this metric — "completion time by device type" — to redesign pages and deploy assisted digital kiosks. Equity, here, was not a lofty ideal but a number on a dashboard highlighting where service design translated into inequality.

Name this approach plainly: differential performance auditing. Explain its purpose. It identifies where systems reproduce or deepen disparities because they are optimised for the median user. The implication is direct. Every AI-enabled service should track at least three equity indicators: uptake by group, completion time variance, and error-rate differences. These cannot be allowed to drift into the decorative margins of annual reports. They are the compass bearings that prevent programmes from drifting into impartiality theatre.

A limitation must be addressed. Equity indicators can be politically charged. Publishing them invites scrutiny local leaders may find uncomfortable. Yet the alternative is to run blind. Reconciliation lies in normalising their presence: including them in routine dashboards makes them less a matter of exception and more a matter of professional practice.

The fifth claim returns us to trust. Trust can be measured indirectly. It appears in repeat engagement after negative experiences, in survey response rates when feedback is optional, and in reduction of adversarial tone in complaints. Show it with a grounded example. In 2021, a London borough redesigned its benefits-appeal letters into plain language and offered a standard evidence pack downloadable from the portal. Appeals rose slightly, but successful appeals rose markedly, and resident satisfaction scores improved. Staff recorded fewer angry calls. Residents trusted the process more because they understood it. Trust became visible in behaviours and metrics: fewer hostile interactions, higher constructive engagement.

Name this shift: procedural clarity. Explain its function. When procedures are clear, people feel respected and informed. The implication is that trust must be tracked not as sentiment but as behaviour. Dashboards should include measures like "percentage of users accessing evidence packs" and "rate of re-engagement within 30 days of adverse decisions".

The counter-example is a warning. When a central agency in Europe replaced phone-based contacts with chatbots, overall contact volume fell. It was misread as increased self-sufficiency. Subsequent audits found that residents with limited literacy struggled, and many abandoned applications midway. The apparent "increase in trust" was actually disengagement. Reconciliation demands paired metrics: contact drop must be evaluated alongside completion rates and appeals. The compass must read true.

With these claims assembled, return to the motif. A compass is useless unless someone commits to a direction. To test whether these indicators hold value, try the exercise that Greater Manchester used after its misleading savings-only dashboard. Pick three metrics you would defend publicly. Choose one that signals equity (for instance, variance in waiting times across wards). Choose one that signals capability (such as successful self-resolution rates). Choose one that signals trust (like re-engagement after negative outcomes). Ask whether you would accept a programme that performs well on these even if its short-term costs rise. If you would, your compass is aligned with public value. If you would not, savings still dominate your field of view.

The unresolved tension remains. Every metric invites the risk of unintended consequences; every dashboard can be weaponised or ignored. But decisions cannot wait for perfect instruments. So a forward test confronts every leader and analyst: will you let cost savings alone set your course, or will you build a compass calibrated to the behaviours that define a fair, effective, and trusted public service?

Chapter 8
Law in the Loop

The queue wrapped around the grey courtyard of the District Administrative Court in Berlin on a cold morning in March 2023. People clutched folders, phones, and letters bearing the same printed phrase: *"Your eligibility has been reassessed."* A housing-support algorithm had shifted thresholds after a software update. Overnight, thousands received notices reducing or removing assistance. No law had changed. No minister had announced a policy shift. Yet a technical adjustment — invisible, unconsulted, and unexplained — had altered people's rights. By midday the court registry had logged more emergency filings than in any single day that winter. A judge, interviewed later, observed dryly: "Policy now travels through code before it reaches Parliament." The remark captured the quiet constitutional truth this chapter explores.

The deeper paradox is sharper still. Democratic states spend years debating proportionality tests, privacy limits, and equality duties; yet a single undocumented parameter push can unwind those protections in seconds. The law moves slowly because it must, building legitimacy through process. Code moves fast because it can, propagating decisions across millions of records at the speed of a deployment script. The mismatch creates a constitutional pressure point: when the two collide, which governs? The people in that Berlin courtyard understood the stakes before many policymakers did. If rights are protected only until the next software update, they are not protected at all.

This tension — between the rule of law and the rule of models — forms the spine of the chapter. Modern governments cannot function without automated systems; nor can they outsource legality to engineers or vendors. The challenge is not merely to regulate algorithms but to weave legal principles into the everyday machinery of administrative decision-making. Rights must survive translation into data schemas, parameters, and protocols. Oversight must travel through release cycles. Accountability must follow the chain from design to deployment to review. Put simply: the law must sit in the loop, not hover above it.

From this starting point, we enter the terrain where constitutional guardrails meet technical design. Equality is not a slogan here but a question of distributions: who is flagged for review, who is denied by default, who waits longer, who is pushed to reapply. Privacy becomes a question of what data a model insists on collecting, how features imply sensitive attributes, and when minimisation is technically possible but procedurally ignored. Proportionality becomes an engineering constraint: does the system use the least intrusive feature set that achieves the legitimate aim? These are legal tests that must be executed through architecture, not simply invoked in ministerial speeches. The hardest mistake for governments to avoid is relying on rights *by policy* — noble statements in guidelines — rather than rights *by law*, which bind systems, operators, and vendors alike.

But statutes alone cannot do the heavy lifting. Standards organise behaviour long before legislation catches up. Documentation norms, audit trails, incident reporting formats, and data-scheme templates shape what engineers build and how managers interpret risk. Soft law — quasi-official guidance, procurement frameworks, voluntary codes — often spreads faster than statutory reform. Its speed makes it powerful, and dangerous. Agencies must decide where to engage: which technical committees they join, which drafts they comment on, which architectures they adopt early. A standard can become an unexamined assumption, then an industry dependency, then a policy constraint. In the hands of astute public leaders, it becomes an instrument of public purpose. In careless hands, it becomes a deregulatory shortcut too subtle to notice until harm accumulates.

Responsibility threads through every layer. When an algorithm misclassifies a benefits claimant, who bears the blame? The designer who trained the model? The vendor who offered it as a turnkey solution? The agency that procured it? The caseworker who clicked "approve"? The reviewer who failed to spot the trend? Legal systems traditionally rely on human actors whose reasoning can be interrogated. Automated systems diffuse both intention and control. The chain of blame becomes a chain of ambiguity. This chapter dissects emerging allocation models: some emphasise design accountability, others centre deployment practices, and others focus on supervisory oversight. The goal is not to assign blame for its own sake, but to ensure that responsibility lands where the power to prevent harm resides.

Cross-border data flows complicate everything. Models hosted in one jurisdiction may be trained on data from another, served through APIs located in a third, and used to make decisions about citizens in a fourth. OECD states face similar dilemmas: which legal regime governs, and what happens when protections conflict? Data minimisation and federated learning offer ways to reduce exposure, but they require strategic decisions about architecture, not last-minute compliance patches. The broader question is one of sovereignty. If a public agency depends on infrastructure operating under another state's laws, where does democratic control sit? The answer will differ across contexts, but the question cannot be deferred.

Threaded through the chapter is a motif: the hinge. Automated systems sit on the hinge between policy and execution, law and code, promise and practice. Hinges work when they carry force smoothly, allowing a door to move without slipping its frame. When misaligned, they warp the structure. Law in the loop is the project of tightening that hinge: ensuring that legal principles translate into technical constraints and operational habits that persist even as systems evolve.

Yet there is a deeper story beneath the technicalities. The rule of law is not a set of doctrines but a lived experience. People understand justice through what they receive: clear notices, reasons they can scrutinise, appeals they can exercise, corrections that actually correct. When automated systems mediate those experiences, they reshape not only administrative outcomes but constitutional expectations. If a model denies a benefit and no one can meaningfully challenge it, the right to appeal is hollow. If a system demands more data than necessary, privacy rights become conditional. If deployment outruns scrutiny, proportionality becomes a footnote. The law, in short, must occupy the same speed and granularity as the systems it oversees.

As governments become hybrid human–machine enterprises, the stakes rise. The systems that score risk, route cases, triage inspections, and flag anomalies increasingly encode policy directly.

They become instruments of state power, subtle yet pervasive. Embedding law within them is not optional. It is the price of legitimacy.

The path forward requires decisions that blend legal clarity with technical fluency. How tightly should purpose statements bind architects? When should soft-law standards be adopted, challenged, or resisted? How far should liability travel up the chain from operational use to design choice? Which cross-border architectures maintain sovereignty without sacrificing collaboration? Each of these questions is a hinge too — decisions that determine whether automated governance bends with democratic oversight or buckles under its own speed.

Turn the page, then, with this in mind. The law must not chase technology. It must inhabit it. The shape of that habitation — sometimes protective, sometimes constraining, sometimes enabling — is the subject of what follows.

Constitutional Guardrails for Code

The French *Conseil d'État* faced an unusual dossier in June 2020. A COVID-19 contact-tracing system, **StopCovid**, had been deployed nationwide weeks earlier. Its stated purpose was narrow, its architecture hastily assembled, its data flows partially documented. Yet the case that reached the court turned on an older question: whether a public health algorithm could demand identifiers beyond what statute permitted. The Ministry argued necessity; privacy groups argued proportionality. After a day of hearings in Paris, the judges issued a pointed observation: *administrative convenience does not create constitutional authority*. The system survived scrutiny only after the Ministry committed to hard limits on retention, feature use, and re-purposing. Code had drifted past its legal mandate. Law pulled it back.

Scenes like that are no longer rare. A procurement officer approves a data pipeline assuming it merely automates existing rules; weeks later, a classifier begins inferring sensitive categories never contemplated in statute. A city deploys a housing inspection triage tool to predict structural risk; its feature list quietly encodes neighbourhood histories that discriminate indirectly. A benefits agency introduces automated re-assessment, triggering mass suspensions without the procedural safeguards guaranteed by law. The pattern is familiar: public systems increasingly embed legal obligations inside architectures that were never designed to express them. Rights become optional configurations. Oversight becomes a post-hoc scramble.

The motif that threads through such cases is a hinge. Constitutional principles must hinge cleanly into technical design, bearing load without shearing. When the hinge misaligns, code begins to govern where law should. The task of this section is to show how equality, privacy, and proportionality — the central guardrails of constitutional democracies — must travel directly into data schemas, model features, deployment conditions, and audit routines.

The starting point is equality. In 2018, the **Dutch SyRI system** (System Risk Indication) was struck down by the District Court of The Hague. Its scoring method flagged households for fraud investigations using opaque correlations between employment records, tax histories, and geographic markers. The state argued that the inputs were lawful and the model impartial. The court disagreed. It emphasised that equal treatment cannot be reduced to the absence of explicitly protected categories; it requires scrutiny of how proxies operate in context. Here, the behaviour was clear: households in certain low-income districts were flagged at disproportionately high rates. The name of this pattern is indirect discrimination. The implication is sharp: a model can operate solely on "neutral" data and still violate equality duties if it maps onto social patterns the law seeks to correct.

Yet there is a counter-example that complicates the picture. In 2021, a Canadian province piloted an automated eligibility screener for disability benefits. Civil society groups warned it would replicate long-standing biases in discretionary assessments. When the pilot results were released, they showed the opposite: approval disparities narrowed because the system removed a layer of inconsistent human judgement. The limitation reveals itself quickly, however. The model performed fairly only while the training distribution remained stable and the appeal process remained active. As appeals behaviour shifted, the system's fairness metrics drifted. The reconciliation is straightforward: equality by design is not a one-off achievement but a monitored condition. Constitutional obligations require continuous measurement — not promises, not intentions.

Privacy operates in a similarly embodied way. It is not an abstraction; it is a set of visible decisions: which features are collected, which are inferred, which are stored, which are shared. The **UK Information Commissioner's Office** highlighted this during its 2019 review of local-authority predictive tools for children's services. Several councils used features like school attendance, housing tenure, and service touchpoints to predict risk of harm. While each feature individually had statutory bases, the *linkage* between them had not been authorised. In effect, metadata became a surveillance system no legislator had debated. The implication is simple: privacy rights must shape architecture. If a model requires a dozen features but statutory purpose justifies only five, the remaining seven cannot be wished into legitimacy through policy guidance. The legal basis must precede the code path.

A limitation occasionally emerges from crisis contexts. Governments facing wildfires, floods, or pandemics sometimes argue that data minimisation is impossible. Historic examples include the rapid geolocation processing used during the 2017 California wildfires to route evacuation traffic. Here, temporary expansions of data scope arguably saved lives. Yet even in such cases, constitutional principles persist. Privacy is not voided by crisis; rather, it must be re-balanced with documented necessity and strict temporal boundaries. The reconciliation lies in controlled exceptionalism: strong activation criteria, logged access, and automatic decommissioning. Rights recover their full force the moment the emergency passes.

Proportionality — the requirement that state interference be necessary and the least intrusive means available — travels into code more directly than officials often expect. Consider the design of eligibility-confirmation models used by several European municipalities. In 2022, **Barcelona City Council** modified the feature set of its housing benefit recommender after independent reviewers demonstrated that half the included variables contributed negligible predictive value. The council removed eight features, many linked to family composition and employment transitions. The revised model retained 94% of its predictive performance. Proportionality here became a matter of feature curation: removing intrusive data that made little difference. The implication radiates outward: if a system achieves its objective without sensitive or excessive data, the law requires the leaner design.

Yet proportionality also governs deployment conditions. A hiring-support algorithm used by a Scandinavian employment agency in 2020 recommended sanctions for claimants who missed digital check-ins. Technically, the system worked. Legally, it faltered. Proportionality required examining the *context* of non-compliance — connectivity issues, disability, unstable housing. Because the system provided no such checks, it amplified minor violations into major penalties. Only after the agency added a human-in-the-loop review for all negative recommendations did the system align with constitutional standards. The hinge again: code without context erodes rights; code with contextual guardrails can reinforce them.

Throughout these examples, a recurring danger emerges: **rights by policy**, rather than **rights by law**. Rights by policy depend on administrative goodwill. A department promises not to use certain data for certain purposes. A vendor promises not to repurpose models. An internal memorandum promises proportionality reviews. These commitments evaporate the moment priorities shift or teams change. Rights by law, in contrast, bind design, procurement, and operation. They make certain architectures unlawful. They enforce reporting obligations. They create remedies when systems behave unlawfully. The difference is visible behaviour: policy rights vanish quietly; legal rights create traceable friction.

That friction is healthy. It forces public bodies to document purpose, justify data flows, and test for discriminatory impacts before deployment. It compels vendors to support auditability and explainability. It slows systems at precisely the points where democratic accountability requires slowness. The chain of implications is clear: constitutional guardrails must be structural, not aspirational.

A quiet motif reappears here: the hinge. Law and code meet at contact points that must not slip — purpose statements written into tenders, feature lists reviewed against statutory limits, fairness metrics monitored over time, appeal pathways integrated into interfaces. Each hinge must bear weight. When they fail, rights fail.

As we move to the closing movement, the unresolved tension surfaces. How should governments decide which legal principles must be "hard-coded" and which may be operationalised through procedures and oversight? How far should a statute reach into technical specificity, and when does over-specification risk freezing innovation? When does privacy minimisation conflict with model robustness? When does equality demand heavier data collection to detect bias? Policymakers face a trade-off: codify too much and systems calcify; codify too little and systems drift.

That is the test ahead. A constitutional democracy must decide where its hinges sit — and how tightly they must lock — before the next generation of automated systems arrives with even greater speed and scale.

Standards, Soft Law, and Hard Problems

In June 2019, engineers at Google in Mountain View quietly updated their internal model documentation template. The change added fields for known limitations, training-data provenance, and "intended user competencies". The template was not a law, nor a contract. It was a house rule. Yet within a year, similar documentation norms appeared in draft technical standards, in guidance from regulators, and, most consequentially, in procurement frameworks issued by governments in the United Kingdom, Canada, and parts of the European Union. Vendors bidding for public-sector contracts were asked to supply "model cards" and "data sheets" tracing lineage and limitations. A tweak in a corporate template had migrated into state practice and regulatory expectation without a single parliamentary vote. This is how standards move: sideways, quietly, fast.

The paradox is unsettling. Constitutions and statutes are designed to channel state power through public deliberation. Yet much of the practical discipline on AI systems comes from standards, guidelines, and procurement norms drafted in committees and working groups most citizens have never heard of. A single line in an ISO draft — say, a definition of "high-risk use case" — can influence insurance products, vendor roadmaps, and agency risk registers long before legislators agree on anything concrete. Soft law, in the form of standards and guidance, often reaches systems before hard law does. That speed is both a benefit and a threat. It can embed responsibility early. It can also lock in assumptions that no court has tested.

The motif that threads this subchapter is *the script*. Standards are scripts for behaviour: they do not compel like statutes, but they script what "good practice" looks like for engineers, buyers, and auditors. Scripts can be rewritten; they can also become invisible. When a script travels from a standards body into a procurement checklist, it begins to shape public systems directly. The question is not whether this will happen, but who is holding the pen.

The first major claim is that standards shape behaviour faster than statutes because they operate at the level of tools, templates, and checklists. Show this clearly. When the IEEE launched its "Ethically Aligned Design" initiative in 2019 and related standards workstreams, it did not produce enforceable law. It produced definitions, process recommendations, and documentation patterns. Within months, several European agencies incorporated those recommendations into funding calls. Applicants were asked to describe impact assessments, stakeholder engagement plans, and bias testing approaches using IEEE language. Behaviour changed because teams wanted grants. The name for this phenomenon is normative cascade: once a standard becomes the default script in technical communities, public bodies copy it rather than invent from scratch.

The implication is immediate. If governments are absent from standards drafting, they still end up living inside the resulting scripts. Their engineers import libraries, follow documentation templates, and adhere to "best practice" that someone else has defined. Law then struggles to catch up because by the time legislators set rules, infrastructure reflects the standards, not the statutes.

A limitation deserves attention. Standards are not inherently virtuous. Some are shallow, drafted quickly to meet market or political timelines. Others are so abstract they provide cover for poor practice. The history of "self-regulatory" privacy seals in the early 2000s is instructive. Many signalled compliance without real constraint. Script without substance. Reconciliation requires a discriminating attitude: agencies cannot treat all standards as equal. They must ask whose interests shaped them, what evidence underpins them, and how they interact with existing legal duties.

The second claim concerns *soft law* — guidelines, frameworks, codes of practice — that occupy the grey zone between voluntary norms and binding regulation. Show how they matter. When the UK's Information Commissioner issued its "AI Auditing Framework" in 2020, it did not create new offences. It set expectations: document lawful bases, trace feature selection decisions, monitor models post-deployment, integrate human review in high-impact settings. Within a year, major public-sector contracts began referencing that framework explicitly. Suppliers were asked how their systems aligned with its recommendations. Soft law had become a procurement filter.

Name this process: regulatory seepage. Explain its mechanics. Regulators publish guidance; public bodies adopt it as a checklist for due diligence; vendors treat it as a de facto requirement. Behaviour shifts before any court invokes the guidance explicitly. The implication is profound. Soft law can extend the reach of legal principles into technical detail without waiting for statutory amendment. It can also overreach, allowing regulators to steer practice beyond what legislators intended if not watched carefully.

A counter-example reveals the danger of over-reliance on soft law. The Dutch childcare benefits scandal, which came to light fully around 2019–2020, involved aggressive fraud detection practices that disproportionately targeted dual-nationality families. Internal guidelines framed these practices as "risk-based" and aligned with fraud-control principles; formal law did not authorise discrimination on nationality grounds. Here, soft internal scripts were presented as responsible management while quietly diverging from constitutional commitments. The lesson is clear. Soft law must be anchored explicitly in hard law, not treated as a replacement for it.

The third claim is that agencies need practical routes of engagement with standards work, not just passive consumption of outputs. Show how this can work. In 2021, Canada's Treasury Board Secretariat created a small, multidisciplinary "standards liaison" team. Its job was straightforward: participate in ISO and OECD AI working groups, report back on emerging drafts, and advise how Canadian law and policy should respond. The team did not approve or veto standards. It translated them. As a result, when the national government updated its "Directive on Automated Decision-Making", it could anticipate where global standards were heading and choose deliberately whether to align, diverge, or push for amendments.

Name this institutional pattern: standards-facing capacity. Explain why it matters. Without such capacity, agencies rely on vendors and consultants to interpret standards. Those interpretations will predictably emphasise commercial convenience, not public purpose. The implication is operational. Even modest governments need at least a minimal bench of people who can read a draft standard, map it to existing duties, and advise where to push back.

There is, again, a limitation. Deep participation in standards committees can be time-consuming and, frankly, tedious. Smaller agencies may feel they cannot spare staff. Reconciliation lies in tiered engagement. Not everyone needs to sit in every working group. A national or regional node can coordinate across many agencies, summarising key developments and providing template positions. The script can be negotiated collectively.

The fourth claim brings us to documentation norms — one of the most visible ways standards migrate into procurement. Show the path. Academic proposals like "model cards" and "datasheets for datasets" began as research artefacts around 2018–2019. Within a few years, they appeared in draft NIST and ISO materials, and then in public-sector guidance. The European Commission's "Ethics

Guidelines for Trustworthy AI" (2019) emphasised documentation of data sources, limitations, and human oversight. Shortly after, some member states began requiring documentation packages describing model purpose, performance on relevant subgroups, monitoring plans, and retraining triggers as part of AI tenders.

Name this convergence: documentation as due process. Explain its function. Documentation norms help convert high-level legal principles — like transparency and accountability — into concrete artefacts that auditors, courts, and citizens can inspect. A "model card" that shows performance dropping sharply for a language minority, for instance, creates an evidential trail that equality bodies can follow. A "datasheet" that lists sensitive proxies pushes privacy officers to question feature inclusion. The implication is legal as well as managerial. When documentation norms are embedded in contracts, failure to comply becomes a contractual breach, not just a bad habit.

A counter-example tempers enthusiasm. Some vendors respond to documentation requirements by generating dense, generic PDFs that satisfy checklists but provide no real insight. Paperwork theatre. To reconcile this, agencies must specify not just *that* documentation is required, but *how it will be used.* If a procurement framework states that model cards will inform impact assessments and that discrepancies will trigger audit, vendors have an incentive to be honest. If documentation sits unread in archives, it becomes a hollow ritual.

The fifth claim touches the hardest problems: when standards risk hardening premature consensus on contested issues. Consider fairness metrics. Technical standards bodies are keen to define "fair AI" in measurable terms. But fairness is context-dependent and politically contested. A single global metric, if enshrined in standards and procurement, could prematurely settle debates that belong in legislatures and courts. Script creep, again. Standards that reach too far into normative territory can constrain democratic choice.

The implication is that agencies must distinguish between *infrastructural* standards (for logging, interoperability, documentation) and *normative* standards (for fairness, risk categories, acceptable error rates). The former are often good candidates for rapid adoption. The latter require slow, public debate. Engagement routes must reflect this difference. Technical staff can negotiate schemas; ministers and parliaments must arbitrate what counts as a just outcome.

The motif of the script returns one more time. Public authorities are already acting from scripts they did not write: vendor playbooks, engineering "best practices", international guidelines. The task is not to discard scripts but to rewrite them consciously. That means choosing which standards to adopt verbatim, which to adapt, and which to resist. It means using procurement to ratify documentation norms that genuinely enable oversight, not tick-box exercises. It means making sure soft law remains anchored to constitutional guardrails, not drifting free as a parallel system of shadow rules.

What remains unresolved is the central trade-off. Should governments move quickly with standards and soft law to rein in risky systems, accepting the chance of overreach? Or should they wait for fully debated statutes, knowing that by then, technical scripts may have hardened practice beyond easy reform? Put differently: who writes the first draft of the rules that public algorithms must obey — engineers in standards rooms, or legislators in public chambers — and how do we keep those drafts from becoming, without anyone noticing, the final version?

Liability and the Chain of Blame

In October 2021, the Dutch Court of Audit reviewed a benefits misclassification that had stripped a Rotterdam mother, Fatma Kaya, of childcare support for nearly a year. The automated risk model used by the Tax and Customs Administration had assigned her a high-fraud score based partly on dual-nationality data. Staff followed the flagged recommendation, suspended her payments, and triggered debt collection. When the error was later overturned, she received an apology and compensation. But what the audit exposed was not simply a faulty model. It revealed a vacuum: no single actor could explain who, precisely, was responsible for the harm — the software vendor that supplied the scoring engine, the civil servants who implemented it, or the supervisors who approved its use. The chain of blame snapped in multiple places, leaving the citizen to assemble the pieces.

The scene became emblematic because it revealed something deeper: automated systems distribute the work of decision-making across designers, deployers, and overseers, while liability regimes still assume a clear, traceable actor. When a benefits officer misfiles a form, responsibility is straightforward. When a model misclassifies a family at scale, the failure is spread through code paths, data pipelines, procurement clauses, and monitoring dashboards. That diffusion makes it easy for every actor to explain why they are not at fault, and harder for citizens to find redress. The motif running through this subchapter is the *broken link*: each actor handles a link in the chain, but unless someone commits to holding the whole chain together, the weakest link defines the citizen's fate.

The first major claim is that responsibility must be unpacked across roles, not personalities. Show the need. In the Kaya case, the audit found that the contractor had delivered the risk model "as specified", including the feature that proxied dual nationality. The deployment team had integrated the model into existing casework flows. Supervisors had approved its roll-out as part of a fraud-control strategy. Each step was formally compliant. Yet the system as a whole created discriminatory outcomes. Name this artefact: distributed causation. Explain why it resists traditional liability tools. Tort and administrative law historically target acts by identifiable agents. But here, harm emerged from how components interacted. The implication is plain. Legal regimes must allocate responsibility in ways that reflect system architecture, not organisational charts.

A counter-example demonstrates the limits of blaming only the model. In 2020, New York City's Automated Decision Systems Task Force reviewed several municipal models. It found that some scoring tools were reasonably built but produced unfair outcomes because frontline staff treated risk bands as binding rather than advisory. The design was sound; the deployment culture was not. Reconciling these examples means accepting a dual truth: better models do not guarantee fair outcomes, and better deployment practices cannot rescue fundamentally flawed designs. Liability must therefore cover both.

The second claim is that clear allocation models reduce ambiguity and help prevent blame shifting. Show this through practice. The UK's "digital by default" programme, active through the mid-2010s, developed what internal guides called a *three-tier responsibility model.* Designers were accountable for documenting assumptions, dataset lineage, and intended use. Deployers were accountable for configuring thresholds, human-in-the-loop points, and escalation paths. Overseers — typically senior responsible owners — were accountable for verifying that the system met legal and policy standards before authorisation. Each group signed off artefacts at their tier. Name this device: role-aligned sign-off. Explain its significance. It forced every actor to articulate and own their part of the chain. The implication is a shift in liability culture. When something breaks, the question is not who touched the system last, but who held which responsibilities.

Limitations remain. Sign-off can become ceremonial. If teams rubber-stamp documents without scrutiny, the chain of blame remains fragile. Reconciliation requires pairing role-aligned sign-off with periodic audits that test whether documents describe actual behaviour. A sign-off stating that a model includes a manual override is meaningless if logs show the override is never used. Liability attaches not to paperwork but to practice.

The third claim concerns the role of procurement as an anchor for liability. Show how this works. When Helsinki's City Executive Office negotiated an analytics contract in 2020, it required vendors to provide model documentation, performance metrics across protected subgroups, and mandatory support during investigations of adverse impacts. The contract made explicit that the city retained final responsibility for decisions, but vendors were accountable for the technical validity of their models and for timely remediation of faults. Name this structure: dual accountability procurement. Explain its logic. It divides responsibility along capability lines. Public authorities own value judgments and outcomes; vendors own technical artefacts and maintenance. The implication is enforceability. Contractual clauses provide mechanisms — penalties, remediation windows, suspension rights — that administrative law alone may not deliver quickly.

A limitation is evident. Small municipalities may lack bargaining power to demand such clauses. Vendors might refuse or provide superficial assurances. Reconciling this requires concerted action: pooled procurement, shared model evaluation services, and transparent reporting that pressures vendors to adhere to higher standards. When multiple authorities specify similar liability clauses, ecosystem norms shift.

The fourth claim is that oversight bodies need adversarial capacities to interrogate failures. Show this through a concrete example. After failures in predictive policing tools, the Los Angeles Police Department's Inspector General in 2020 reviewed the system's auditability. The review concluded that insufficient logs made it impossible to trace model decisions or assess officer interventions. Without trace data — timestamps, override events, reclassification metrics — the oversight body could not assign responsibility. Name this essential infrastructure: traceability. Explain its purpose. Traceability produces evidence, and evidence grounds liability. The implication is operational. Public systems must treat logging and monitoring not as technical chores but as democratic safeguards.

To show a counterpoint, consider a case where traceability exists but is underused. Several European welfare agencies introduced audit logs for automated scoring engines around 2021. Logs captured input features, scores, and overrides. Yet internal auditors struggled to analyse them because staff lacked training and tools. The system was transparent on paper but opaque in practice. Reconciliation lies in capacity building. Logs are only as useful as the people able to interpret them. Oversight bodies need dedicated analysts who can reconstruct decision paths and identify fault lines.

The fifth claim concerns remedies. Liability is not solely about identifying blame; it is about repairing harm. Show this. In the Kaya case, the Court of Audit emphasised that compensation should not depend solely on litigation. Agencies must maintain administrative redress channels that are accessible, responsive, and well-publicised. Name this principle: administrative reparation. Explain its logic. Litigation is slow; welfare is immediate. Administrative channels that can reverse automated errors quickly reduce harm and demonstrate institutional responsibility. The implication is a shift towards proactive remediation. Systems should include built-in mechanisms to identify and compensate groups affected by systematic model errors, not just individuals who complain loudly.

A limitation emerges. Remediation can be uneven. In some jurisdictions, people with legal representation secure corrections faster than those without. Reconciliation demands standard evidence packs, plain-language notices, and appeal interfaces that prompt users to supply specific information. Responsibility includes designing systems that lower the barrier to redress.

The sixth claim addresses the chain itself: responsibility must be layered, not singular. Show how this appears in practice. The Canadian government's 2021 update to its "Directive on Automated Decision-Making" introduced three layers of accountability: technical (model integrity), operational (decision workflow), and supervisory (policy alignment and risk). Each layer had named owners and explicit duties. Name this architecture: layered accountability. Explain its significance. It reflects the reality that no single actor controls everything. The implication is resilience. When one layer fails — a data pipeline error, a mis-set threshold — other layers should detect and correct it. Liability becomes a shared fabric rather than a hunt for an individual culprit.

The motif of the broken link returns. Many public failures occur not because the link is weak but because no one realises the link exists. A misclassification harming benefits often sits at the junction between two layers — technical and operational — with neither group seeing the full picture. To mend the chain, systems must include explicit maps of which team owns which link, and oversight bodies must trace harm back through each link, not just the last touchpoint.

The closing tension remains unresolved. Should liability follow the code, tracing fault back to design decisions, or follow the decision, fixing fault wherever the human officer validated the result? Should vendors bear more responsibility when their models influence rights, or should public authorities shoulder it because they authorise and deploy? The chain of blame cannot remain ambiguous, but every allocation creates incentives. Designing those incentives wisely determines whether we build systems that protect citizens — or ones where every link defers to another, leaving the broken chain in the citizen's hands.

Cross-Border Data and Jurisdiction

In July 2020, the Court of Justice of the European Union annulled the EU–US Privacy Shield framework in a case now shorthand as *Schrems II*. A Viennese lawyer, Max Schrems, had argued that Facebook Ireland's transfers of Europeans' data to servers in the United States exposed them to surveillance powers incompatible with EU fundamental rights. The Court agreed. Overnight, thousands of European organisations found themselves relying on contractual clauses that might or might not be lawful, depending on how data moved and which foreign authorities could access it. No server had physically relocated. Yet a judgment in Luxembourg altered the legal climate of cloud data centres in Oregon and Virginia.

The paradox was stark for public agencies. A health authority in France running analytics on hospital readmissions through a US-based cloud provider, a labour ministry in Germany using a global fraud-detection service, a provincial government in Canada consuming European-hosted APIs — all discovered that jurisdiction was not where they thought it was. Legal duties followed people's data across borders, but technical architectures had been designed as if geography no longer mattered. The problem was not simply that data moved. It was that the map of law and the map of infrastructure no longer overlapped.

The quiet motif that underpins this subchapter is the *misaligned map*: where the legal borders that allocate rights and duties fail to match the network paths that route packets and gradients. Automated public systems, and the AI models embedded within them, now routinely draw on services and storage located outside their home jurisdiction. Yet constitutional guarantees, administrative law, and sectoral regulations remain largely domestic. To govern responsibly, public institutions must understand how cross-border data flows alter both their legal exposure and their capacity to honour commitments made to citizens.

The first major claim is that cross-border data transfers are not an exotic corner case but part of the default stack of public AI. Show this concretely. A social security agency in an OECD country contracts a vendor to provide an employment-risk model. The vendor trains on anonymised historical records in a data centre located in a neighbouring state with similar legal standards. The agency assumes that because the data are "anonymised" and the neighbour is an ally, jurisdictional issues are minor. Yet once the model is deployed as a cloud API, operational logs containing quasi-identifiers, IP addresses, and sometimes raw inputs start flowing back to the vendor's main platform, which is hosted in a third country. The name for this pattern is *secondary transfer*. It often occurs through monitoring, debugging, or feature telemetry rather than the initial training pipeline.

The implication is sobering. Even when initial data exports are tightly controlled, subsequent operational uses can create new flows governed by different law. A data minimisation principle that looked robust on the training side may fracture under the weight of implementation. Citizens' rights to access, correction, or deletion become harder to exercise when their data — or inferences about them — sit in parallel stores across jurisdictions. The misaligned map grows more tangled.

The second claim concerns extraterritorial reach. Many OECD jurisdictions extend their data protection or consumer laws beyond their borders when their residents are affected, but they do so differently. The EU's General Data Protection Regulation asserts authority based on data subjects' location; the United States often grounds jurisdiction in corporate presence or infrastructure; Canada blends federal and provincial regimes. Show how this bites. A welfare agency in a European member state deploys a US-developed triage model via a European subsidiary. Under EU law, the agency remains a controller; under US law, certain national security instruments can compel access to data held by the parent company, even if physically stored in Europe.

Name this friction: *conflicting obligations*. The same data may be subject to secrecy requirements in one jurisdiction and disclosure duties in another. The implication for public bodies is structural. They must design systems with an understanding that foreign powers' legal tools can reach into their infrastructures indirectly, via vendors and sub-processors. Trust is no longer just about how an agency itself behaves; it is about the legal ecosystem in which its suppliers operate.

A counter-example offers nuance. Some cross-border collaborations have strengthened, rather than weakened, protections. Nordic states' joint work on X-Road and shared interoperability services, for example, rests on mutual legal frameworks and explicit agreements that restrict secondary use. Here, cross-border architecture was designed with law in mind from the outset. The misaligned map was redrawn before deployment. The reconciliation between these cases lies in design intention. Where cross-border flows are treated as a legal design parameter, constitutional guardrails can travel with the data. Where they are treated as a technical convenience, law arrives late and awkwardly.

The third claim introduces data minimisation as a concrete response when jurisdiction is uncertain. Data minimisation is not a slogan; it is a set of visible decisions: how many fields are exported, at what granularity, for how long, and with what linkage keys. Show it in action. A transport authority in an OECD city wishes to use a global vendor's optimisation engine for bus scheduling. Rather than export complete passenger records, it aggregates boarding events into hourly counts by stop, strips exact timestamps, and removes card identifiers. The model still learns peak patterns and route pressures, but it cannot be straightforwardly reverse-engineered to reconstruct individuals' journeys.

Name this pattern: *reduced attack surface*. Explain its legal effect. By reducing identifiability, the authority lowers the likelihood that foreign legal instruments or data breaches will meaningfully expose individuals. The implication is that minimisation acts as a buffer against jurisdictional ambiguity. When nobody holds more data than strictly necessary — and when exported data are genuinely less sensitive — the stakes of cross-border conflict are lower.

A limitation must be confronted. Some AI models perform best with fine-grained, longitudinal data. For example, early-intervention systems in health or social care may require detailed histories to detect deterioration. Minimisation, if applied bluntly, can erode model utility. Reconciling this requires tiered strategies: keep rich identifiable data within the home jurisdiction; export only the aggregated statistics or model updates needed for collaborative learning; reserve direct cross-border access for narrowly defined, logged, and exceptional cases. The misaligned map is adjusted rather than ignored.

The fourth claim brings federated learning to the foreground as a structural answer to jurisdictional messiness. Federated learning allows models to train across data held by multiple parties without centralising the raw data. Show how this might work in an OECD welfare context. Several regional employment agencies wish to build a shared model to predict long-term unemployment risk. Legal concerns hinder pooling of individual-level data in a single data centre, especially across borders. Instead, a central coordinator sends an initial model to each agency. Local systems train on their own data, compute parameter updates, and send only those updates back. The central model aggregates them to improve performance, then redistributes.

Name this architecture: *data-local, model-global.* Explain why it matters. Raw records never leave the jurisdiction or agency that collected them; yet the system still learns from patterns across regions. The implication is pragmatic. Federated learning does not remove all legal risk — gradients can sometimes leak information, and coordination nodes still raise questions — but it shifts the locus of risk from raw data movement to controlled parameter exchange. For agencies facing unclear cross-border rules, this may be the difference between acting and stalling.

A counter-example adds necessary caution. Early deployments of federated learning in healthcare have shown that heterogeneity in local data quality and coding practices can degrade model performance. Some participants benefit less, or even regress, because local biases persist. Moreover, governance agreements about who can update the global model, how conflicts are resolved, and what happens when one party withdraws are often underdeveloped. The misaligned map shows up again: technical architecture outruns institutional arrangements. Reconciling this requires treating federated learning not as a purely technical fix but as a governance project. Data-protection officers, legal teams, and frontline managers must help define participation rules, audit rights, and exit conditions.

The fifth claim returns to jurisdiction through the lens of accountability. Citizens typically know which government body they can complain to when a local service fails. But what happens when harm arises from a cross-border model? Show the difficulty. A resident in an OECD capital city is denied a housing benefit after a scoring system hosted abroad assigns them a low priority. They appeal. The local agency explains that the model is provided by an external partner and that parameters are proprietary. Supervisory authorities investigate and collide with foreign secrecy laws or trade protections. The resident experiences a practical denial of jurisdiction: legally, they have rights; operationally, no authority can fully exercise them.

Name this condition: *opaque extraterritoriality*. Explain its nature. Formal jurisdiction over decisions remains domestic, but effective control over the tools influencing those decisions is shared, constrained, or shifted abroad. The implication is constitutional. If a state cannot fully scrutinise, explain, or correct the systems that affect rights, its claim to sovereignty is weakened.

Some OECD states have responded by requiring that certain "high-risk" public systems run on infrastructure subject only to domestic or tightly aligned law. Data localisation for critical registers, judiciary systems, or security services is one manifestation. Yet localisation is blunt. It can raise costs, limit access to best-of-breed tools, and damage interoperability with neighbouring states. A more targeted approach combines localisation for core identifiers and registers with carefully architected cross-border collaboration for analytics, using minimisation and federated models as described earlier.

Throughout these debates, the motif of the misaligned map recurs. Engineers often start from a network map — latency, redundancy, capacity. Lawyers start from a sovereignty map — territory, jurisdiction, mutual assistance. Decisions about cross-border AI draw both maps on top of each other. Where they overlap, design is easy. Where they diverge, hard choices appear.

Those choices coalesce into an unresolved tension. Should public institutions privilege legal certainty by keeping sensitive data and critical models firmly within their jurisdiction, even if that slows adoption and limits international collaboration? Or should they embrace cross-border infrastructures and models to gain capability and scale, relying on technical mitigation like minimisation and federated learning to manage legal fog? Put differently: when the maps of law and infrastructure fail to match, which should move first — the cables or the constitution?

Chapter 9
Design for Dignity

The queue formed at dawn outside an employment centre in Birmingham during the winter of 2018. Frost clung to railings, breath hung briefly in the air, and every few minutes another person pressed a gloved hand against the locked glass doors to check whether the automatic sensor might mercifully stir. Most were there for a single task: to complete an identity verification step that the new benefits portal required before payments could resume. The portal itself worked. The algorithm assessing eligibility had been tuned; the risk flags behaved. Yet the journey felt punishing. For many, the fairness of the final decision was immaterial. They had already been worn down by a sequence of hurdles that treated their time, mobility, and bandwidth as if these were inexhaustible. A mother with a pushchair murmured that she had taken two buses and missed a shift. A man with arthritis quietly hoped the office lifts were working. The service was lawful. But it did not feel humane.

That morning captured a wider truth about the state's digital turn. Public institutions can invest in technically sound models, beautifully drafted policies, and crisp statutory safeguards, and still leave people feeling unseen. The distance between procedural fairness and lived fairness is sometimes no more than a screen that explains too little, a form that hides the "why", or an interface that traps a person in loops without a way to raise their hand. Each touchpoint can carry the residue of care or the impression of indifference. People know the difference instantly.

Dignity is not ornamental. It is the quiet infrastructure that supports legitimacy. When a citizen taps through a service journey, they are encountering the state's stance towards them — its posture, its patience, its curiosity about their circumstances. That posture is shaped long before a model computes a score or a caseworker reads a file. It emerges from the pathways, prompts, silences, and recovery routes designed by teams who may never meet the people they affect. If power hides in code, dignity hides in design.

This chapter takes that claim seriously. It begins with end-to-end service journeys, because the state's decisions do not occur in isolation; they sit within sequences of tasks, waits, and verifications that can either compound disadvantage or gently remove it. A verification stage that requires passports when half the intended population cannot easily produce them; an address check that assumes private broadband; a timed-out session that forces someone to restart from zero — these are not marginal irritations. They are signals about whose time counts. By mapping entire journeys rather than single decisions, public designers can see where friction piles up and where remedies must be placed. The Birmingham queue stands as a reminder: a fair algorithm is meaningless inside an unfair journey.

The narrative then moves to interfaces that explain and invite challenge. The public increasingly engages with the state through screens, not counters. Yet screens can mislead through brevity. They strip voice from complex assessments. A notice that says "your submission is incomplete" without specifying which field; an appeal link buried in a menu; evidence upload that only accepts a narrow file type — these patterns weaken procedural justice. Reasons, in the administrative sense, must be reasons a person can act upon. Explanations are not decorative summaries; they are tools for challenge. In multilingual contexts, translations and readability levels are equity levers. If an interface cannot be understood by those who depend on it most, it is the design that has failed, not the user.

The same holds for the shift from behavioural nudges to choice architecture with rights. For years, digital government borrowed lightly from behavioural economics: pre-selected defaults, suggestive prompts, and encouraging micro-copy. Some of that helped people navigate complexity. Yet persuasion is not the state's core purpose. Protection is. Interfaces must therefore embed rights prompts — clear routes to escalation, visible paths to independent review, explicit statements that a person may disagree, provide additional information, or speak to a human. This repositioning alters the moral geometry of digital services. The centre of gravity moves from steering to safeguarding.

The chapter also confronts measurement. Satisfaction scores, smiley-button widgets, and star ratings offer comforting numerics, but they often capture mood rather than justice. Dignity is sensed in the grain of experience: whether someone could complete a task without unnecessary repetition, whether an appeal was acknowledged promptly, whether a remedy arrived when a mistake was found. Completion rates, appeal rates, and remedy times are not soft metrics; they are the pulse of administrative justice. They resist gaming because they reveal failure modes that matter.

Across these themes runs a consistent motif: dignity as design discipline. It is the discipline of mapping experiences rather than assuming them; of offering reasons that illuminate rather than obscure; of enabling choice rather than nudging by default; of measuring what enables a life rather than what flatters a dashboard. It is also the discipline of humility. Public designers wield extraordinary power over those with less. Each decision — where to place a button, how many steps to require, whether to time out a session at five minutes or fifteen — can shift that balance.

What follows in this chapter is not nostalgia for paper forms or an argument against digital transformation. It is a claim that transformation without dignity is hollow. The techniques explored here — journey mapping, explanatory interfaces, rights-based paths, meaningful metrics — are not aesthetic enhancements. They are mechanisms through which the state reveals its regard for people who rely on it. If the twentieth century's administrative challenge was scale, the twenty-first century's is empathy at scale. That is harder. And more necessary.

As you turn the page, the question lingers: when systems grow smoother and faster, will they also become kinder? Or will speed and scale conceal their own forms of silence?

Service Journeys, Not Single Decisions

The morning rush at the Glasgow Southside Jobcentre in February 2019 did not look unusual at first: a queue of fifteen people, some clutching envelopes, others scrolling through cracked phone screens, waiting for the identification booth to open. Yet the outcome of that day mattered. A new digital identity verification requirement had been rolled out nationally the week before, and the Department for Work and Pensions (DWP) had assured ministers that the decision logic behind benefit approvals was fair, accurate, and consistent. It probably was. But the process wrapped around it was anything but. One man, a warehouse picker, had taken an unpaid hour off to travel across the city because the mobile upload step repeatedly rejected his photographs. A student on a bridging loan had returned for the third time because she lacked the right form of address proof; her tenancy agreement, though valid, was not in the system's dropdown list. By noon, eight out of the fifteen had been told to return another day. The algorithm's fairness did not soften the blow of an unfair journey.

Scenes like this reveal the deeper structure of administrative experience: the state often designs its technical components with precision, yet neglects the connective tissue that determines how people encounter them. A decision can be lawful, proportionate, and procedurally correct, while the pathway leading to it exhausts, confuses, or penalises the very people it intends to support. When we ask why a citizen feels mistreated, the answer usually lies not in the decision itself but in the journey's seams — the waits, the loops, the missing explanations, the misplaced steps that compound harm. Fairness collapses when it is not experienced as such. This is the quiet failure of many digital reforms.

The motif that runs through this subchapter — *the seam* — is not decorative. Every journey contains seams: points at which systems meet, tasks switch, or responsibilities hand over. When a seam is smooth, the person barely notices. When it is jagged, the entire service feels broken. Dignity is carried or compromised at these points. The state, therefore, must design with seams in mind.

The case of Glasgow shows the first claim: end-to-end mapping is indispensable. It is not enough to scrutinise the eligibility criteria, the model behind a risk flag, or the logic of a compliance rule. Designers must watch how a person moves from one step to the next. Show the journey, then name what it exposes. The DWP verification rollout showed a system that assumed smartphone literacy, stable broadband, and a portfolio of documentary ID that many low-income claimants do not possess. Explain the implication: even if 95 per cent of decisions that reached the algorithm were accurate, the journey filtered out people on the basis of their circumstances rather than their needs. Implication: fairness confined to a corridor within the larger building is not fairness at all.

A second example reinforces this pattern. In 2021, the city of Utrecht introduced a digital scheduling tool for housing inspections aimed at reducing overcrowding and fire risk. The model prioritised addresses based on signals: complaints, sudden energy spikes, and building characteristics. The prioritisation logic was transparent and defensible. But the booking process that followed required residents to select time slots through an online portal that used two-factor authentication by SMS. Many of the addresses flagged were in migrant neighbourhoods where phone contracts were pay-as-you-go and numbers changed frequently. Inspectors reported that dozens of households missed appointments not because they refused inspection but because the authentication step failed. The seam, not the model, created the friction. Utrecht eventually added a human-callback pathway and reported a measurable drop in no-shows. The decision logic remained the same; the journey changed.

The counter-example matters too. In 2020, Estonia's e-Residency programme — often cited as a gold standard of digital statecraft — updated its application flow. The decision-making model for granting residency status had long been criticised for being somewhat opaque. Yet the journey surrounding it was markedly smoother than most public digital services: predictable timelines, multilingual instructions, real-time progress dashboards, and a guaranteed human review if no progress occurred after 30 days. Even with imperfect internal logic, users consistently reported high satisfaction. This limitation shows that a streamlined journey can compensate for some weaknesses in the decision engine. Reconcile it carefully: an elegant journey cannot justify flawed or discriminatory decision logic, but it demonstrates that people experience fairness holistically, not modularly.

The seam motif appears again when we examine why journeys fail. Many systems embed invisible expectations about time, mobility, or cognitive effort. A digital housing-allowance form that formally takes "only 20 minutes" may require two hours when someone must gather utility bills scattered across emails, decipher jargon, or crop images to fit maximum upload sizes. The metric of completion time hides the lived metric: labour. When systems take labour for granted, dignity frays.

Administrative researchers frequently observe that people tolerate bad news more readily than bad process. If the journey respects them, they accept an unfavourable outcome with less resentment. Show this with a concrete behaviour: the Scottish Social Security Agency reported in 2022 that claimants who received clear reasons and a prompt appeal route were 40 per cent less likely to lodge a complaint about treatment even when their appeal failed. Name the implication: fairness is not an isolated virtue but a relational one. The state earns trust through each step, not only through the final decision.

Designing journeys requires technical decisions that often appear mundane but have deep ethical weight. Consider session timeouts. A five-minute timeout may protect security, but it also punishes people with slower typing speed, those switching between childcare and forms, or anyone working from shared devices. Extending it to fifteen minutes shifts the seam from hostile to humane. Or consider identity verification: allowing a wider range of documents, permitting in-person alternatives, or enabling community attestation mechanisms directly affects whether a journey includes or excludes. Systems are experienced physically — in bus fares, in waiting-room hours, in the heat of a kitchen where parents try to upload documents while a pot boils. That physicality is part of the journey and must be mapped.

We must also recognise the structural causes of unfair journeys. Public services often evolve through accretion. A new model is bolted onto an old portal. A privacy safeguard introduces an extra step without reconsidering the overall route. A historic division between two agencies creates a handoff that nobody owns. These seams accumulate. A journey that once made sense becomes labyrinthine. Naming this helps prevent a common administrative delusion: believing that fairness can be localised. It cannot. Fairness is architectural.

Technically, end-to-end mapping is not complicated. Teams walk through the journey as if they were citizens, tracking every click, every form field, every wait. They measure drop-offs, time spent per step, and rates of repeat contact. They interview people who give up or never reach the decision stage. When ministries in British Columbia conducted such a mapping exercise for disability assistance applicants in 2020, they found that nearly 30 per cent of unsuccessful applicants had abandoned the process before their case had ever been reviewed. The problem was not the model for eligibility. It was the journey's demands: medical forms that required three appointments, proof-of-condition documents that had to be reprinted despite already being stored in government systems, and unclear guidance about mandatory versus optional steps. Mapping made the seams visible.

Journey mapping is not a soft skill. It is a method for making power visible. Each checkpoint, verification, reminder, and redirect expresses a policy stance. If a system requires four forms of ID to replace a lost benefit card, it expresses suspicion. If it provides an unconditional "speak to a human now" button after two failed attempts, it expresses care. These are design choices that carry normative weight. And they are measurable: number of steps, load times, rejection rates at each stage, count of forced restarts. Metrics reveal where dignity is strained.

Two further examples — one successful, one instructive — show how journeys can be redesigned around fairness. In 2022, the London Borough of Camden restructured its homelessness triage workflow. Rather than forcing applicants through an online triage questionnaire that often misclassified them due to missing context, Camden introduced a hybrid approach: a preliminary digital checklist followed by a guaranteed human conversation within 48 hours for anyone flagged as potentially eligible. The conversation, not the model, became the anchor of the journey. Camden reported not only more accurate triage but also a drop in repeat presentations. The success lay in treating the journey as a whole rather than trusting the model alone.

Contrast that with a regional transport subsidy in New South Wales whose digital renewal form required applicants to upload proof of income annually, even though their income records were already held by the state revenue office. The unfairness was not the decision to reassess eligibility; it was the needless journey. People with lower digital literacy or unstable documentation faced higher dropout rates. The remedy was simple: an inter-agency data exchange that removed the redundant step. Fairness flowed not from revising the model but from repairing the journey's seam.

Journeys also matter because they shape expectations. A person who encounters friction early becomes defensive later. By the time they reach the formal decision point, they may have lost faith. Trust is cumulative. So is mistrust. A journey that repeatedly signals "we expect you to fail" becomes a self-fulfilling prophecy, as users disengage or provide incomplete information. Conversely, a journey that signals clarity and respect encourages cooperation. These behavioural effects are well documented in administrative studies and are visible in metrics such as call-centre escalations, rework rates, and appeal volumes.

Where digital government aspires to scale, the stakes heighten. A single poorly designed seam can degrade the experiences of thousands daily. This is why modular systems must be matched with modular journeys. When one module changes — identity checks, evidence uploads, scheduling — the journey must be re-mapped. Otherwise, new frictions slip in unnoticed. A fair decision nested in an unfair journey is like a sturdy beam holding up a sinking floor: admirable in isolation but insufficient overall.

The unresolved question is whether governments will treat journeys as seriously as they treat algorithms. Will they invest in mapping, testing, iterating, and measuring the seams where dignity is won or lost? Or will they continue to celebrate fair decisions while ignoring the miles of administrative terrain people must cross to reach them?

Interfaces that Explain and Invite Challenge

The turning point came in September 2017, when the UK's HM Courts & Tribunals Service (HMCTS) piloted a redesigned online tax-appeal form in London. The old interface had buried the reason for refusal three screens deep; the new version placed a plain-language explanation at the top, offered a templated "evidence pack" checklist, and showed a single, unmissable route to challenge the decision. Within three months, HMCTS staff reported a fall in incomplete appeals and a rise in successful submissions — not because the law had changed, but because the interface finally said what it meant and invited citizens to answer back. A form became a dialogue. A bureaucratic wall became a navigable doorway.

That pilot revealed something subtle yet structural: clarity is not a cosmetic improvement. It is a procedural right. When an interface withholds reasons, buries evidence routes, or hides alternatives behind jargon, it quietly shifts power away from citizens. When it explains and invites challenge, it redistributes that power. The interface becomes the front line of administrative justice, not an afterthought.

The motif that threads through this subchapter — *the doorframe* — captures this shift. A doorframe shapes who enters, how they enter, and whether they stumble. A well-designed interface frames the journey so that challenge is not an act of defiance but an ordinary, intelligible step. A poorly designed one makes the citizen feel as if they are forcing their way in. Doorframes set expectations before a single decision is made.

Consider the first major claim: reasons matter only when they are readable. The HMCTS pilot showed that a reason that can be read at a glance — "We could not verify your income with the documents provided" — grounds the citizen in reality. Show the pattern, then name it: this is the global trend towards *readability as equity*. The OECD's 2020 survey on government digital services noted that average reading levels among public-service users often align with Year 8 or 9. Explain the implication: if reasons require A-level literacy, they cease to be reasons and become barriers. Forcing citizens to decode dense prose is a design choice, not an inevitability. Design teams that measure reading age, track comprehension rates, and test clarity with real users commit to procedural fairness in a visible, quantifiable way.

A second example underscores this point. In 2022, Service Canada restructured its Employment Insurance portal by replacing legalistic reasons with structured explanations written in three short statements: the rule, the evidence gap, and how to fix it. Completion times fell. Appeal rates stabilised. More importantly, caseworkers observed fewer panicked calls because citizens understood what had happened without needing translation. The interface acted like a steady doorframe: visible, stable, honest.

A credible counter-example reminds us that clarity alone is not salvation. In New South Wales in 2021, a mobility-parking permit renewal site adopted clear reasoning but placed the evidence-upload step behind a mandatory mobile app that older citizens struggled to install. The reason made sense; the route to challenge did not. A citizen presented with a clear explanation but an unusable challenge pathway will still feel stonewalled. Reconcile this: clarity must be paired with accessibility. A doorframe without a floor still trips those who approach it.

The second major claim centres on evidence. Upload mechanisms are not technical footnotes; they are procedural levers that determine whether a citizen can act on their rights. Interfaces that demand high-resolution images, that timeout after five minutes, or that reject documents without explanation manufacture procedural failure. These systems *perform* fairness while quietly blocking it. A visible metric clarifies the point: when the municipality of Amsterdam introduced a redesigned evidence-upload component for housing-benefit applications in 2020, upload failure rates dropped from 42 per cent to under 10 per cent. The improvement did not come from changing the rules; it came from treating evidence as a civic juncture, not a file-management chore.

The doorframe motif returns here. Evidence steps frame the citizen's ability to respond. If poorly built, they narrow the threshold so that only the digitally fluent can step through. If well built, they widen it through multiple options: scanned documents, photographs, declarations, or human-assisted uploads in local offices. Each option is a widening of the frame.

The third major claim turns to alternative paths. The assumption that a single interface can accommodate all users is administratively convenient but ethically hollow. People's circumstances differ: language, disability, broadband stability, device availability, confidence, and fear of making mistakes. A well-designed interface recognises this pluralism and embeds alternatives. Show the behaviour, then name it: "choose another way" buttons, human-callback requests, and printable forms delivered by post or community hubs. Explain the implication: alternatives are not inefficiencies; they are equity instruments. They recognise that digital is not destiny for everyone.

A telling example comes from Helsinki's 2021 social-assistance portal redesign. Alongside the main digital flow, the city introduced a "Request a Helper Call" button that guaranteed a call within two hours. Uptake was high among older residents and those with limited Finnish. Crucially, appeal success rates rose in these groups because the helper-call pathway allowed them to articulate their case properly. The system's fairness improved not by automating challenge but by embedding respectful alternatives.

Yet limitations must be acknowledged. Pure multiplicity can breed confusion. A 2020 audit of multilingual welfare notices in California found that offering twelve languages without clear selection guidance led to mis-sequenced journeys and increased abandonment. Too many doorframes can feel like a maze. The reconciliation lies in structured choice: offer meaningful alternatives, but guide the citizen with simple prompts and a single "start again safely" route.

Readability and translation are not decorative features but civic equalisation tools. If a citizen cannot understand a notice, the state has failed before any substantive decision is made. Translation quality is measurable: error rates, consistency across languages, and back-translation tests. A rigorous translation pipeline signals respect. Municipal governments from Barcelona to Montreal have shown that co-designing translations with community groups increases comprehension far more effectively than contractor-led bulk translations.

A further example from the UK demonstrates that challenge must be actively welcomed. When the Northern Ireland Social Security Agency trialled a new "challenge this" banner on its assessment letters in 2019, placed prominently above the fold, appeals rose but so did speed of resolution. Caseworkers reported that early, well-framed challenges made final decisions more accurate. Citizens responded to the signal that challenge was an expected part of the process, not a sign of troublemaking. The doorframe widened again.

Interfaces also require an ethic of reversibility. Users make mistakes. They upload wrong files. They select incorrect categories. Systems that punish these mistakes with restarts erode confidence and disproportionately harm those with low digital skills. Conversely, systems that highlight "fix this now" options, provide immediate feedback, and retain partially entered information reinforce dignity. Metrics show this clearly: British Columbia's Family Benefit portal recorded a 25 per cent reduction in abandoned applications after introducing inline correction messages instead of post-submission errors.

The deeper truth, revealed across these examples, is that interfaces are not neutral. They encode institutional attitudes. A terse, opaque notice communicates suspicion. A clear, courteous explanation communicates fairness. A single narrow route conveys indifference to diversity; a structured array of alternatives conveys recognition of varied lives. Interfaces teach citizens what the state thinks of them.

The unresolved question is how far governments will go to build doorframes worthy of the people who walk through them. Will they adopt readability standards, invest in translation pipelines, measure upload failure rates, and design alternative routes as first-class components? Or will they continue to rely on interfaces that claim fairness while quietly constricting it?

From Nudge to Choice Architecture with Rights

The shift began quietly in March 2019, when the Danish Tax Agency tested a redesigned digital consent screen in Copenhagen. For years, most citizens had accepted the default option allowing the system to prefill their employment data. Acceptance rates hovered around 94 per cent. Then the agency inserted a new prompt above the button, written in plain Danish: *"You may decline. Your decision will not affect your benefits or future filings."* The default stayed the same, but the rights prompt altered the frame. Within two months, the proportion of citizens choosing manual review doubled. Nothing about the underlying tax calculation had changed; what changed was the interface's willingness to acknowledge the citizen's autonomy. A nudge became a choice.

That moment captured a wider paradox: governments invest heavily in accurate algorithms yet often neglect the basic fairness of the screens that surround them. A system may compute correctly and still pressure citizens into outcomes they neither intend nor understand. The promise of digital government lies not in persuasion but in protection — designing journeys that assume citizens can think, should choose freely, and deserve a route to challenge decisions without fear. It is here, in the quiet logic of the interface, that rights become operational rather than ceremonial.

The motif for this subchapter — *the handrail* — reflects that moral shift. A handrail does not push or steer; it supports. It gives stability without dictating direction. Choice architecture with rights functions in the same way: it provides clarity, visibility of options, and safe escalation paths. It replaces the psychology of nudging with the civics of empowerment.

The first major claim concerns the limits of nudging in public administration. A nudge, when used responsibly, simplifies a task. Show the point: the UK's 2015 organ-donation opt-out model increased enrolment by setting a sensible default. Then name the deeper issue: *default sensitivity*. In administrative settings, defaults can exploit cognitive shortcuts. Explain the consequence: a citizen who accepts a default to maintain speed or avoid confusion has not meaningfully chosen. The implication is blunt — when rights are at stake, nudges easily become coercive. A government committed to procedural fairness must measure comprehension rates, track default acceptance by socio-economic group, and monitor whether disadvantaged users disproportionately follow the path of least resistance.

A concrete example sharpens this claim. In 2021, New Zealand's Ministry of Social Development rebuilt its hardship-assistance request flow. The previous version preselected the lowest-value support option. It aimed to control expenditure, but the resulting pattern was predictable: families who most needed the higher allowance were the least likely to challenge the default. The redesigned interface made the options equal in visual weight, added a "compare entitlements" prompt, and inserted a short explanation clarifying that choosing the higher amount would not trigger an audit. Outcomes shifted. Use became more even across demographics, and caseworkers reported fewer distress calls. The handrail held firm: support, not steer.

A credible counter-example shows why this is difficult. In 2022, a health appointment portal in Ontario replaced nudges with a rights-based explanation screen. The interface now required users to read three short statements before booking. Completion time increased, and some users abandoned the process. The rights prompt was accurate but too heavy-handed. The lesson is not to dilute information but to refine its delivery. Rights prompts must be concise, positioned at decision points, and written in language that does not intimidate. A handrail should steady, not impose weight.

The second major claim addresses escalation. A system that encourages choice but blocks escalation undermines itself. Show the behaviour: error messages that simply say "Your request cannot be processed" without any route to speak to a human or submit revised evidence. Name the pattern: *closed loops*. These loops are efficient for administrators yet hostile to citizens. Explain the consequence: users stuck in closed loops feel trapped rather than served. Implication: escalation must be embedded as a first-class element of the interface — a visible "seek review" option, a documented route to human intervention, and a clear statement that requesting review does not reset or delay entitlements.

A strong example comes from Scotland's 2020 revisions to its Adult Disability Payment pilot interface. The system introduced three escalation choices: request clarification, request reconsideration, and request caseworker call-back. Uptake varied — the call-back option was the most used — but appeal quality improved. Caseworkers noted that early clarifications often resolved issues that would otherwise have become formal disputes. The interface protected citizens from procedural drift without overburdening the system. The handrail, again, gave balance.

A third major claim concerns transparency. An interface cannot support rights if it conceals the logic guiding its recommendations. Show the current reality: automated systems that suggest support plans or allocate appointments without explaining their basis. Name the requirement: *reason tokens* — short, structured statements that explain why the system presented this option. Explain: a reason token need not reveal proprietary detail; it must simply give meaning. "Appointments are shown based on your postcode and service-load forecasts for next week" does more to support autonomy than an unexplained calendar. Implication: transparency need not paralyse design. It must provide enough information for a citizen to make a reasoned decision and recognise when something is off.

Two examples illuminate this. First, Estonia's 2022 expansion of its X-Road services introduced a rule that all automated recommendations must include a one-line explanation and a link to extended information. Users were not overwhelmed; they were grounded. Second, a regional housing portal in Queensland added a "Why this?" button beside recommendation tiles. Use of the button correlated with higher satisfaction — not because the outcomes changed, but because citizens felt oriented.

But transparency can fail. A German benefits portal briefly experimented with long-form explanations, drawing directly from policy manuals. Users were flooded with complexity, and satisfaction plummeted. The reconciliation is simple: transparency must be digestible. The handrail must fit the hand, not tower above it.

The fourth major claim concerns mini-patterns — small, reusable design elements that turn rights into routine steps. These include consent reframers, alternative-path selectors, reason tokens, escalation buttons, and evidence guides. Naming them makes them teachable. Showing them makes them reproducible. Explaining them reveals their logic: they stabilise the citizen's journey without constraining choice. Implication: a rights-based system is not heavy;

it is modular. Agencies can adopt patterns incrementally, starting with the decisions that most affect people's lives.

A practical example comes from the 2020 redesign of São Paulo's childcare-allocation portal. The city adopted a mini-pattern library developed with local NGOs: structured reasons, multi-path submissions, and "speak to a coordinator" escalation routes. Measured outcomes followed: appeal rates stabilised, error corrections improved, and parents reported higher confidence in the fairness of the process. The handrail was installed in sections, each one reinforcing dignity.

Throughout these examples, choice architecture with rights reveals a shift from behavioural economics to administrative ethics. Nudging emerged as a way to help people navigate complexity. It often worked. But rights-oriented choice architecture recognises that citizens are not consumers in need of subtle steering; they are rights-holders entitled to clarity, options, and review. The goal is not to optimise compliance but to support agency.

The unresolved tension lies here: will states invest in the discipline needed to maintain these handrails? It is easier to default to nudges — cheaper to build, faster to deploy. Rights prompts, alternative paths, and escalation routes require maintenance, monitoring, and humility. The question is whether governments will choose the path of persuasion or protection. The choice will show whether their systems honour citizens' autonomy or merely gesture towards it.

Measuring Experience with Meaning

The warning came from an unlikely place: the front desk of Service NSW's Parramatta centre in May 2019. Throughout the spring, the agency had enjoyed satisfaction scores above 90 per cent, a figure proudly displayed on posters and dashboards. Yet on one Tuesday afternoon, a floor manager noticed something odd. A woman who had waited almost an hour to resolve a licence renewal tapped the "Very Satisfied" button before walking away visibly irritated. When a staff member followed and asked why, she replied, "If I press anything else, doesn't it make your day harder?" The metric glowed green. The experience did not.

That small exchange captured a quiet truth about public services: people often inflate satisfaction responses because they sympathise with staff, fear repercussions, or simply want to exit quickly. A feel-good number masks the lived reality it claims to measure. In the digital state, where interfaces rather than counters mediate most interactions, the gap widens. A click, a tap, or a short emoji rating can hide the fact that a citizen struggled to upload evidence, repeated a task three times, or abandoned a form to seek help elsewhere. If experience is to mean anything — if it is to signal dignity rather than décor — governments need metrics that reveal friction, not camouflage it.

The motif for this subchapter is *the seam.* A seam marks the point where two pieces meet. In service journeys, seams signal the points where clarity, support, or fairness can fray. Measuring experience with meaning requires tracing these seams, not polishing the surface.

The first major claim concerns the emptiness of vanity metrics. Show the problem: the "smiley terminal" satisfaction stations used across airports, councils, and benefits offices. Name the issue: *response bias.* Explain its mechanics: people rate the interaction, not the system; they rate their relief at completion, not the difficulty of the journey. Implication: a high score may reflect exhaustion, gratitude, or resignation — anything but true ease. Agencies that rely on vanity metrics risk misallocating resources because the numbers falsely suggest stability.

A stark example emerged in 2020 when Chicago's Department of Family and Support Services analysed satisfaction scores alongside system logs. The logs revealed that nearly 28 per cent of applicants for utility-support grants had made more than one attempt to submit the required documents. Yet the satisfaction scores remained above 85 per cent. Why? Staff suggested that applicants wished to avoid seeming ungrateful. When the department shifted to measuring *first-attempt task completion*, the picture sharpened: the true bottleneck lay in the photo-upload step for proof of residency. Only by abandoning the sheen of satisfaction could the department see the seam.

A credible counter-example complicates the point. In some emergency services, such as London's 999 call centres, satisfaction scores correlate strongly with life-impacting performance. People rate the service harshly when response times lag. But this is the exception, not the pattern. Satisfaction correlates with outcomes when situations are high-stakes, time-critical, and personally consequential. For routine administrative journeys, it correlates with almost anything else. Reconciling the tension requires simple honesty: keep satisfaction as a coarse, supplementary indicator, but treat it as insufficient for system improvement.

The second major claim addresses task completion. Show the behaviour: citizens repeating the same form section because the interface fails to save progress or validate documents correctly. Name the metric: *completion-through friction*, measured as the number of steps taken relative to the optimal path. Explain the insight: high friction means wasted human energy. Implication: agencies should measure not only whether tasks finish but how they finish — how many prompts, retries, or detours were required.

Estonia's 2021 pension reform portal illustrates this well. Logs showed that the average successful pension-switch request took seven minutes. But deeper analysis revealed that a third of users needed to re-enter personal identification numbers twice or more. Only when the agency introduced a friction map — tracking retries, reversions, and abandoned attempts — did developers realise the form validation logic was failing silently. Fixing it cut retries by 60 per cent. The seam tightened.

A second example appears in British Columbia's childcare benefit system. In 2022, the province introduced segmented tracking: "time to clarity", "time to submit", and "time to remedy". These measures exposed something satisfaction never could: parents struggled not with the benefit calculation but with assembling the evidence required to prove employment status. The government responded by publishing evidence templates and allowing employers to submit confirmation directly. Submission rates rose; remedy times fell. Experience improved because the seams were mapped, not because citizens clicked "happy".

The third major claim concerns appeal rates as indicators of invisible strain. Show the pattern: a benefits system with low appeal rates may appear stable. Name the risk: *suppressed challenge*. Explain its root causes: confusing notices, fear of reprisal, or simple exhaustion. Implication: rising appeal rates can signal clarity and empowerment, not system failure — provided appeals are handled with care.

A compelling example comes from Scotland's shift to Social Security Scotland in 2018. Before the redesign, appeal rates were low but so were claimant confidence scores. After the agency introduced clearer reasons, multiple review routes, and plain-language notices, appeal rates rose modestly. Instead of panicking, the agency interpreted the increase as a sign of restored agency. And they were right: subsequent tribunal decisions aligned more closely with entitlements. Measuring appeals as seams, not burdens, allowed the system to improve its moral geometry.

The credible limitation emerges in policing. In 2021, some Canadian police services piloted digital complaint pathways. Appeal rates spiked sharply, stretching oversight bodies. Yet investigations found that many new complaints were minor issues previously resolved in person. Reconciling this requires nuance: appeal metrics must distinguish between procedural correction and grievance expression. Not all appeals reveal system strain; some simply reflect the ease of clicking a form. Agencies must measure appeal quality — evidence completeness, reason clarity, and resolution time — not just volume.

The fourth major claim shifts to remedy times. Show the problem: citizens receiving decisions but waiting weeks for corrections. Name the key metric: *mean time to remedy* (MTTR). Explain its role: MTTR measures how quickly errors become justice. Implication: a system that resolves cases slowly erodes confidence even when initial decisions are fair.

A revealing case comes from Belgium's Kruispuntbank van de Sociale Zekerheid, which in 2017 began tracking remedy times as a core performance metric. Before the shift, data-entry errors affecting benefits could take up to 45 days to correct. After introducing automated alerts for inconsistent records and granting caseworkers authority to apply provisional remedies, MTTR dropped to under a week. Citizens' reported confidence increased accordingly. The improvement did not stem from more accurate algorithms but from faster repair of human seams.

Each of these examples underscores the central motif: the seam tells the truth. Experience metrics that illuminate seams — retries, remedies, detours, escalations — produce a more honest picture of public service quality. Metrics that obscure them create a façade that flatters systems while failing citizens.

The final question is unresolved: will governments commit to measuring what matters, even when it reveals uncomfortable truths? Task-completion logs can expose unreliable vendor tools. Remedy times can pressure agencies to invest in staffing. Appeal rates can reveal weaknesses in automated decisions. The tension lies in whether leaders prefer the comfort of green dashboards or the clarity of visible seams. The choice will shape not only measurement but the lived dignity of those who rely on public systems.

Chapter 10
Building the Playbook

Two floors above a busy market in Rotterdam in October 2016, a small team gathered around a whiteboard scarred with the residue of half-erased diagrams. Their task was deceptively simple: redesign the housing-allocation process for a neighbourhood where demand outstripped supply three to one. They had a single week, a patchwork of legacy databases, and a set of political commitments that could not be diluted. What they produced by Friday was not a system, nor even a prototype, but a one-page diagram. Six boxes. Arrows in pencil. A sketch of mandate, data sources, model logic, oversight steps, remedies, and metrics. The room fell quiet when one planner said, "If we cannot explain the system on one page, we are not ready to build it." The work that followed reshaped more than housing allocation; it reshaped how the city governed its digital tools. The map came before the machinery.

This chapter begins with that image—the whiteboard as a civic instrument. It captures a deeper shift taking hold across governments wrestling with artificial intelligence: policy is no longer only written in statutes or guidance but also in data schemas, model features, thresholds, and escalation routes. Designing these elements demands a playbook, one sturdy enough to guide teams and flexible enough to adapt. When institutions lack such a playbook, they drift from pilot to pilot, accumulating tools without direction. When they build one, even a modest council can exert strategic power, temper vendor dominance, and align technology with public purpose. The stakes are structural. So are the opportunities.

The need becomes clearest when observing how fragmented most public-service efforts remain. A benefits office might run a predictive model without a clear mandate about what it should optimise. A transport team may contract for analytics without securing rights to the underlying data. A procurement unit might buy a decision-support tool without having a plan for monitoring its performance. Each action makes sense in isolation yet frays when placed within the broader fabric of accountability. What governments require is not only capacity but coherence—an operating architecture that turns good intentions into repeatable practice.

This chapter introduces that architecture by starting with a simple premise: governance improves when it is made visible. Visibility is the motif threading through the pages that follow. Visibility of purpose, visibility of risk, visibility of control. A playbook gives shape to that visibility. It forces teams to answer questions that often go unasked. What is the public mandate for this system? Who is accountable for oversight? What is the path of remedy? Which metrics track harm rather than convenience? The governance canvas, the first pillar of this chapter, provides one method of structuring those answers. The Rotterdam team discovered that naming each element early prevented the usual drift into opaque technical complexity. Their lesson travels far.

But tools alone do not govern. People do. That is why the chapter turns next to capability and culture—not as abstract virtues but as practical disciplines. Many governments suffer from the same organisational fragility: siloed teams, transient staff, and delivery cycles that reward short-term launches over long-term stewardship. Building a durable playbook means cultivating roles that anchor good judgement—product managers who translate mandates into features, data scientists who understand legal constraints, legal advisors who are literate in model behaviour, ethicists who read logs as carefully as case law, and delivery teams who embed reflection into rhythm. Rituals such as pre-mortems and decision logs matter because they preserve memory in institutions that leak knowledge with every election and turnover cycle. Culture shapes capability; capability shapes outcomes.

For a playbook to influence real systems, it must also contend with time—political time, budgetary time, crisis time. That is why the chapter examines roadmaps and reform windows. Far too often, a promising pilot collapses under the weight of scaling or loses momentum when its champions move on. Sequencing becomes its own craft. A small, low-risk pilot in housing eligibility might prepare the ground for a later reform in disability assessments. A funding cycle might offer a rare moment to replace brittle infrastructure. A change of leadership might open political space to embed new governance norms. The most effective public innovators are not just builders; they are watchers of windows. They understand that reform is not a straight line but a rhythm, and a playbook must teach teams how to move with that rhythm rather than fight it.

The chapter closes with the hardest challenge: turning projects into institutions. Public sectors are littered with pilots that worked once but never again, because the scaffolding that made them possible was dismantled rather than absorbed. An institution becomes wiser when good practices are codified—lightly at first, then more firmly as evidence accumulates. Norms become standards. Standards become policy. Policies become law. And yet law itself needs maintenance, which is why sunset reviews and iterative codification matter. Without mechanisms for pruning and renewal, even the best rules ossify. The vignette of a city that learned to learn—by anchoring feedback, reforming its governance canvas, and adjusting its rituals—illustrates how institutions can accumulate competence rather than merely age.

What holds these threads together is a belief that the public sector can design its own future rather than inherit one from vendors or crises. Building the playbook is not an administrative exercise but a democratic one. It determines who sets the agenda, who bears responsibility, and who gets to correct course when systems fall short. It demands clarity and humility in equal measure. And it invites every reader to consider not only how systems should function, but how their organisations should learn.

The chapters ahead offer no templates for imitation; they offer scaffolds for adaptation. Whether you work in a ministry, a small council, a regulator, or a service delivery team, the playbook you help build will determine whether AI strengthens public purpose or steers it. The question is not whether governments can rise to this moment. It is whether they will commit to the slow, deliberate work of drawing the map before building the machine.

The Governance Canvas

In March 2019, the municipal council of Utrecht faced an uncomfortable truth. Months into its new housing-allocation system, complaints were climbing despite a decision engine that—on paper—was scrupulously fair. Allocation scores were calculated consistently. Waiting times had not lengthened. Yet residents were furious. At a tense public meeting, a caseworker held up a folder containing the journey of one applicant, Fatima Khalil. The decision denying her priority status was correct; the path leading to it was not. She had been asked to verify her identity four separate times across three portals, submit the same tenancy documents twice, and navigate an appeal process that assumed fluency in bureaucratic Dutch. The system had made a fair decision inside an unfair journey. That evening, officials sketched their first version of a governance canvas on a wall: mandate, data, model, oversight, remedy, metrics. It became their compass for rebuilding trust.

The Utrecht case captures a wider dilemma facing public institutions deploying algorithmic tools. They often build the engine before they define the roadway around it. Without a structured way to articulate what a system is for, what it relies on, how it behaves, and who can intervene when something goes wrong, governments produce brittle services—ones that meet technical specifications yet fracture under real civic pressure. A governance canvas offers a different starting point: one sheet that forces teams to confront the full lifecycle of a system, from authority to remedy. It is less a template than a discipline, and its discipline matters precisely because governments operate under legal and moral obligations that commercial product teams seldom face.

The canvas begins with mandate, the box many teams assume they have already filled. Show the mandate clearly, and the rest of the canvas tightens. In Utrecht's case, the mandate was not simply "allocate housing fairly"; it included statutory duties on equal treatment, obligations to prevent discriminatory impacts on families with disabilities, and political commitments to support those facing sudden displacement. Name these requirements early, and engineers understand the guardrails. Explain them poorly, and the model might optimise for administrative convenience rather than lawful purpose. The implication is simple but far-reaching: clarity of mandate shapes every downstream decision, from training data selection to user-interface prompts during appeals.

Data comes next, though many teams treat it as an afterthought. The canvas forces specificity. What data is used? Who maintains it? How often is it updated? In 2021, Helsinki's social-services department confronted the limits of an elegant model intended to prioritise urgent childcare applications. The model itself functioned well, but the underlying address data had a lag of up to seven days, meaning families who had recently moved—often the most vulnerable—were systematically mis-scored. When the department mapped its data box on the canvas, the visible behaviour was stark: seven days meant seven days of potential harm. They implemented same-day data synchronisation and added a flag for addresses not yet validated. The implication rippled across the system: a reliable model is useless if its data substrate is stale.

Model logic occupies the third box, but not as pseudo-code. It describes how decisions are formed, what features matter most, and where judgment remains human. The governance canvas asks teams to write these elements in plain language, enabling legal, policy, and frontline staff to interrogate them. Montreal's 2020 audit of its rental-inspection triage tool found that a seemingly neutral feature—distance from city centre—over-weighted older neighbourhoods inhabited predominantly by low-income residents. Displaying this logic on a canvas forced a reconsideration of weighting and the introduction of a constraint ensuring inspection capacity was distributed proportionally across districts. The implication was the emergence of a more transparent city-wide planning rationale.

Oversight forms the fourth box: who watches, how often, and with what authority. Visibility is the quiet motif of the canvas, and nowhere is it more consequential than in oversight. A strong oversight design shows where logs are stored, names the team with review powers, explains triggers for escalation, and identifies which patterns—disparity, accuracy drift, unexplained denials—should prompt investigation. In practice, oversight separates accountable systems from opaque ones. The UK's Driver and Vehicle Licensing Agency, during a 2022 review of its vision-assessment model, introduced quarterly fairness checks and an external observer seat drawn from a disability rights organisation. The visible behaviour changed quickly: declines that clustered in particular regions surfaced earlier, and remediation happened faster. The implication is that oversight, when embedded from the outset, makes accountability routine rather than reactive.

Remedy occupies the canvas's most neglected territory. Show it clearly, and systems become humane. Name who can appeal, what evidence counts, and how corrections propagate. During Utrecht's redesign, remedy revealed the fragility of the old system: appeals were technically possible but practically inaccessible, buried behind jargon-heavy instructions and a 14-day deadline that penalised shift workers and non-native Dutch speakers. The new canvas required multiple pathways—digital submission, in-person support, and a telephone route—and mandated that successful appeals feed back into model calibration. The implication reached beyond fairness: remedy turned lived experience into system improvement.

Metrics close the canvas, but they must resist performative behaviour. A team tempted to measure success through satisfaction ratings or response times risks mistaking smoothness for justice. The canvas requires measures that reveal reality: appeal rates, error corrections, demographic parity across decisions, time to resolution for remedies. In 2022, Lisbon's transport authority tested a routing model to optimise school-bus journeys. Their initial metrics—mileage reduction and on-time arrivals—made the pilot look successful. When the canvas forced inclusion of a fairness metric—number of times children with special needs were required to change buses—the picture shifted. The model saved fuel but increased transfers for those least able to tolerate them. That metric, once visible, redirected the project. The implication is that metrics determine morality: what you count influences whom you serve.

To see the canvas in full, return to Utrecht and walk through a simplified worked example of the redesigned housing-allocation system. The mandate is explicit: prioritise applicants facing statutory vulnerability, respect equal-treatment obligations, and promote stability for families with young children. The data section records sources—income statements, tenancy records, care-plan indicators—and their update cycles. It names custodians and flags fields prone to error. The model logic section describes a scoring function with bounded weights and a human override when a sudden change, such as domestic violence, disrupts formal indicators. Oversight details a quarterly review panel combining housing officers, data specialists, and a civil-society representative; it lists triggers including spikes in appeals or anomalies in neighbourhood-level allocations. Remedy outlines three routes of appeal, maximum review times, support for translation, and an explicit rule: every upheld appeal forces a pattern check. Metrics track distributional equity across districts, percentage of expedited cases processed within target time, and number of model adjustments prompted by appeals. In one page, the system becomes legible.

Every canvas, however, meets limits. A credible counter-example comes from a mid-sized regional government in Australia in 2020 that adopted the canvas but used it perfunctorily. Their child-support triage model had a clear mandate and transparent logic, but the oversight box was left vague and the remedy box collapsed into "standard appeals." Months later, when a miscalibrated threshold delayed urgent interventions for dozens of families, the absence of strong oversight mechanisms left managers scrambling. The limitation is obvious: a canvas is only as strong as the seriousness with which it is completed. Yet reconciling that limitation leads to a practical insight. Even an imperfect canvas surfaces gaps sooner than a fully unconstrained process. In the Australian case, the presence of a half-filled oversight box sped the retrospective review: officials knew exactly where to strengthen the next iteration.

Across these examples, the governance canvas does more than structure thinking; it alters behaviour. A service team that writes its metrics down commits to being judged by them. A policy team that states its mandate openly invites public scrutiny. A data team that documents update cycles signals responsibility. And a model team that names its oversight partners accepts shared authority. This is visibility at work: small disciplines producing large shifts in how institutions act.

The unresolved tension at the heart of the canvas is this: simplicity is its strength and its vulnerability. One page can force clarity, but one page can also tempt oversimplification. The forward test for every government, then, is whether they can treat the canvas not as a form to be completed, but as a living framework—updated as models evolve, enriched as data improves, and hardened as oversight matures. The next decision is yours: will the governance canvas become a ritual that shapes systems, or a document filed and forgotten?

Capability and Culture

In September 2020, the Welsh Government's Digital Health and Care team gathered in a nondescript meeting room in Cardiff to understand why a seemingly modest referral-triage tool had produced such uneven results across health boards. The model itself was not at fault; an external audit found it stable and within expected error margins. The problem lay elsewhere. Product managers had interpreted clinical guidelines one way, data engineers another. Legal advisers had been consulted only after deployment, and ethics reviewers had not been invited at all. When the team reconstructed the timeline on a whiteboard, the pattern was unmistakable: capability gaps had hardened into cultural habits. Decisions that should have been taken together had been taken alone. The rollout was paused. A cross-functional group was assembled. And for the first time, the team ran a structured pre-mortem before their next release. "We must learn as one team, not five," their director said that morning. The result, six months later, was a smoother service and a verified reduction in referral delays across three health boards. One place. One date. One reminder: governance lives or dies in its people.

The Cardiff episode illustrates a wider truth. Governments racing to introduce algorithmic tools often imagine capability as a list of roles to recruit, not as a culture to build. Yet technical systems do not fail because of a missing data scientist; they fail because the people who hold different pieces of the puzzle never learn to work with shared purpose. Capability is relational. Culture is cumulative. And public institutions, more than any other sector, depend on both to steer complex socio-technical systems safely.

Show the capability challenge in concrete form and its contours sharpen. A product manager drafts a service flow that assumes instant data availability. The data team points out that two critical sources refresh weekly. The legal adviser cites proportionality requirements that limit data linkage. The ethics specialist warns that a particular feature may amplify disparities for a minority group. The delivery manager stresses that frontline teams cannot support new workflows without proper training. Name this ensemble—product, data, legal, ethics, delivery—and the system becomes legible. Explain it and the implication becomes clear: capability is not the sum of experts but the choreography of their judgments.

The most resilient public teams share a motif of deliberate pause. They slow down before they speed up. Pre-mortems, for example, are not rituals of pessimism but exercises in clarity. In Copenhagen's municipal digital unit in 2022, a pre-mortem for a housing-maintenance prioritisation tool exposed a fault line between engineering assumptions and union-negotiated workflows. The visible behaviour was simple: maintenance crews had fixed time blocks that could not be rearranged by an optimisation routine. By imagining the project's failure in advance, the team redesigned the model to accept these constraints rather than bend them. The implication was profound: culture protected both labour rights and system performance.

Decision logs serve a similar purpose. They anchor institutional memory in a world where staff turnover can erase context in months. In 2018, New Zealand's Social Investment Agency introduced decision logs for all analytical models used in early-years intervention planning. Each log entry captured the decision itself, the evidence behind it, and the dissenting views—if any—expressed during deliberation. When, a year later, an external reviewer questioned the choice of a poverty indicator as a proxy for vulnerability, the decision log revealed the trade-offs considered at the time, including constraints imposed by privacy laws and the unavailability of certain linked datasets. The behaviour that followed was instructive: the agency revised the indicator but preserved the reasoning pathway. The implication is that culture, when documented, becomes transmissible.

Yet capability cannot be built by ritual alone. Two named examples show this. In 2021, the City of Amsterdam created a dedicated Algorithmic Oversight Team, combining engineers, legal scholars, and social scientists. Its mandate extended beyond audits. Members rotated into service teams, shadowed caseworkers, and ran workshops on feature sensitivity. This immersion shifted attitudes; frontline staff began to flag data inconsistencies proactively, while data scientists learned to phrase model outputs in language service staff could defend. In contrast, a mid-sized provincial government in Canada attempted to build capability by establishing separate "centres of excellence"—one for data, one for ethics, one for digital delivery—but kept teams largely siloed. A later review of their inspections-triage tool revealed avoidable errors: inconsistent data cleaning, misalignment with statutory mandates, and an appeal route that contradicted the province's own administrative-law guidance. The limitation is that structure without culture breeds brittleness. Reconciling the limitation leads to a deeper point: capability centralisation can help, but only when cross-functional habits become daily practice rather than occasional ceremony.

Governments also confront a visible tension in skill scarcity. Many local agencies lack the luxury of building five specialised teams. Capability must, therefore, be grown as well as bought. Small councils in Scotland, for example, addressed this in 2020 by forming shared analytics units across neighbouring authorities. They set metrics: number of staff trained in data-literacy programmes, frequency of joint code reviews, and time to resolve data-quality issues. These indicators grounded the abstract notion of "capacity building" in behaviours that could be measured. Over time, councils reduced dependency on single vendors and improved model transparency because more staff understood the underlying mechanics. The implication is that capability is not a fixed asset; it is a living practice that can be nurtured even under constraint.

The quiet motif of visibility returns when one examines how teams communicate during crises. A strong culture commits publicly to decisions. During the 2022 outage of a licensing system in Victoria, Australia, the cross-functional team published a rolling decision log every two hours, documenting fallback triggers, manual overrides, and upcoming choices. Customers saw transparency rather than silence. Managers saw accountability rather than confusion. When the system came back online, analysts used these logs to identify where resilience had succeeded and where it had faltered. A counter-example—Italy's 2019 welfare-claims processing glitch—reveals the alternative. There, fragmented communication across product, policy, and IT teams created contradictory public messages and delayed remedies. The reconciliation lies in acknowledging that culture cannot be improvised in a crisis; it must be built long before pressure arrives.

The ethical dimension of capability is equally grounded in action. Consider the visible decision in Manchester's 2021 youth-support triage pilot: when the ethics adviser proposed a rule requiring models to surface "uncertainty prompts" whenever confidence scores fell below a threshold, engineers integrated them within a fortnight. Caseworkers reported higher comfort because the system signalled when human judgment mattered most. The metric that followed—percentage of cases overridden due to uncertainty—became a regular item in review meetings. The implication is that ethics, when operationalised, moves from principle to practice.

There remains, however, a credible limitation: rituals such as pre-mortems and decision logs can degenerate into theatre if leadership treats them as compliance rather than commitment. A European ministry's 2020 digital-identity project demonstrated this risk. Although teams dutifully completed pre-mortem templates, they rarely challenged core assumptions, and management never returned to the logs during reviews. The project later encountered predictable issues—unverified datasets, inconsistent legal interpretations, and misaligned service flows—that the rituals had theoretically anticipated. Reconciling this limitation requires leaders to inhabit, not merely endorse, the culture they wish to build. When directors attend pre-mortems, ask uncomfortable questions, and visibly adapt plans based on what they hear, rituals regain their power.

Taken together, capability and culture form the operating system of algorithmic governance. They determine whether technical tools become civic assets or sources of harm. They reveal whether multidisciplinary teams learn to measure what matters, compare evidence honestly, and commit to shared purpose. But the unresolved tension at the centre of this subchapter persists: can institutions sustain these practices when leadership rotates, budgets tighten, and political priorities shift? The forward test is deceptively simple. Look at your next project and ask: who needs to be in the room for this decision, how will we document what we choose, and what will we examine in the pre-mortem we have not yet run?

Roadmaps and Reform Windows

In March 2016, New York City's Mayor's Office of Data Analytics launched a modest pilot to predict building fire-risk across the boroughs, using inspection histories, complaint logs, and building-age data. The pilot worked. In its first season, the Fire Department reported a measurable uptick in identifying high-risk structures before incidents occurred. Yet success alone did not carry it into stable policy. The pilot stalled for nearly a year until a budget negotiation opened a narrow window in late 2017, allowing the city to fold the capability into a multi-year capital plan. One technical proof, several bureaucratic detours, and a moment of institutional opportunity later, a pilot became part of the city's long-term inspection strategy. The scene was unremarkable: a cramped office near City Hall, a team clutching spreadsheets, a deputy commissioner insisting that "timing is half the work." But the outcome revealed something essential—good ideas need windows.

The rhythm of that story repeats across governments. A pilot—often elegant, often fragile—demonstrates value but cannot yet carry the weight of law or permanent funding. Sequencing pilots into policy requires a roadmap that is neither naïve nor fatalistic. It demands an understanding of how leadership transitions, budget cycles, and crises create openings and close them again. And it requires the discipline to prepare for these openings so that when they arrive, reformers move with speed rather than scramble with haste. *The window shifts.*

A roadmap begins with clarity about what the pilot proved and what it merely hinted at. Show the lesson, name its context, explain its force, and the implication becomes visible. When the Greater Manchester Combined Authority tested a homelessness-prevention triage model in 2019, the visible behaviour that convinced councillors was not accuracy alone but repeat performance: frontline staff reported that the tool cut their triage time by an average of 11 minutes per case, allowing earlier interventions. Accuracy mattered; workflow change mattered more. The implication was immediate: the roadmap needed to preserve speed gains while designing stronger oversight before scaling across councils. A pilot had produced both evidence and constraints.

Reform windows then shape the order of moves. Leadership changes can accelerate reform if reformers present options early. After the 2022 local elections in Helsinki, the incoming deputy mayor for social services requested a "system map" of ongoing algorithmic projects. The map showed fragmentation—seven pilots with no shared oversight. The legal team seized that window to propose a minimal viable reform: a joint review panel to assess data protection, error impacts, and appeal routes across tools. It was small enough to pass; large enough to shift incentives. The metric that mattered was not scale but coordination, measured by the number of projects reviewed and the average time to issue recommendations. Within six months, the panel's work informed the city's budget hearings. A window had become a wedge.

Funding cycles provide another predictable opening. They reward teams who prepare. In 2021, the Government of New South Wales sought to scale a successful road-traffic analytics pilot. Rather than ask for a full programme budget, the delivery team framed its request as a two-year transition plan tied to explicit metrics: reduction in average data-processing time, number of integrated datasets, and frequency of cross-agency coordination meetings. By presenting quantifiable, intermediate steps, the team kept political risk low and institutional learning high. The implication is straightforward: reform windows favour teams who present sequences, not events.

Crises, by contrast, generate involuntary windows. The risk is that speed eclipses structure. During the 2018 wildfires in British Columbia, emergency planners deployed an improvised data-sharing protocol between transport, forestry, and police services to coordinate evacuations. It worked under extreme pressure. But when the crisis subsided, a review revealed the limitation: none of the protocols had legal footing, and several bypassed privacy safeguards that should not be suspended lightly. The reconciliation came through a minimal viable reform—formalising a small subset of emergency data-sharing rules with clear sunset clauses. This act preserved agility while preventing temporary improvisations from hardening into permanent, unexamined practice. *The window warns.*

Two further examples show how sequencing shapes outcomes. In 2020, the Flemish Government piloted an employment-matching model across three municipalities. Rather than push for region-wide adoption immediately, officials sequenced a refinement phase: measuring mismatch rates, comparing outcomes against control cohorts, and embedding a new appeal process. By 2022, the programme was scaled with legislative backing because evidence had undone resistance. Contrast this with a provincial digital-identity initiative in 2019 that raced from prototype to mandate without adjusting for frontline reality. Here the counter-example reveals the cost of poor sequencing: authentication failure rates rose in rural areas, and service uptake dropped. The limitation underscores the need for a roadmap that respects capability gaps and distributional effects. Reconcile the limitation, and the deeper lesson emerges: policy is the final stage of learning, not the first.

Roadmaps acquire authority when they include friction—deliberate checkpoints that stop momentum from becoming dogma. A good sequence forces teams to measure what matters. If a pilot aims to reduce claim-processing time, the roadmap should track median resolution times across demographic groups, not just overall averages. If a pilot promises fewer appeals, the roadmap should measure appeal quality and remedy time. Behaviour, not aspiration, proves reform. And when reform windows open, these measurements equip leaders with arguments grounded in observed outcomes rather than promises of future efficiency.

The quiet motif of *the window* threads through the human side of reform. Officials preparing for leadership change compare notes weeks in advance. Data teams rehearse explanations for model behaviour so that when a budget committee asks how error rates vary across groups, they respond with clarity rather than jargon. Service teams prepare stories—documented, verified—showing how a pilot altered their workday. These practices accumulate into readiness. Windows reward those who are ready.

Capability shapes these roadmaps, but so does culture. Sequencing pilots into policy requires institutions willing to revisit early assumptions. One city's housing-allocation pilot in 2021 introduced a fairness constraint that improved equity but inadvertently slowed assignment speeds. The roadmap team confronted the trade-off directly, tested model variants during a scheduled budget window, and validated a hybrid approach that preserved the fairness constraint while adapting queue algorithms. The implication was stark: only institutions that learn aloud can legislate wisely.

Still, an unresolved tension remains. Reform windows rarely align neatly with technical learning cycles. A pilot may mature just as political attention shifts elsewhere; an incoming leader may demand rapid scaling without time for sufficient refinement; a crisis may pressure teams to act before guardrails are in place. The forward test therefore sits with every reader stewarding such reforms: when the next window opens—predictable or forced—will you have prepared a sequence that protects the public, respects the limits of your pilot, and earns the trust your roadmap claims to build?

From Projects to Institutions

In September 2014, the City of Boston launched a small experiment: a mobile app, *City Hall to Go*, allowing residents to request pothole repairs, report graffiti, and lodge service complaints. The app was ordinary in appearance but radical in consequence. Within a year, Boston had processed thousands of requests through a workflow that blended automated triage with human review. The concrete outcome was a reduction in average pothole repair time from twelve to eight days, reported in the city's 2015 Public Works briefing. Yet the deeper shift occurred quietly: teams began documenting their own decisions, refining escalation paths, and tracking remedy times in weekly huddles. A project had planted the behaviours of an institution. By 2017, these practices were codified into departmental standard operating procedures, and, in 2019, the city council adopted portions of the workflow into a municipal ordinance governing digital service standards. The arc was unmistakable—prototype, habit, norm, law.

That progression is neither guaranteed nor linear. Many pilots remain orphans: funded once, admired briefly, then abandoned. The pattern is depressingly familiar—an innovation lab produces a promising model, a press release celebrates its novelty, and nothing in the host institution shifts. The scene in Boston mattered precisely because it showed the opposite: officials recognised that sustaining improvement required more than software. It required codification. It required a culture that documented uncertainty as rigorously as success. And it required sunset reviews to prevent early assumptions from ossifying into brittle rules. *The thread must hold.*

The transformation of practice into norm begins with visibility. Show the work, name its provenance, and the implications become legible. Consider the case of Wellington City Council in 2018, when it introduced a predictive maintenance tool for its water network. Engineers initially treated the model as a decision-support layer rather than a determinant, verifying predictions through manual inspection logs. Over the first year, they recorded the variance between the model's risk ranking and field observations, finding that the model consistently overestimated risk for pipes older than ninety years. This visible behaviour did two things. It exposed a systematic bias and prompted the data team to create a correction factor. And it established an expectation—each model iteration required explicit validation against field data. By 2020, this check had become a documented requirement for all algorithmic tools used in infrastructure planning. What began as a technical anomaly matured into a governance norm.

But norms cannot rest on technical teams alone. They demand organisational rituals. A pre-mortem, for example, forces teams to imagine failure before it occurs, naming weak points and examining trade-offs. When the Government Digital Service in the United Kingdom trialled this ritual across departments in 2016, project leads reported a measurable change in meeting behaviour: risk discussions began earlier, and decision logs grew more detailed. That detail—who decided what, on what evidence, and at what moment—proved invaluable for later audits. The implication is clear: institutions grow not through dramatic redesigns but through repeated, modest actions that accumulate into discipline. *The thread strengthens.*

Yet codification carries its own risk. Over-codify, and institutions become defensive, closed to learning. Under-codify, and reforms remain fragile. The tension is visible in a counter-example from a Canadian provincial agency that adopted strict model governance rules in 2020 following a high-profile benefits misclassification case. The rules mandated extensive documentation for even minor model updates, including small parameter tweaks. The result was paradoxical: innovation slowed, error corrections lagged, and teams circumvented the rules through informal workarounds. The limitation was obvious—rigour had hardened into rigidity. The reconciliation came when the agency revised the policy in mid-2022 to differentiate between high-impact and low-impact changes. Documentation remained mandatory, but the burden became proportional to risk. Codification regained flexibility without losing accountability.

The journey from project to institution hinges on one repeated question: *What do we keep?* Projects generate artefacts—templates, workflows, logs, performance dashboards. Institutions decide which artefacts to elevate. For example, when Edinburgh's housing services tested a new allocation algorithm in 2021, a central component of the pilot was a "fairness table" comparing wait times across demographic groups. Although initially created as an internal diagnostic, councillors requested regular publication. Over time, this table evolved into a publicly reported equity metric, reviewed during budget cycles and referenced in parliamentary committee discussions. Its elevation into an institutional metric altered incentives: housing officers began monitoring disparities monthly, and model updates required demonstrating improvement or explaining stagnation. A pilot's internal tool had become a public accountability instrument.

The impulse to codify is strongest when teams learn visibly. That learning depends on systematic sunset reviews. These reviews require teams to ask whether a rule still makes sense given new data, new tools, or new expectations. In 2023, Copenhagen's digital mobility unit conducted a sunset review of its congestion-pricing algorithm. Traffic patterns had shifted post-pandemic; commuter flows were flatter; and cyclists represented a larger share of road users. The review revealed that the algorithm's weighting assumptions no longer reflected lived reality. City officials revised the model, updated documentation, and reissued guidelines for data collection. The behaviour mattered: rather than treat initial assumptions as fixed, the city demonstrated a willingness to revisit its own logic. The implication is profound—institutions that embed sunset reviews legislate humility.

Institution-building also requires narrative consistency. Staff must understand why a practice matters before they are asked to repeat it. Here, leadership plays a crucial role. In 2017, the City of Amsterdam appointed a Chief Algorithm Officer. The role had limited formal power but significant symbolic authority. By repeatedly articulating the principle that "automated decisions must be explainable to the people they affect," the officer helped translate abstract rights into operational norms. Departments began crafting plain-language explanations for model outputs, testing them with residents, and adjusting interfaces accordingly. This narrative consistency shaped behaviours: engineers wrote clearer documentation; product teams created challenge pathways; legal teams linked explanations to data protection obligations. Words became practice; practice became culture.

Culture, however, must meet capability. Institutions cannot inherit behaviours they cannot execute. A small-town council seeking to adopt AI-driven triage for citizen services may lack the in-house data expertise required to sustain governance norms. Here, shared service hubs offer a bridge. In 2020, several regions in Finland formed joint analytics units to support municipalities. These units provided technical validation, model monitoring, and documentation templates. Crucially, they also facilitated peer learning—municipal teams compared decisions, metrics, and failure modes. The behaviour of shared reflection created coherence across fragmented institutions. The implication: institutionalisation is often a regional project, not a solitary one.

Institutionalisation also demands attention to political rhythm. Leadership changes disrupt patterns; new administrations bring different priorities, sometimes dissolving ongoing reforms. Yet reforms survive when norms embed deeply enough that reversal becomes costly. Toronto's open data programme, launched in 2010, survived three mayoral transitions because it built routines—monthly dataset releases, public documentation, and community feedback sessions. By the time open data entered municipal ordinance in 2018, the law was merely recognising what practice had already established. This is the crux of institutionalisation: law formalises what norms have already stabilised.

Still, a core tension persists. Institutions must protect against harm without stifling invention. They must set rules without freezing behaviours that should evolve. They must preserve memory without allowing precedent to overpower evidence. *The thread resists and bends.*

The chapter closes with a city that learned to learn. In 2015, Medellín's planning department began experimenting with data-driven zoning tools to anticipate the effects of development proposals. Early pilots were clumsy; data gaps produced misleading outputs; residents mistrusted the interface. But the city persisted. Officials created a public log of errors, invited universities to challenge assumptions, and embedded sunset reviews into each seasonal update. By 2020, the tool's accuracy had improved, and residents could trace decisions through clearer explanations. In 2022, the city council adopted a zoning governance framework requiring iterative review, public documentation, and explainability audits. The law did not impose learning; it recognised learning that had already taken root.

The unresolved question for every reader is straightforward and uncomfortable: when your next project succeeds, will it remain a project—or will you build the behaviours, codifications, and review cycles that allow it to become an institution?

About the Author

Zinedine Calvori helps governments and civic organisations build technology that serves public purpose. Across roles in policy design, digital delivery, and service transformation, he has worked at the seam where law meets code and where citizen experience meets institutional constraint. His mission is simple: make state capability visible, legible, and humane. A long-standing interest in Mediterranean civic traditions informs his view that legitimacy flows from participation as much as performance. Drawing on projects with city halls, regulators, and non-profits, he translates dense debates on algorithms, data rights, and accountability into practical choices about mandates, metrics, and methods. He writes and teaches widely on digital public infrastructure, institutional design, and administrative justice.

www.ingramcontent.com/pod-product-compliance
Lightning Source LLC
Chambersburg PA
CBHW031342230926
51848CB00002B/346